A MODERN APPROACH TO
LOGIC
REASONING

(Fully Solved)

For entrance examinations for:
* M.B.A.; C.A.T.; Hotel Management
* Bank P.O.; R.B.I.; S.B.I.P.O.; NABARD
* B.S.R.B. Recruitment
* Railway Recruitment, S.C.R.A.
* L.I.C.A.A.O.; G.I.C.A.A.O.; Asstt. Grade
* S.S.C.; U.D.C.; L.D.C.
* I. Tax & Central Excise, C.B.I.; C.P.O.
* I.A.S.; P.C.S.; I.F.S.
* B.Ed.; M.B.B.S.

R.S. AGGARWAL
VIKAS AGGARWAL

S. CHAND
AN ISO 9001 : 2000 COMPANY
2005

S. CHAND & COMPANY LTD.
RAM NAGAR, NEW DELHI - 110 055

S. CHAND & COMPANY LTD.

(An ISO 9001 : 2000 Company)

Head Office : 7361, RAM NAGAR, NEW DELHI - 110 055
Phones : 23672080-81-82; Fax : 91-11-23677446
Shop at: **schandgroup.com**
E-mail: **schand@vsnl.com**

Branches :

- 1st Floor, Heritage, Near Gujarat Vidhyapeeth, Ashram Road, **Ahmedabad**-380 014. Ph. 27541965, 27542369.
- No. 6, Ahuja Chambers, 1st Cross, Kumara Krupa Road, **Bangalore**-560 001. Ph : 22268048, 22354008
- 152, Anna Salai, **Chennai**-600 002. Ph : 28460026
- S.C.O. 6, 7 & 8, Sector 9D, **Chandigarh**-160017, Ph-2749376, 2749377
- 1st Floor, Bhartia Tower, Badambadi, **Cuttack**-753 009, Ph-2332580; 2332581
- 1st Floor, 52-A, Rajpur Road, **Dehradun**-248 011. Ph : 2740889, 2740861
- Pan Bazar, **Guwahati**-781 001. Ph : 2522155
- Sultan Bazar, **Hyderabad**-500 195. Ph : 24651135, 24744815
- Mai Hiran Gate, **Jalandhar** - 144008 . Ph. 2401630
- 613-7, M.G. Road, Ernakulam, **Kochi**-682 035. Ph : 2381740
- 285/J, Bipin Bihari Ganguli Street, **Kolkata**-700 012. Ph : 22367459, 22373914
- Mahabeer Market, 25 Gwynne Road, Aminabad, **Lucknow**-226 018. Ph : 2226801, 2284815
- Blackie House, 103/5, Walchand Hirachand Marg , Opp. G.P.O., **Mumbai**-400 001. Ph : 22690881, 22610885
- 3, Gandhi Sagar East, **Nagpur**-440 002. Ph : 2723901
- 104, Citicentre Ashok, Govind Mitra Road, **Patna**-800 004. Ph : 2671366, 2302100

Marketing Offices :

- 238-A M.P. Nagar, Zone 1, **Bhopal** - 462 011. Ph : 5274723
- A-14 Janta Store Shopping Complex, University Marg, Bapu Nagar, **Jaipur** - 302 015, Phone : 0141-2709153

© *Copyright Reserved*

All rights reserved. No part of this publication may be reproduced, stored in a retrieval system or transmitted, in any form or by any means, electronic, mechanical, photocopying, recording or otherwise, without the prior permission of the Publisher.

S. CHAND'S Seal of Trust

In our endeavour to protect you against counterfeit/fake books we have put a Hologram Sticker on the cover of some of our fast moving titles. The hologram displays a unique 3D multi-level, multi-colour effect of our logo from different angles when tilted or properly illuminated under a single source of light.

Background artwork seems to be "under" or "behind" the logo, giving the illusion of depth. **A fake hologram does not give any illusion of depth.**

First Edition 1999
Reprints 2000, 2001, 2002, 2003, 2004
Reprint 2005

ISBN : 81-219-1905-3

PRINTED IN INDIA

By Rajendra Ravindra Printers (Pvt.) Ltd., 7361, Ram Nagar, New Delhi-110 055 and published by S. Chand & Company Ltd., 7361, Ram Nagar, New Delhi-110 055.

PREFACE TO THE FIRST EDITION

Hereby we proudly announce the presentation of this unique book "Logic Reasoning". Now-a-days success in every single competitive examination (Bank Clerical, Bank P.O., LIC, GIC, M.B.A., Assistant Grade, Excise & Income Tax, IAS, IFS, A.A.O., Railways, Hotel Management and others) depends much on the candidate's performance in the Reasoning Paper. So a much comprehensive and intelligent approach to it is the need of the day. This book serves the purpose.

It is unique in the following aspects:

(i) Its coverage of all types of questions asked in the exams and all the study material available on these;

(ii) Its huge collection of practisable questions;

(iii) Fully solved examples and explanatory answers.

Question Papers and references given on memory basis shall help to know the types of questions asked in a particular examination.

May I request the, student readers, worthy friends, and valuable colleagues to further suggest any change for improvement of the book.

I am thankful to M/s. S. Chand & Company Ltd. for bringing out this book well in time with such a nice get up.

AUTHORS

CONTENTS

LOGICAL DEDUCTION

1. LOGIC

The word 'Logic' is derived from the Greek noun 'logos' meaning both 'thought' and 'the word expressing thought'.

Thus, LOGIC is the 'science of thought as expressed in language'. This means that the questions on logic are to be solved as per the information given without any concern of the formal validity or truth of the statements *i.e.* conclusion should follow directly from the statements given.

With this unique characteristic, the Logic Test becomes an instrument of teaching the candidates to follow the rules and work as per the instructions without an error. Thus, it prepares the mind for all types of reasoning practices and teaches how to detect and avoid mistakes in the same.

LOGICAL REASONING

In Logic, any statement is termed as the **Proposition.** Thus, *a Proposition is a statement expressing certain relation between two or more terms,* analogous to a sentence in grammar.

The Proposition consists of three parts :

1. **Subject :** The Subject is that about which something is said.
2. **Predicate :** The Predicate is the part of the Proposition denoting that which is affirmed or denied about the subject.
3. **Copula :** The Copula is that part of the Proposition which denotes the relation between the Subject and the Predicate.

Consider the Proposition *'Man is cultured'.*

Here an information is given about the man. So 'Man' is the Subject.

'Cultured' is the quality affirmed for this Subject. So it is the Predicate.

'is' denotes the relation between the Subject and the Predicate. So, it is the Copula.

Four Fold Classification of Propositions :

'Propositions' can be classified into four types :

1. Universal Affirmative Proposition (denoted by A) : It distributes *only the subject i.e.,* the Predicate is not interchangeable with the subject while maintaining the validity of the Proposition. *e.g.,*

All men are animals.

This is Proposition A since we cannot say 'All animals are men.'

2. Universal Negative Proposition (denoted by E) : It distributes *both the Subject and the Predicate i.e.,* an entire class of predicate term is denied to the entire class of the subject term, as in the proposition. *e.g.*

No boy is intelligent.

3. Particular Affirmative Proposition (denoted by I) : It distributes *neither the Subject nor the Predicate. e.g.*

Some people are foolish.

1

Here, the subject term 'Some people' is used not for all but only for some men and similarly the predicate term 'foolish' is affirmed for a part of subject class. So, both are undistributed.

4. Particular Negative Proposition (denoted by O) :

It distributes *only the Predicate. e.g.,*

Some animals are not wild.

Here the subject term 'some animals' is used only for a part of its class and hence is undistributed while the predicate term 'wild' is denied in entirety to the subject term and hence is distributed.

These facts can be summarised as follows :

Proposition	Type
(a) (A) distributes subject only.	All S is P.
(b) (E) distributes subject and predicate both.	No S is P.
(c) (I) distributes neither.	Some S is P.
(d) (O) distributes predicate only.	Some S is not P.

SYLLOGISM : In Logic, we are required to deal with a particular type, termed as Syllogism. It was introduced by Aristotle.

In Syllogism, a *conclusion* has to be drawn from two propositions, referred to as the Premises.

Example : 1. All lotus are flowers.

2. All flowers are beautiful.

3. All lotus are beautiful.

Clearly, the propositions 1 and 2 are the Premises and the proposition 3, which follows from the first two propositions, is called the Conclusion.

Term : In Logic, a TERM is a word or a combination of words, which by itself can be used as a subject or predicate of a proposition.

Syllogism is concerned with three terms :

1. Major Term : It is the *predicate of the conclusion* and is denoted by P (first letter of 'Predicate.)

2. Minor Term : It is the *subject of the conclusion* and is denoted by S (first letter of 'Subject').

3. Middle Term : It is the *term common to both the premises* and is denoted by M (first letter of 'Middle').

Note that the middle term does not occur in the conclusion.

Example : Premises :   1. All dogs are animals.

2. Tiger is a dog.

Conclusion :   Tiger is an animal.

Here, 'animal' is the predicate of the conclusion and so, it is the Major Term, P. 'Tiger' is the subject of the conclusion and so, it is the Minor Term, S. 'Dog' is the term common to both the premises and so, it is the Middle Term, M.

Major and Minor Premise : Of the two premises, the *major premise* is that in which the middle term is the subject and the *minor premise* is that in which the middle term is the predicate.

Rules for deriving the conclusion :

1. *The conclusion does not contain the middle term.*

Example :   *Statements :*   1. All men are girls.

2. Some girls are students.

              Conclusions :   1. All girls are men.
                                   2. Some students are girls.

Since both the conclusions 1 and 2 contain the middle term 'girls', so neither of them can follow.

2. *No term can be distributed in the conclusion unless it is distributed in the premises.*

   Example :   *Statements :*   1. Some dogs are goats.
                                   2. All goats are cows.
              Conclusions :   1. All cows are goats.
                                   2. Some dogs are cows.

Statement 1 is an I type proposition which distributes neither the subject nor the predicate. Statement 2 is an A type proposition which distributes the subject. i.e. 'goats' only.

Conclusion 1 is an A type proposition which distributes the subject 'cow' only.

Since the term 'cow' is distributed in conclusion 1 without being distributed in the premises, so conclusion 1 cannot follow.

3. *The middle term (M) should be distributed at least once in the premises. Otherwise, the conclusion cannot follow.*

For the middle term to be distributed in a premise,

      (*i*) M must be the Subject if premise is an A proposition.

     (*ii*) M must be Subject or Predicate if premise is an E proposition.

   (*iii*) M must be Predicate if premise is an O proposition.

Note that in an I proposition, which distributes neither the Subject nor the Predicate, the middle term cannot be distributed.

   Example :   *Statements :*   1. All fans are watches.
                                   2. Some watches are black.
              Conclusions :   1. All watches are fans.
                                   2. Some fans are black.

In the premises, the middle term is 'watches'. Clearly, it is not distributed in the first premise which is an A proposition as it does not form its subject. Also, it is not distributed in the second premise which is an I proposition. Since the middle term is not distributed at least once in the premises, so no conclusion follows.

4. *No conclusion follows*

   (a) *if both the premises are particular*

      Example :   *Statements :*   1. Some books are pens.
                                       2. Some pens are erasers.
                 Conclusions :   1. All books are erasers.
                                        2. Some erasers are books.

Since both the premises are particular, no conclusion follows.

   (b) *if both the premises are negative*

      Example :   *Statements :*   1. No flower is mango.
                                       2. No mango is cherry.
                 Conclusions :   1. No flower is cherry.
                                        2. Some cherries are mangoes.

Since both the premises are negative, neither conclusion follows.

(c) if the major premise is particular and the minor premise is negative.

Example :   *Statements :*   1. Some dogs are bulls.
                                  2. No tigers are dogs

                Conclusions :   1. No dogs are tigers.
                                  2. Some bulls are tigers.

Here the first premise containing the middle term 'dogs' as the Subject is the major premise and the second premise containing the middle term 'dogs' as the Predicate is the minor premise. Since the major premise is particular and the minor premise is negative, so no conclusion follows.

5. If the middle term is distributed twice, the conclusion cannot be universal.

Example :   *Statements :*   1. All fans are chairs.
                                  2. No tables are fans.

                Conclusions :   1. No tables are chairs.
                                  2. Some tables are chairs.

Here, the first premise is an A proposition and so, the middle term 'fans' forming the subject is distributed. The second premise is an E proposition and so, the middle term 'fans' forming the predicate is distributed. Since the middle term is distributed twice, so the conclusion cannot be universal.

6. If one premise is negative, the conclusion must be negative.

Example :   *Statements :*   1. All grasses are trees.
                                  2. No tree is shrub.

                Conclusions :   1. No grasses are shrubs.
                                  2. Some shrubs are grasses.

Since one premise is negative, the conclusion must be negative. So, conclusion 2 cannot follow.

7. If one premise is particular, the conclusion is particular.

Example :   *Statements :*   1. Some boys are thieves.
                                  2. All thieves are dacoits.

                Conclusions :   1. Some boys are dacoits.
                                  2. All dacoits are thieves.

Since one premise is particular, the conclusion must be particular. So, conclusion 2 cannot follow.

8. If both the premises are affirmative, the conclusion would be affirmative.

Example :   *Statements :*   1. All women are mothers.
                                  2. All mothers are sisters.

                Conclusions :   1. All women are sisters.
                                  2. Some women are not sisters.

9. If major premise be affirmative, the conclusion must be particular.

Example :   *Statements :*   1. All plays are stories.
                                  2. Some poems are plays.

                Conclusions :   1. Some poems are stories.
                                  2. All stories are poems.

The first premise containing the middle term 'plays' as the subject is the major premise. Also, it is affirmative. So, the conclusion must be particular. Hence, conclusion 2 cannot follow.

EXERCISE 1A

Directions : *In each question below are given two statements followed by two conclusions numbered I and II. You have to take the given two statements to be true even if they seem to be at variance from commonly known facts. Read the conclusions and then decide which of the given conclusions logically follows from the two given statements, disregarding commonly known facts.*

Give answer (a) if only conclusion I follows; (b) if only conclusion II follows; (c) if either I or II follows; (d) if neither I nor II follows and (e) if both I and II follow.

1. Statements   : All planets are moons.
                    All moons are stars.   **(Bank P.O. 1996)**
   Conclusions   : I. All moons are planets.
                    II. All planets are stars.

2. Statements   : All men are dogs.
                    All dogs are cats.   **(M.B.A. 1997)**
   Conclusions   : I. All men are cats.
                    II. All cats are men.

3. Statements   : All tubes are handles.
                    All cups are handles.   **(Bank P.O. 1997)**
   Conclusions   : I. All cups are tubes.
                    II. Some handles are not cups.

4. Statements   : All bags are cakes.
                    All lamps are cakes.
   Conclusions   : I. Some lamps are bags.
                    II. No lamp is bag.

5. Statements   : All flowers are stems.
                    All stems are roots.   **(Bank P.O. 1993)**
   Conclusions   : I. All roots are flowers.
                    II. All stems are flowers.

6. Statements   : All puppets are dolls.
                    All dolls are toys.
   Conclusions   : I. Some toys are puppets.
                    II. All toys are puppets.

7. Statements   : All apples are oranges.
                    Some oranges are papayas.   **(M.B.A. 1998)**
   Conclusions   : I. Some apples are papayas.
                    II. Some papayas are apples.

8. Statements   : Some players are singers.
                    All singers are tall.   **(Bank P.O. 1998)**
   Conclusions   : I. Some players are tall.
                    II. All players are tall.

9. Statements   : All coins are crows.
                    Some crows are pens.   **(Bank P.O. 1997)**
   Conclusions   : I. No pen is coin.
                    II. Some coins are pens.

10. **Statements**   : All men are married.
    Some men are educated.   **(M.B.A. 1997)**
    Conclusions : I. Some married are educated.
    II. Some educated are married.

11. **Statements**   : All cars are tables.
    Some children are tables.   **(Hotel Management, 1992)**
    Conclusions : I. Some cars are children.
    II. Some children are cars.

12. **Statements**   : All windows are needles.
    Some trees are windows.   **(Bank P.O. 1996)**
    Conclusions : I. Some trees are needles.
    II. Some trees are not needles.

13. **Statements**   : Some dogs bark.
    All dogs bite.
    Conclusions : I. Those dogs who do not bark, also bite.
    II. Those dogs who do not bark, not necessarily bite.

14. **Statements**   : Some fools are intelligent.
    Some intelligent are great.   **(Bank P.O. 1998)**
    Conclusions : I. Some fools are great.
    II. All great are intelligent.

15. **Statements**   : Some papers are files.
    Some files are pens.   **(Bank P.O. 1997)**
    Conclusions : I. Some files are not pens.
    II. Some pens are papers.

16. **Statements**   : Some bottles are pencils.
    Some pencils are glasses.   **(Bank P.O. 1996)**
    Conclusions : I. No glass is bottle.
    II. Some bottles are glasses.

17. **Statements**   : Some soldiers are famous.
    Some soldiers are intelligent.
    Conclusions : I. Some soldiers are either famous or intelligent.
    II. Some soldiers are neither famous nor intelligent.

18. **Statements**   : All boys are honest.
    Sachin is honest.
    Conclusions : I. Sachin is a boy.
    II. All honest persons are boys.

19. **Statements**   : Lawyers married only fair girls.
    Shobha is very fair.
    Conclusions : I. Shobha was married to a lawyer.
    II. Shobha was not married to a lawyer.

20. **Statements**   : Sohan is a good sportsman.
    Sportsmen are healthy.
    Conclusions : I. All healthy persons are sportsmen.
    II. Sohan is healthy.

21. Statements : All students in my class are intelligent.
Rohit is not intelligent. **(Asstt. Grade, 1992)**

Conclusions : I. Rohit is not a student of my class.

II. Rohit must work hard.

22. Statements : All hill stations have a sun-set point.
X is a hill station.

Conclusions : I. X has a sun-set point.

II. Places other than hill stations do not have sun-set points.

23. Statements : Some sticks are bolts.
Kite is a stick.

Conclusions : I. Some bolts are sticks.

II. Some kites are bolts.

24. Statements : Some men are educated.
Educated persons prefer small families.

Conclusions : I. All small families are educated.

II. Some men prefer small families.

25. Statements : Some nurses are nuns.
Madhu is a nun. **(M.B.A. 1998)**

Conclusions : I. Some nuns are nurses.

II. Some nurses are not nuns.

26. Statements : All lamps are hooks.
No hook is coloured. **(Bank P.O. 1996)**

Conclusions : I. Some lamps are coloured.

II. No lamp is coloured.

27. Statements : All windows are doors.
No door is wall.

Conclusions : I. No window is wall.

II. No wall is door.

28. Statements : All locks are keys.
No key is a spoon.

Conclusions : I. No lock is a spoon.

II. No spoon is a lock.

29. Statements : All young scientists are open-minded.
No open-minded men are superstitious.

Conclusions : I. No scientist is superstitious.

II. No young people are superstitious.

30. Statements : All plants are trees.
No tree is green.

Conclusions : I. Some plants are green.

II. Those plants which are not trees are green.

31. Statements : No magazine is cap.
All caps are cameras. **(Bank P.O. 1997)**

Conclusions : I. No camera is magazine.

II. Some caps are magazines.

32. Statements : Some shirts are biscuits.
                     No biscuit is book.

Conclusions : I. Some shirts are books.
                   II. Some books are biscuits.

33. Statements : Some books are pens.
                     No pen is pencil.   **(Bank P.O. 1998)**

Conclusions : I. Some books are pencils.
                   II. No book is pencil.

34. Statements : No women can vote.
                     Some women are politicians.

Conclusions : I. Male politicians can vote.
                   II. Some politicians can vote.

35. Statements : Some books are toys.
                     No toy is red.   **(Bank P.O. 1997)**

Conclusions : I. Some books are red.
                   II. Some books are not red.

36. Statements : All birds are dogs.
                     Some dogs are cats.   **(C.B.I. 1997)**

Conclusions : I. Some cats are not dogs.
                   II. All dogs are not birds.

37. Statements : Many books are rocks.
                     All rocks are clips.

Conclusions : I. Some books are clips.
                   II. No rock is a book.

38. Statements : Most clocks are fans.
                     Some fans are walls.

Conclusions : I. Some walls are fans.
                   II. Some clocks are walls.

39. Statements : No man is a donkey.
                     Rahul is a man.

Conclusions : I. Rahul is not a donkey.
                   II. All men are not Rahul.

40. Statements : All poles are guns.
                     Some boats are not poles.   **(M.B.A. 1997)**

Conclusions : I. All guns are boats.
                   II. Some boats are not guns.

ANSWERS

1. (*b*) : Since both the statements are affirmative, the conclusion must be affirmative. However, conclusion I cannot follow as it contains the middle term. So, only conclusion II follows.

2. (*a*) : Since both the premises are affirmative, the conclusion must be affirmative. However, conclusion II being an A type proposition, distributes the term 'goats'. Since the term 'goats' is distributed in II without being distributed in any of the premises, so conclusion II cannot follow. Thus, only I follows.

3. (*d*) : Both the premises are A type propositions. So, in either, the middle term 'handles' forming the predicate is not distributed.

Since the middle term is not distributed even once in the premises, so no conclusion follows.

4. (*d*) : Both the premises being A type propositions, the middle term 'cakes' forming the predicate is not distributed in any of them.

Since the middle term is not distributed even once in the premises, so no conclusion follows.

5. (*d*) : Conclusion I being an A type proposition, distributes the term 'roots'. Since the term 'roots' is distributed in I without being distributed in any of the premises, so conclusion I cannot follow. Conclusion II cannot follow as it contains the middle term.

6. (*a*) : Conclusion II, being an A type proposition, distributes the term 'toys'. Since the term 'toys' is distributed in II without being distributed in any of the premises, so conclusion II cannot follow. So, only I follows.

7. (*d*) : The first premise is A type and distributes the subject. So, the middle term 'oranges' which forms its predicate, is not distributed.

The second premise is I type and does not distribute either subject or predicate. So, the middle term 'oranges' forming its subject is not distributed.

Since the middle term is not distributed even once in the premises, so no conclusion follows.

8. (*a*) : Since one premise is particular, the conclusion must be particular. So, only conclusion I follows.

9. (*d*) : Since the middle term 'crows' is not distributed even once in the premises, so no conclusion follows.

10. (*e*) : Since one premise is particular, the conclusion must be particular. So, both I and II follow.

11. (*d*) : The first premise is an A type proposition, So, the middle term 'tables' forming the predicate is not distributed.

The second premise is an I type proposition. So, the middle term forming the predicate is not distributed. Since the middle term is not distributed even once in the premises, so no conclusion follows.

12. (*a*) : Since one premise is particular, so the conclusion must be particular. Also, since the term 'needles' is distributed in II (O type proposition) without being distributed in the premises, so, conclusion II cannot follow. Thus, only I follows.

13. (*a*) : Clearly, conclusion I follows from the statements.

14. (*d*) : Since both the premises are particular, no conclusion follows as the middle term is not distributed even once in the premises.

15. (*d*) : Since both the premises are particular, so no conclusion follows.

16. (*d*) : Since both the premises are particular, so no conclusion follows.

17. (*d*) : Since both the premises are particular, so no conclusion follows.

18. (*d*) : Both the premises are A type propositions. So, the middle term 'honest' forming the predicate in each is not distributed in either.

Since the middle term is not distributed even once, no conclusion follows.

19. (*c*) : The data does not mention whether all fair girls were married to lawyers. So, either of the two conclusions may follow.

20. (*b*) : Conclusion I cannot follow as it contains the middle term, So, only conclusion II follows.

21. (*a*) : Since one premise is negative, the conclusion must be negative. So, only conclusion I follows.

22. (*a*) : Since both the premises are affirmative, the conclusion must be affirmative. So, only conclusion I follows.

23. (*d*) : The middle term 'sticks' forming the subject is not distributed in the first premise which is an I type proposition. The middle term forming the predicate is not distributed in second premise as it is an A type proposition and distributes subject only.
Since middle term is not distributed even once, no conclusion follows.

24. (*b*) : Since one premise is particular, the conclusion must be particular. So, only conclusion II follows.

25. (*d*) : Since the middle term is not distributed even once in the premises, so no conclusion follows.

26. (*b*) : Since one premise is negative, the conclusion must be negative. So, only conclusion II follows.

27. (*a*) : Since one premise is negative, the conclusion must be negative. Conclusion II cannot follow as it contains the middle term. So, only conclusion I follows.

28. (*a*) : Since one premise is negative, the conclusion must be negative. So, I follows. But the reverse is not necessarily true. So, II does not follow.

29. (*d*) : The subject in both the conclusions is vague. The true conclusion is 'No young scientist is superstitious'. So, neither conclusion follows.

30. (*d*) : Since one premise is negative, the conclusion must be negative. So, neither conclusion follows.

31. (*d*) : Since one premise is negative, the conclusion must be negative. So, II cannot follow. Also, the term 'camera' is distributed in I without being distributed in any of the premises. So, conclusion I also does not follow.

32. (*d*) : Since one premise is negative, so conclusion must be negative. So, neither I nor II follows.

33. (*d*) : Since one premise is negative, the conclusion must be negative. So, conclusion I cannot follow.
Since one premise is particular, the conclusion must be particular. Also, the term 'books' is distributed in II without being distributed in any of the premises. So, II also cannot follow.

34. (*d*) : Since one premise is negative, the conclusion must be negative. So, neither conclusion follows.

35. (*b*) : Since one premise is negative, the conclusion must be negative. So, I cannot follow. Thus, only II follows.

36. (*d*) : Since the middle term is not distributed even once in the premises, no conclusion follows.

37. (*a*) : Since the first premise is particular, the conclusion must be particular. So, only conclusion I follows.

38. (*d*) : Since both the premises are particular, no conclusion follows.

39. (*a*) : Since one premise is negative, the conclusion must be negative. Conclusion II cannot follow as it contains the middle term. So, only conclusion I follows.

40. (*d*) : Clearly, the term 'guns' is distributed in both the conclusions without being distributed in any of the premises. So, no conclusion follows.

EXERCISE 1B

Directions : *In each questions below are given two statements followed by two conclusions numbered I and II. You have to take the given two statements to be true even if they seem to be at variance from commonly known facts. Read the conclusions and then decide which of the the given conclusions logically follows from the two given statements, disregarding commonly known facts.*

Give answer (a) if only conclusion I follows; (b) if only conclusion II follows; (c) if either I or II follows; (d) if neither I nor II follows and (e) if both I and II follow.

1. **Statements** : All dogs are jackals.
   Some jackals are crows. **(Bank P.O. 1994)**

   Conclusions : I. Some dogs are crows.
   II. All dogs are crows.

2. **Statements** : Some children are adults.
   Some adults are old.

   Conclusions : I. Some children are not old.
   II. Some adults are not old.

3. **Statements** : All keys are locks.
   All locks are screws. **(Bank P.O. 1998)**

   Conclusions : I. All screws are keys.
   II. Some locks are keys.

4. **Statements** : All poets are readers.
   No reader is wise.

   Conclusions : I. No poet is wise.
   II. All readers are poets.

5. **Statements** : Some kites are horses.
   All horses are dogs.

   Conclusions : I. All dogs are horses.
   II. Some dogs are horses.

6. **Statements** : Some calendars are sticks.
   No stick is flower. **(Bank P.O. 1996)**

   Conclusions : I. Some calendars are flowers.
   II. No calendar is flower.

7. **Statements** : Most crops are machines.
   Some machines are fools.

   Conclusions : I. Some fools are machines.
   II. Some crops are fools.

8. **Statements** : Some flies are ants.
   All insects are ants.

   Conclusions : I. All flies are ants.
   II. Some ants are insects.

9. **Statements** : Some stones are cups.
   Some cups are black.

   Conclusions : I. Some black are not cups.
   II. Some cups are stones.

10. **Statements** : All goats are wolves.
    Some wolves are tigers.

    Conclusions : I. Some goats are tigers.
    II. Tigers which are wolves are not goats.

11. **Statements** : Some phones are watches.
    All watches are guns. **(Bank P.O. 1992)**

    Conclusions : I. All guns are watches.
    II. Some guns are phones.

12. **Statements** : All teachers are good.
    Some women are teachers.
    Conclusions : I. All good teachers are women.
    II. Some women are good.

13. **Statements** : All roads are poles.
    No pole is house.
    Conclusions : I. Some roads are houses.
    II. Some houses are poles.

14. **Statements** : Some pastries are toffees.
    All toffees are chocolates. **(R.B.I. 1997)**
    Conclusions : I. Some chocolates are toffees.
    II. Some toffees are not pastries.

15. **Statements** : Some chairs are stools.
    Table is a chair.
    Conclusions : I. Some stools are chairs.
    II. Table is not a stool.

16. **Statements** : All tigers are ships.
    Some ships are cupboards.
    Conclusions : I. Some tigers are cupboards.
    II. Some cupboards are tigers.

17. **Statements** : Some vegetables are fruits.
    No fruit is black. **(Bank P.O. 1998)**
    Conclusions : I. Some fruits are vegetables.
    II. No fruit is black.

18. **Statements** : Some aeroplanes are living beings.
    Some non-living beings are ghosts.
    Conclusions : I. Some aeroplanes are ghosts.
    II. Some aeroplanes are not ghosts.

19. **Statements** : All dresses are shoes.
    No shoe is brown.
    Conclusions : I. No dresses are brown.
    II. Some shoes are dresses.

20. **Statements** : Some boys are men.
    No man is black. **(Bank P.O. 1997)**
    Conclusions : I. Some boys are not black.
    II. Some men are boys.

21. **Statements** : All stones are diamonds.
    Some diamonds are pearls.
    Conclusions : I. Some pearls are stones.
    II. All diamonds are pearls.

22. **Statements** : Some parrots are crows.
    No crow is green.
    Conclusions : I. No parrot is green.
    II. No crow is white.

23. Statements : All cows are Rambha.
Some buffaloes are Rambha.

Conclusions : I. All Rambhas are not cows.

II. Some Rambhas are not buffaloes.

Directions (*Questions 24-25*) : *In the following questions, select one alternative in which the third statement is implied by the first two statements.*

(Assistant Grade, 1994)

24. (*a*) All elephants are wild. All lions are wild. So, all lions are elephants.

(*b*) All mangoes are red. Some apples are mangoes. So, all apples are red.

(*c*) All roads are boxes. All foxes are roads. So, all boxes are foxes.

(*d*) All XYZ can run. All ABC are XYZ. So, all ABC can run.

25. (*a*) All dogs are mad. All sick persons are mad. So, all sick persons are dogs.

(*b*) All oranges are black. All figs are oranges. So, all figs are black.

(*c*) All windows are dogs. Some doors are dogs. So, all windows are doors.

(*d*) No man can fly. No kite can fly. So, all men are kites.

Directions (*Questions 26 to 30*) : *In each of the following questions, two statements P and Q are given. They may look factually absurd. You have to ignore this absurdity and concentrate only upon the logic involved in each statement.*

Mark your answer as

(*a*) *if both P and Q are true;*

(*b*) *if both P and Q are false or doubtful;*

(*c*) *if P is true and Q is false or doubtful;*

(*d*) *if P is false or doubtful and Q is true.*

26. P : Jackals live in forests. Cities are in forests. Therefore jackals live in cities.

Q : Some tables are grass. All stools are grass. Therefore all tables are stools.

27. P : Cups play chess. Chess is a difficult game. Therefore cups play a difficult game.

Q : Reena is a girl. All girls are timid. Therefore Reena is timid.

28. P : Some musicians are not rich. All musicians are polite. Therefore not all polite persons are rich.

Q : All musicians are rich. No rich person is polite. Therefore musicians are not polite.

29. P : Some mangoes are apples. All grapes are mangoes. Therefore all apples are grapes.

Q : Some mangoes are apples. All apples are grapes. Therefore some mangoes are grapes.

30. P : All fish can fly. Some fish are birds. All birds are naughty. Therefore some naughty can fly.

Q : Some fish are birds. All birds are naughty. Therefore all fish are naughty.

ANSWERS

1. (*d*) : Since the middle term is not distributed even once in the premises, no conclusion follows.

2. (*d*) : Since both the premises are particular, no conclusion follows.

3. (*d*) : The term 'screws' is distributed in conclusion I without being distributed in any of the premises. So, I cannot follow. Also, conclusion II cannot follow as it contains the middle term.

4. (*a*) : Since one premise is negative, the conclusion must be negative. So, only conclusion I follows.

5. (*d*) : None of the conclusions follows as both contain the middle term.

6. (*d*) : Since one premise is particular, the conclusion must be particular. So, II cannot follow. Since one premise is negative, the conclusion must be negative. So, I cannot follow.

7. (*d*) : Since both the premises are particular, no conclusion follows.

8. (*d*) : Since the middle term is not distributed even once in the premises, no conclusion follows.

9. (*d*) : Since both the premises are particular, no conclusion follows.

10. (*d*) : Since the middle term is not distributed even once in the premises, no conclusion follows.

11. (*b*) : Since one premise is particular, the conclusion must be particular. So, only conclusion II follows.

12. (*b*) : Since one premise is particular, the conclusion must be particular. So, only conclusion II follows.

13. (*d*) : Since one premise is negative, the conclusion must be negative. So, neither conclusion follows.

14. (*d*) : Neither conclusion I nor II follows as both contain the middle term.

15. (*d*) : The first premise is an I type proposition. So, the middle term 'chairs' forming the subject is not distributed.
The second premise is an A type proposition. So, the middle term 'chairs' forming the predicate is not distributed.
Since the middle term is not distributed even once, no conclusion follows.

16. (*d*) : Since the middle term is not distributed even once in the premises, no conclusion follows.

17. (*d*) : Since one premise is particular, the conclusion must be particular. So, II cannot follow. Since one premise is negative, the conclusion must be negative. So, I cannot follow.

18. (*d*) : Since both the premises are particular, no conclusion follows.

19. (*a*) : Since one premise is negative, the conclusion must be negative. So, only conclusion I follows.

20. (*a*) : Since one premise is negative, the conclusion must be negative. So, II does not follow and only I follows.

21. (*d*) : Since the middle term is not distributed even once in the premises, no conclusion follows.

22. (*d*) : Since one premise is particular, the conclusion must be particular. So, neither I nor II follows.

23. (*d*) : Since the middle term is not distributed even once in the premises, no conclusion follows.

24. (*d*)   25. (*b*)   26. (*b*)   27. (*a*)   28. (*a*)   29. (*d*)   30. (*c*)

TYPE 2
(When more than two conclusions are given)

In this type of questions, two statements called premises are given, followed by four conclusions. The candidate is required to find out which of the conclusions logically follow from the given premises. More than one conclusion may also follow. In such questions, first the given statements are analysed. If the middle term is not distributed even once, no conclusion follows. Thus, the middle term must be distributed at least once. To derive the correct conclusions, we usually take the help of Venn diagrams. Also, no conclusion follows in the following cases :

(*i*) If both the premises are particular

(*ii*) If both the premises are negative

However, in some cases, more than one Venn diagrams may be possible. In such cases, all the possible Venn diagrams are drawn and the solution is derived from each of these separately. Finally, the solution common to all the diagrams is taken as the answer.

ILLUSTRATIVE EXAMPLES

Ex. 1. Statements : All books are cakes.

All cakes are apples.

Conclusions :   I. Some cakes are books.

II. No cake is book.

III. Some apples are books.

IV. All apples are books.

(a) Only I follows   (b) Only either I or II follows

(c) Only I and III follow   (d) Only either III or IV follows

(e) None follows

Sol. For the given statements, the Venn diagram is as shown where B indicates books, C indicates cakes and A indicates apples.

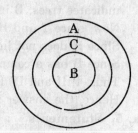

Now, since B has a common area with C, so I follows while II does not. Also, B has a common area with A but does not entirely lie within A. So III follows while IV does not.

Thus, only I and III follow.

Hence, the answer is (c).

Ex. 2. Statements : Some flowers are apples.

Some apples are stones.

Conclusions :   I. No flower is stone.

II. All apples are stones.

III. Some stones are flowers.

IV. No apple is flower.

(a) Only either I or III follows   (b) Only I and IV follow

(c) Only II and III follow   (d) Only I, III and IV follow

(e) None follows

Sol. Since both the statements or premises are particular, no conclusion follows.

Hence, the answer is (e).

Ex. 3. Statements : All leaves are papers.

Some papers are pictures.

Conclusions :   I. All pictures are papers.

II. All pictures are leaves.

III. Some leaves are pictures.

IV. No leaf is a picture.

(a) Only I, III and IV follow   (b) Only II and III follow

(c) Only III and IV follow   (d) Only III follows

(e) None of these

Sol. Clearly, here the middle term is 'papers'. Now, the first premise is an A type proposition and distributes the subject only. So, the middle term 'papers' forming the predicate, is not distributed. The second premise is an I type proposition and distributes neither the subject nor the predicate. So, the middle term 'papers' forming the subject, is not distributed.

Since the middle term is not distributed even once in the premises, no conclusion follows.

Hence, the answer is (e).

Ex. 4. Statements : Some trees are buses.
All buses are hats. **(S.B.I.P.O. 1997)**

Conclusions : I. Some trees are hats.
II. Some hats are trees.
III. All hats are buses.
IV. Some buses are hats.

(*a*) None follows (*b*) Only I, II and IV follow
(*c*) Only II, III and IV follow (*d*) All follow
(*e*) None of these

Sol. Clearly, the Venn diagram is as shown where T indicates trees, B indicates buses and H indicates hats. Now, since T and H have a common area, so I follows. Since H does not lie entirely within B, so III does not follow. Since B has a common area with H, so III follows. Thus, I, II and IV follow.

Hence, the answer is (*b*).

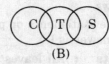

Ex. 5. Statements : Some trucks are scooters.
No scooter is cycle. **(Bank P.O. 1996)**

Conclusions : I. No truck is cycle.
II. No scooter is truck.
III. Some trucks are cycles.
IV. Some scooters are trucks.

(*a*) None follows (*b*) Only I and III follow
(*c*) Only IV follows (*d*) Only I, II and IV follow
(*e*) All follow

Sol. Clearly two Venn diagrams are possible :

(A)   (B)

From (A), only I and IV follow.
From (B), only III and IV follow.
The solution common to both the above diagrams is 'Only IV follows'.
Hence, the answer is (*c*).

Ex. 6. Statements : All papers are bags.
No bag is green. **(Bank P.O. 1995)**

Conclusions : I. No paper is green.
II. Some papers are green.
III. Some green are papers.
IV. Some bags are papers.

(*a*) Either I or II follows (*b*) Either II or III follows
(*c*) Only I and III follow (*d*) Only I and IV follow
(*e*) None of these

Sol. Clearly, the Venn diagram is as shown.

Since P and G are disjoint, so I follows, while
II and III do not.

Since P and B have a common area, so IV follows.

Thus, I and IV follow.

Hence, the answer is (*d*).

Ex. 7. **Statements** : All apples are brinjals.
　　　　　　　　　　All brinjals are ladyfingers.
　　　　　　　　　　All ladyfingers are oranges.

　　　　Conclusions : I. Some oranges are brinjals.
　　　　　　　　　　II. All brinjals are apples.
　　　　　　　　　　III. Some apples are oranges.
　　　　　　　　　　IV. All ladyfingers are apples.

(*a*) None follows　　　　(*b*) All follow　　　　(*c*) Only I and III follow

(*d*) Either I or III follows　(*e*) None of these　　　　(S.B.I.P.O. 1995)

Sol. Clearly, there are following three possible Venn diagrams :

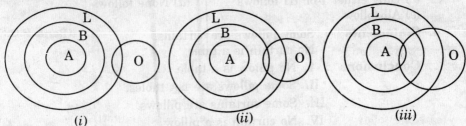

　　　(*i*)　　　　　　　　　(*ii*)　　　　　　　　　(*iii*)

From (*i*), none of the conclusions follows.

From (*ii*), only conclusion I follows.

From (*iii*), only conclusions I and III follow.

Thus, the combined solution is : None follows.

EXERCISE 1C

Directions : *In each question below are given two statements followed by four conclusions numbered I, II, III, and IV. You have to take the two given statements to be true even if they seem to be at variance from the commonly known facts. Read all the conclusions and then decide which of the given conclusions logically follows from the two given statements, disregarding commonly known facts.*

1. **Statements** : All green are blue.
　　　　　　　　　All blue are white.　　　　　　　(S.B.I.P.O. 1994)

　　　Conclusions : I. Some blue are green.
　　　　　　　　　　II. Some white are green.
　　　　　　　　　　III. Some green are not white.
　　　　　　　　　　IV. All white are blue.

(*a*) Only I and II follow　　　　(*b*) Only I and III follow

(*c*) Only I and IV follow　　　　(*d*) Only II and IV follow

(*e*) All follow

2. Statements : All windows are rods.
Some rods are frames.

Conclusions : I. All frames are rods.
II. All frames are windows.
III. Some windows are frames.
IV. No window is a frame.

(a) Only I follows (b) Only II and III follow
(c) Only either II or III follows (d) Only either I or IV follows
(e) None follows

3. Statements : Some clothes are marbles.
Some marbles are bags.

Conclusions : I. No cloth is a bag.
II. All marbles are bags.
III. Some bags are clothes.
IV. No marble is a cloth.

(a) Only either I or IV follows (b) Only either I or II follows
(c) Only either I or III follows (d) None follows
(e) All follow

4. Statements : Some pillows are curtains.
No curtain is a table.

Conclusions : I. No pillow is a table.
II. Some pillows are not tables.
III. Some curtains are pillows.
IV. No curtain is a pillow.

(a) Only I and III follow (b) Only II and III follow
(c) None follows (d) All follow
(e) Only either I or IV follows

5. Statements : Some frogs are bricks.
All bricks are cakes. **(S.B.I.P.O. 1997)**

Conclusions : I. Some cakes are not frogs.
II. Some cakes are frogs.
III. No cake is frog.
IV. All frogs are cakes.

(a) None follows (b) Only I and II follow
(c) Only I, II and IV follow (d) Only II, III and IV follow
(e) All follow

6. Statements : No parrot is crow.
All crows are bats. **(Bank P.O. 1994)**

Conclusions : I. Some bats are parrots.
II. All bats are parrots.
III. Some bats are crows.
IV. Some bats are not crows.

(a) None follows (b) Only I and II follow
(c) Only I, II and III follow (d) Only II, III and IV follow
(e) Only III and IV follow

7. Statements : Some students are brilliant.
                    Sushma is a student.

Conclusions : I. Some students are dull.
                   II. Sushma is brilliant.
                   III. Sushma is dull.
                   IV. Students are usually brilliant.

(a) Only I follows   (b) Only I and II follow
(c) Only II follows   (d) None follows
(e) All follow

8. Statements : All rats are cows.
                    No cow is white.   **(Bank P.O. 1997)**

Conclusions : I. No white is rat.
                   II. No rat is white.
                   III. Some whites are rats.
                   IV. All cows are rats.

(a) None follows   (b) Only I and IV follow
(c) Only II and IV follow   (d) Only IV follows
(e) None of these

9. Statements : Some camels are ships.
                    No ship is a boat.

Conclusions : I. Some ships are camels.
                   II. Some boats are camels.
                   III. Some camels are not boats.
                   IV. All boats are camels.

(a) Only I follows   (b) Only II and III follow
(c) Only I and III follow   (d) Only I and II follow
(e) Only either III or IV follows

10. Statements : Some trees are pens.
                     All pens are erasers.   **(Bank P.O. 1995)**

Conclusions : I. All erasers are pens.
                   II. All trees are pens.
                   III. Some trees which are not pens are erasers.
                   IV. Some erasers are trees.

(a) All follow   (b) Only I and II follow
(c) Only III and IV follow   (d) Only IV follows
(e) None of these

11. Statements : All chairs laugh.
                     Some birds laugh.

Conclusions : I. All chairs are birds.
                   II. Some birds are chairs.
                   III. Those who do not laugh are not chairs.
                   IV. Some birds do not laugh.

(a) Only II follows   (b) Only I follows
(c) Only II and IV follow   (d) Only IV follows
(e) None follows

20 *Reasoning*

12. Statements : No educationists are researchers.
All researchers are teachers.　　　　**(Bank P.O. 1996)**
Conclusions : I. No teacher is researcher.
II. No teacher is educationist.
III. Some researchers are teachers.
IV. Some teachers are researchers.

(a) Only II follows　　　　　　　　(b) None follows
(c) Either I or III follows　　　　　(d) Only III and IV follow
(e) All follow

13. Statements : All bags are chalks.
All chalks are bottles.　　　　**(S.B.I.P.O. 1997)**
Conclusions : I. Some bottles are bags.
II. All bags are bottles.
III. All bottles are bags.
IV. Some chalks are not bags.

(a) Only I, II and IV follow　　　　(b) Only I, III and IV follow
(c) Only II, III and IV follow　　　(d) All follow
(e) None of these

14. Statements : No fan is shirt.
All shirts are trousers.
Conclusions : I. All fans are trousers.
II. No fan is trouser.
III. Some trousers are shirts.
IV. All trousers are shirts.

(a) Only I follows　　　　　　　　(b) Only II follows
(c) Only either I or II follows　　　(d) Only III and IV follow
(e) None of these

15. Statements : Some cubs are tigers.
Some tigers are goats.　　　　**(Bank P.O. 1994)**
Conclusions : I. Some cubs are goats.
II. No cub is goat.
III. All cubs are goats.
IV. All goats are cubs.

(a) Only either I or II follows　　　(b) Only either II or III follows
(c) Only either I or IV follows　　　(d) Only either II or IV follows
(e) None of these

16. Statements : Some coolers are watches.
No watch is bed.
Conclusions : I. No watch is cooler.
II. No cooler is watch.
III. Some watches are beds.
IV. Some coolers are beds.

(a) None follows　　　　　　　　(b) Only I and IV follow
(c) Only either II or III follows　　(d) Only either III or IV follows
(e) Only either II or IV follows

17. Statements : Some men are goats.

All goats are jackals. **(Bank P.O. 1995)**

Conclusions : I. Some men are jackals.

II. Some jackals are men.

III. All jackals are goats.

IV. Some goats are men.

(a) Only I and II follow

(b) Only III and IV follow

(c) Only IV follows

(d) All follow

(e) None of these

18. Statements : All sparrows are koels.

No koel is parrot.

Conclusions : I. No sparrow is parrot.

II. Some sparrows are parrots.

III. All koels are sparrows.

IV. Some parrots are sparrows.

(a) Only I follows

(b) None follows

(c) Only II and III follow

(d) Only II and IV follow

(e) None of these

19. Statements : All typists are stenographers.

Some stenographers are boys.

Conclusions : I. All boys are stenographers.

II. All boys are typists.

III. Some typists are boys.

IV. No typist is a boy.

(a) Only I follows

(b) Only II and III follow

(c) Only either II or III follows

(d) Only either I or IV follows

(e) None follows

Directions (*Questions 20 to 26*) : *In each question below are given two statements followed by five conclusions numbered (a), (b), (c), (d) and (e). You have to take the two given statements to be true even if they seem to be at variance from the commonly known facts. Read the conclusions and then decide which of the given conclusions logically follows from the two given statements.*

20. Statements : All novels are stories.

All stories are songs.

Conclusions : (a) All novels are songs.

(b) Some novels are songs.

(c) Some songs are novels.

(d) All stories are not songs.

(e) None of these

21. Statements : All belts are socks.

All shirts are belts.

Conclusions : (a) All shirts are socks.

(b) Some belts are shirts.

(c) No shirt is socks.

(d) Some socks are shirts.

(e) None of these

22. Statements : Some tables are curtains.

Some tables are toys.

Conclusions : (a) All tables which are not curtains are toys.

(b) Some curtains are toys.

(c) There are some tables which are neither curtains nor toys.

(d) All tables are either curtains or toys.

(e) None of these

23. Statements : Manas is a player.

All the players are tall.

Conclusions : (a) Manas is tall.

(b) All tall men are players.

(c) Tall men are not players.

(d) Manas is not tall.

(e) None of these

24. Statements : All businessmen are dishonest.

All businessmen are fraudulent.

Conclusions : (a) Either all fraudulent persons are dishonest or all dishonest

are fraudulent.

(b) Some dishonest persons are fraudulent.

(c) Generally fraudulent persons are dishonest.

(d) Fraud and dishonesty go together.

25. Statements : All men are vertebrates.

Some mammals are vertebrates.   **(Assistant Grade, 1993)**

Conclusions : (a) All men are mammals.

(b) All mammals are men.

(c) Some vertebrates are mammals.

(d) All vertebrates are men.

(e) None of these

26. Statements : All knowledge is good.

All knowledge is difficult.

Conclusions : (a) Some good things are difficult.

(b) All difficult things are knowledge.

(c) All good things are difficult.

(d) Easy things are not knowledge.

27. If the statement 'Some teachers are not learned' is false, which of the following is false ?

(a) All teachers are learned.   (b) Some learned beings are teachers.

(c) Some teachers are learned.   (d) All learned beings are teachers.

(e) None of these

Directions (Questions 28 to 35) : *In each question below, there are some statements followed by four conclusions numbered I, II, III and IV. Read all the conclusions and then decide which of the given conclusions logically follows from the given statements, disregarding commonly know facts.*

28. Statements : All teachers are doctors.
All doctors are engineers.
All engineers are students.   **(Bank P.O. 1995)**

Conclusions : I. Some students are teachers.
II. All doctors are students.
III. Some engineers are teachers.
IV. All doctors are teachers.

(*a*) Only I and II follow   (*b*) Only I and III follow
(*c*) Either I or II, and III follow   (*d*) Either II or IV follows
(*e*) None of these

29. Statements : Some birds are insects.
All birds are butterflies.
All insects are snakes.   **(S.B.I.P.O. 1995)**

Conclusions : I. Some snakes are birds.
II. Some butterflies are insects.
III. Some snakes are butterflies.
IV. Some insects are birds.

(*a*) None follows   (*b*) Either I or III follows
(*c*) All follow   (*d*) Only IV follows
(*e*) None of these

30. Statements : Some bananas are apples.
All apples are tomatoes.
Some potatoes are tomatoes.

Conclusions : I. Some bananas are tomatoes.
II. Some potatoes are bananas.
III. Some apples are potatoes.
IV. Some apples are bananas.

(*a*) Only I follows   (*b*) Only I and II follow
(*c*) Only I and IV follow   (*d*) Either II or III, and I follow
(*e*) None of these

31. Statements : All boxes are pans.
Some boxes are jugs.
Some jugs are glasses.

Conclusions : I. Some glasses are boxes.
II. No glass is box.
III. Some jugs are pans.
IV. No jug is pan.

(*a*) Only I and II follow   (*b*) Either I or II, and III follow
(*c*) Only III follows   (*d*) Either I or II, and either III or IV follow
(*e*) None of these

32. Statements : Some books are papers.
Some papers are cars.
No car is white.   **(Bank P.O. 1996)**

Conclusions : I. Some papers are not white.

II. All papers are not white.

III. Some papers are white.

IV. Some books are white.

(a) Only I follows

(b) Only I and IV follow

(c) Only I, III and IV follow

(d) Either II or III follows

(e) None of these

33. Statements : All trolleys are pulleys.

Some pulleys are chains.

All chains are bells.

Conclusions : I. Some bells are trolleys.

II. No bell is trolley.

III. Some pulleys are bells.

IV. All chains are pulleys.

(a) None follows

(b) Either I or II follows

(c) Only III and IV follow

(d) Either I or II, and III follow

(e) I and II, and either III or IV follow

34. Statements : Some newspapers are radios.

Some radios are televisions.

No television is a magazine. **(S.B.I.P.O. 1995)**

Conclusions : I. No newspaper is a magazine.

II. No radio is a magazine.

III. Some radios are not magazines.

IV. Some newspapers are televisions.

(a) None follows

(b) Only I and II follow

(c) Either I or II follows

(d) Only III follows

(e) None of these

35. Statements : Some doors are windows.

All windows are black.

Some black are brown. **(Bank P.O. 1995)**

Conclusions : I. Some windows are brown.

II. All doors are black.

III. Some doors are black.

IV. No window is brown.

(a) Only II follows

(b) Only III follows

(c) Only IV follows

(d) Either I or IV, and III follow

(e) None of these

ANSWERS

1. (a) : G and B have some area in common.

So, I follows.

G and W have some area in common.

So, II follows.

III does not always hold.

Since B lies within W, so IV does not follow.

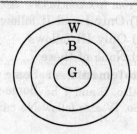

2. (*e*) : Here the first premise is an A type proposition and distributes only the subject. So, the middle term 'rods' forming its predicate is not distributed. The second premise is an I type proposition and distributes neither the subject nor the predicate. So, the middle term 'rods' forming the subject is not distributed. Since the middle term is not distributed even once in the premises, no conclusion follows.

3. (*d*) : Since both the premises are particular, no conclusion follows.

4. (*b*) : Clearly, for the given data two Venn diagrams A and B are possible.

From diagram A, conclusions I, II and III follow.
From diagram B, conclusions II and III follow.
The solution common to the two diagrams is : II and III follow.

5. (*b*) : Clearly, it follows from the Venn diagram that some cakes are frogs and some are not *i.e.* conclusions I and II follow but conclusions III and IV cannot follow.

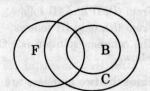

6. (*e*) : Clearly, two Venn diagrams (*i*) and (*ii*) are possible as shown.
From diagram (*i*), conclusions III and IV follow.
From diagram (*ii*), conclusions I, III and IV follow.
The common solution is : Only III and IV follow.

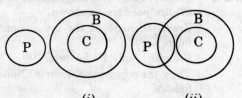

7. (*a*) : Clearly the area not common to Students and Brilliant will represent the dull students in the Venn diagram. So, conclusion I follows.

8. (*e*) : Clearly, in the adjoining Venn diagram, since R and W are disjoint, so I and II follow while III does not.
Since C does not lie entirely within R, so IV does not follow.

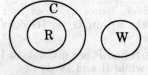

9. (*c*) : Clearly, two Venn diagrams (i) and (ii) are possible as shown :

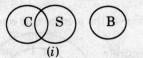 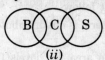

From (*i*), conclusions I and III follow.
From (*ii*), conclusions I, II and III follow.
The common solution is : Only I and III follow.

10. (*c*) : Since E and T do not lie entirely within P, so neither I nor II follows. Since some area common to T and E lies outside P, so III follows.
Also, E and T have a common area.
So, IV also follows.

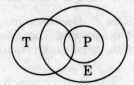

11. (*e*) : Since the middle term is not distributed even once in the premises, no conclusion follows.

12. (*d*) : Clearly, two Venn diagrams (*i*) and
(*ii*) are possible as shown.
From (*i*), II, III and IV follow.
From (*ii*), III and IV follow.
The common solution is : Only III
and IV follow.

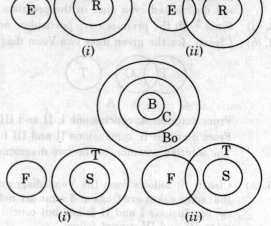

13. (*a*) : Clearly, it follows from the Venn
diagram that only conclusions I, II
and IV follow.

14. (*e*) : Clearly, two Venn diagrams (*i*) and
(*ii*) are possible as shown.
From (*i*), II and III follow.
From (*ii*), only III follows.
The common solution is : Only III
follows.

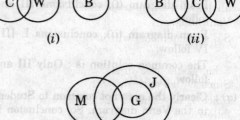

15. (*e*) : Since the two premises are particular, no conclusion follows.

16. (*a*) : Clearly, two Venn diagrams (*i*) and
(*ii*) are possible as shown.
From (*i*), none of the conclusions
follows.
From (*ii*), only IV follows.
Thus, the common solution is : None
follows.

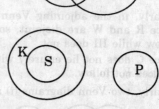

17. (*e*) : Since J and M have a common area,
so both I and II follow.
Since G and M have a common
area, so IV follows.
However, since J does not lie
entirely within G, so III does not
follow.

18. (*a*) : Since S and P are disjoint, so I fol-
lows while II and IV do not.
Since K does not lie entirely within
S, so III does not follow.

19. (*e*) : Since the middle term is not distributed even once in the premises, no conclusion follows.

20. (*a*) : Clearly, since the area for novels (N) lies entirely
within the area for songs (So), it follows that all
novels are songs. So, some songs are novels. But only
one conclusion has to follow and the most logical
conclusion is 'All novels are songs'. So, (*a*) follows.

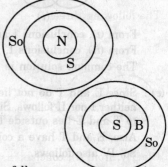

21. (*a*) : Here S denotes shirts, B denotes belts and So
denotes socks. Then, clearly conclusion (*a*) follows
with the same explanation as in Q. 20.

22. (*e*) : Since both the premises are particular, no conclusion follows.

23. (a) : Again, from the Venn diagram, conclusion (a) follows with the same
explanation as in Q. 20.

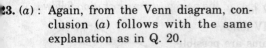

24. (b) : Clearly, being dishonest and fraudulent is a common quality of a particular
class of people. So, the Venn diagram
is as shown. Thus, (b) alone is the
logical conclusion that follows.

25. (c) : Clearly, from the given data, either
of the Venn diagrams (i) or (ii) can
follow. So, conclusion (c) which follows
from both, is the most logical conclusion.

26. (a) : Clearly, (a) is the most logical conclusion from the same explanation as in
Q. 24.

27. (d) : 'Some teachers are not learned' is false means 'All
teachers are learned'. But this does not mean that
all learned beings are teachers, as shown in the
Venn diagram.
So, statement (d) will be false.

28. (e) : S has some area in common with T. So, I follows.
Since D lies entirely within S, so II follows.
Since E has some area in common with T, so III
follows.
Since D does not lie entirely within T, IV does not
follow.

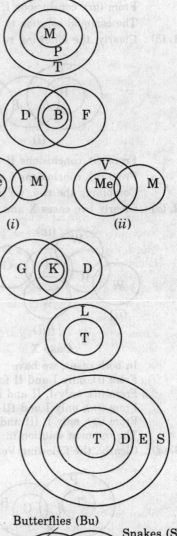

29. (c) : Since S and B, Bu and I, S and Bu, I and B have
some area in common, so all the four conclusions
follow.

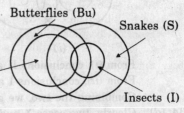

30. (c) : The following three Venn diagrams are possible :

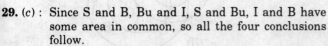

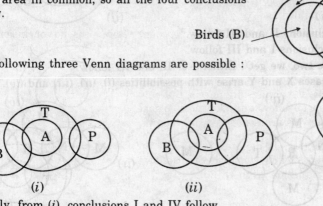

Clearly, from (i), conclusions I and IV follow.
From (ii), conclusions I, III and IV follow.

From (*iii*), conclusions I, II, III and IV follow.

The common solution is : Only I and IV follow.

31. (*b*) : Clearly, the following two Venn diagrams are possible :

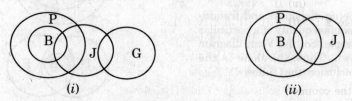

(*i*)   (*ii*)

From, (*i*), conclusions II and III follow.

From (*ii*), conclusions I and III follow.

Combining the two, we have : Either I or II, and III follow.

32. (*a*) : Clearly two cases X and Y arise with possibilities (*i*), (*ii*), (*iii*) and (*iv*).

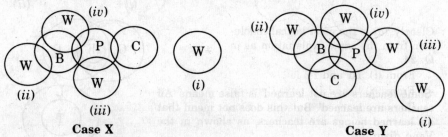

Case X   **Case Y**

In both cases, we have :

From (*i*), only I and II follow.

From (*ii*), only I, II and IV follow.

From (*iii*), only I and III follow.

From (*iv*), only I, III and IV follow.

The common solution in all the above is : Only I follows.

33. (*d*) : Clearly, the following Venn diagrams are possible :

(*i*)   (*ii*)

From (*i*), conclusions II and III follow.

From (*ii*), conclusions I and III follow.

Combining the two, we get : Either I or II, and III follow.

34. (*d*) : Clearly, two cases X and Y arise with possibilities (*i*), (*ii*), (*iii*) and (*iv*).

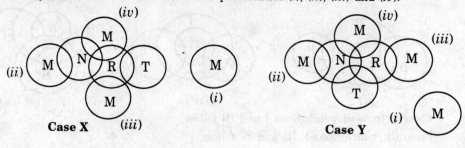

Case X   **Case Y**

Case X :   (*i*) I, II and III follow
          (*ii*) II and III follow
          (*iii*) I and III follow
          (*iv*) III follows

Case Y :   (*i*) I, II, III and IV follow
          (*ii*) II, III and IV follow
          (*iii*) I, III and IV follow
          (*iv*) III and IV follow

Thus the common solution is : Only III follows.

35. (*a*) : Clearly, the following Venn diagrams are possible :

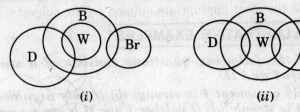

(*i*)   (*ii*)

From (*i*), III and IV follow.
From (*ii*), I and III follow.
Combining the two, we get : Either I or IV, and III follow.

2. STATEMENT — ARGUMENTS

In this type of questions, a statement concerned with a political, social or economic issue is given, followed by two arguments, generally one in favour of and one against the statement. The candidate is required to analyse first the statement, then the arguments in context of the statement and decide which of the arguments holds strong, and helps, formulate the most appropriate opinion on the subject.

ILLUSTRATIVE EXAMPLES

Directions : *Each of the following questions consists of a statement followed by two arguments I and II.*

Give answer (a) if only argument I is strong; (b) if only argument II is strong; (c) if either I or II is strong; (d) if neither I nor II is strong and (e) if both I and II are strong.

Ex. 1. Statement : Should number of holidays of government employees be reduced ?

Arguments : I. Yes. Our government employees are having maximum number of holidays among the other countries of the world.

II. Yes. It will lead to increased productivity of government offices.

(Bank P.O. 1998)

Sol. Clearly, a comparison with the system in other countries is no strong a criteria for taking a decision on the issue. So, argument I does not hold. Also, reducing the number of holidays implies more working hours which will surely increase productivity.

Hence, the answer is (b).

Ex. 2. Statement : Should foreign films be banned in India ?

Arguments : I. Yes. They depict an alien culture which adversely affects our values.

II. No. Foreign films are of a high artistic standard.

Sol. Clearly foreign films depict the alien culture but this only helps in learning more. So, argument I does not hold. Also, the reason stated in argument II is not strong enough in contradicting the ban. So, it also does not hold.

Thus, the answer is (d).

Ex. 3. Statement : Should there be reservation of seats and posts on communal basis ?

(M.A.T. 1997)

Arguments : I. Yes. It will check most of the inter-communal biases.

II. No. Ours is a secular state.

Sol. Clearly, reservations on communal basis will increase inter communal biases. So, argument I is vague. Also, it will be against the secular policy, according to which no communal group is given preference over the others. So, only argument II holds.

Hence, the answer is (b).

Ex. 4. Statement : Should young entrepreneurs be encouraged ?

    Arguments :   I. Yes. They will help in industrial development of the country.

              II. Yes. They will reduce the burden on employment market.

Sol. Clearly, encouraging the young entrepreneurs will open up the field for the establishment of new industries. Thus, it shall help in industrial development and not only employ the entrepreneurs but create more job opportunities for others as well. So, both the arguments hold strong.

Hence, the answer is (e).

Ex. 5. Statement : Should government stop spending huge amounts of money on international sports ?   **(Bank P.O. 1996)**

    Arguments :   I. Yes. This money can be utilised for upliftment of the poor.

              II. No. Sportspersons will be frustrated and will not get international exposure.

Sol. Clearly, spending money on sports cannot be avoided merely because it can be spent on socio-economic problems. So, argument I does not hold. Also if the expenses on sports are curtailed, the sportspersons would face lack of facilities and training and our country will lag behind in international sports competitions.

Hence, the answer is (b).

Ex. 6. Statement : Should octroi be abolished ?

    Arguments :   I. Yes. It will eliminate an important source of corruption.

              II. No. It will adversely affect government revenues.

Sol. 'Octroi' is a custom duty. If octroi is abolished, the practice of bringing in things from foreign countries illegally will be abolished. So, argument I holds strong. If octroi is abolished, the income to the government in the way of the duty paid shall be diminished. So, argument II also holds strong.

Hence, the answer is (e).

Ex. 7. Statement : Should taxes on colour television be further increased ?

    Arguments :   I. Yes. Colour television is a luxury item and only rich people buy them.

              II. No. Televisions are bought by the poor too.

Sol. Clearly, taxes on an item cannot be increased or decreased on the basis of the financial position of the people who buy it. So, both arguments I and II do not hold strong.

Hence, the answer is (d).

Ex. 8. Statement : Should English be the medium of instruction for higher education in India ?

    Arguments :   I. Yes. Even in advanced countries like England and U.S.A., the medium of instruction is English for higher education.

              II. Yes. English is a much widely spoken language in the world.

Sol. Clearly, the pursuance of a policy in India cannot be based on the pretext that it is followed in other advanced countries because every country has its own environment, situations and resources. So, argument I is vague. Clearly, English needs to be pursued in higher education because being widely spoken it shall ensure uniformity and prepare the students better. So, argument II holds.

Hence, the answer is (b).

EXERCISE 2A

Directions : *Each question given below consists of a statement, followed by two arguments I and II. You have to decide which of the arguments is a 'strong' argument and which is a 'weak' argument.*

Give answer (a) if only argument I is strong; (b) if only argument II is strong; (c) if either I or II is strong; (d) if neither I nor II is strong and (e) if both I and II are strong.

1. **Statement** : Should there be a ban on product advertising ?
   Arguments : I. No. It is an age of advertising. Unless your advertisement is better than your other competitors, the product will not be sold.
   II. Yes. The money spent on advertising is very huge and it inflates the cost of the product. **(S.B.I.P.O. 1995)**

2. **Statement** : Should a total ban be put on trapping wild animals ?
   Arguments : I. Yes. Trappers are making a lot of money.
   II. No. Bans on hunting and trapping are not effective.

3. **Statement** : Should telecasting feature films be stopped ?
   Arguments : I. Yes. Young children are misguided by the feature films.
   II. No. This is the only way to educate the masses.

4. **Statement** : Should school education be made free in India ? **(S.B.I.P.O. 1997)**
   Arguments : I. Yes. This is the only way to improve the level of literacy.
   II. No. It would add to the already heavy burden on the exchequer.

5. **Statement** : Is paying ransom or agreeing to the conditions of kidnappers of political figures, a proper course of action ?
   Arguments : I. Yes. The victims must be saved at all cost.
   II. No. It encourages the kidnappers to continue their sinister activities.

6. **Statement** : Should government jobs in rural areas have more incentives ?
   Arguments : I. Yes. Incentives are essential for attracting government servants there.
   II. No. Rural areas are already cheaper, healthier and less complex than big. So, why offer extra incentives !

7. **Statement** : Should India stop missile development ?
   Arguments : I. Yes. The U.S.A. desires so.
   II. No. The nation must always remain up-to-date in its defence preparedness.

8. **Statement** : Should we scrap the 'Public Distribution System' in India ?
   Arguments : I. Yes. Protectivism is over, everyone must get the bread on his/her own.
   II. Yes. The poor do not get any benefit because of corruption.
   (Bank P.O. 1998)

9. **Statement** : Should India go in for computerisation in industry ?
   Arguments : I. No. Computerisation demands a lot of money. We should not waste money on it.
   II. Yes. When advanced countries are introducing computers in India, how can India afford to lag behind ?

10. **Statement** : Is unemployment allowance justified ?
    Arguments : I. Yes. It provides financial aid to the unemployed.
    II. No. It might promote idleness among the unemployed youth.

11. **Statement** : Is buying things on instalments profitable to the customer ?
    Arguments : I. Yes. He has to pay less.
    II. No. Paying instalments upsets the family budget.

12. **Statement** : Should an organisation like UNO be dissolved ?
    Arguments : I. Yes. With cold war coming to an end, such organisations have no role to play.
    II. No. In the absence of such organisations there may be a world war. **(Bank P.O. 1996)**

13. **Statement** : Is monarchy better than democracy ?
    Arguments : I. Yes. If the chair has one confirmed ruler, there are no ambitious aspirants fighting for it.
    II. No. People are more contented and happy in democracy.

14. **Statement** : Should Doordarshan be given autonomous status ?
    Arguments : I. Yes. It will help Doordarshan to have fair and impartial coverage of all important events.
    II. No. The coverage of events will be decided by a few who may not have healthy outlook.

15. **Statement** : Should there be a complete ban on strike by government employees in India ? **(M.A.T. 1997)**
    Arguments : I. Yes. This is the only way to teach discipline to the employees.
    II. No. This deprives the citizens of their democratic rights.

16. **Statement** : Should agriculture in rural India be mechanised ?
    Arguments : I. Yes. It would lead to higher production.
    II. No. Then many villagers would be left unemployed.

17. **Statement** : Should the illiterate be debarred from voting ?
    Arguments : I. Yes. They are easily misguided.
    II. No. It is their constitutional right.

18. **Statement** : Should luxury hotels be banned in India ? **(Bank P.O. 1991)**
    Arguments : I. Yes. They are places from where international criminals operate.
    II. No. Affluent foreign tourists will have no place to stay.

19. **Statement** : Should there be students' union in college/university ?
    Arguments : I. No. This will create a political atmosphere in the campus.
    II. Yes. It is very necessary. Students are the future political leaders.

20. **Statement** : Should new big industries be started in Bombay ?
    Arguments : I. Yes. It will create job opportunities.
    II. No. It will further add to the pollution of the city.

21. **Statement** : Should internal assessment in colleges be abolished ?
    Arguments : I. Yes. This will help in reducing the possibility of favouritism.
    II. No. Teaching faculty will lose control over students.
    (Bank P.O. 1996)

22. Statement : Can pollution be controlled ?

     Arguments :   I. Yes. If everyone realises the hazard it may create and co-operates to get rid of it, pollution may be controlled.

              II. No. The crowded highways, factories and industries and an ever growing population eager to acquire more and more land for constructing houses are beyond control.

23. Statement : Should military service be made compulsory in our country ?

     Arguments :   I. No. It is against the policy of non-violence.

              II. Yes. Every citizen should protect his country.

24. Statement : Should all the remote parts of a country be connected by road ?

     Arguments :   I. No. It will disturb peaceful simple life of the villagers.

              II. Yes. It must be done immediately.

25. Statement : Should we impart sex education in schools ?   **(S.B.I.P.O. 1995)**

     Arguments :   I. Yes. All the progressive nations do so.

              II. No. We cannot impart it in co-educational schools.

26. Statement : Should colleges be given the status of a university in India ?

     Arguments :   I. Yes. Colleges are in a better position to assess the students' performance and therefore the degrees will be more valid.

              II. No. It is utopian to think that there will not be nepotism and corruption in awarding degrees by colleges.

27. Statement : Should adult education programme be given priority over compulsory education programme ?

     Arguments :   I. No. It will also help in success of compulsory education programme.

              II. Yes. It will help to eliminate the adult illiteracy.

28. Statement : Should the health care service be nationalised ?

     Arguments :   I. Yes. It has been done elsewhere also.

              II. No. the quality of health care service will deteriorate.

29. Statement : Should fashionable dresses be banned ?   **(Bank P.O. 1991)**

     Arguments :   I. Yes. Fashions keep changing and hence consumption of cloth increases.

              II. No. Fashionable clothes are a person's self expression and therefore his/her fundamental right.

30. Statement : Should all the legislators be forced to resign from their profession ?

     Arguments :   I. Yes. They will be able to devote more time for the country.

              II. No. Nobody will contest election.

31. Statement : Is ragging in colleges a good practice ?

     Arguments :   I. Yes. A sensible ragging helps the school boys to step into manhood and teaches them to take trifles in a good humour.

              II. No. The tortures inflicted in the name of ragging and the humiliation suffered by young boys and girls often go beyond limits.

32. **Statement** : Should India manufacture atom bombs ?
    Arguments : I. Yes. It is imperative to protect the sovereignty and integrity of the country.
    II. No. This will create imbalance in the power of nations in this region.

33. **Statement** : Should computers be used in all possible sectors in India ?
    Arguments : I. Yes. It will bring efficiency and accuracy in the work.
    II. No. It will be an injustice to the monumental human resources which are at present underutilised.

34. **Statement** : Should family planning be made compulsory in India ?
    Arguments : I. Yes. Looking to the miserable conditions in India, there is no other go.
    II. No. In India there are people of various religions and family planning is against the tenets of some of the religions.
    (Hotel Management, 1992)

35. **Statement** : Should films be included in the Concurrent List ?
    Arguments : I. Yes. It will give respect to the views of the states.
    II. No. It will deteriorate the standard of films.

36. **Statement** : Should there be only one university throughout India ?
    Arguments : I. Yes. This is the only way to bring about uniformity in the educational standards.
    II. No. This is administratively impossible.

37. **Statement** : Should there be a world government ?   **(M.B.A. 1996)**
    Arguments : I. Yes. It will help in eliminating tensions among the nations.
    II. No. Then, only the developed countries will dominate in the government.

38. **Statement** : Should workers be allowed to participate in the management of factories in India ?
    Arguments : I. Yes. It is the present management theory.
    II. No. Many workers are illiterate and so their contributions will not be of any value.

39. **Statement** : Are educational institutions responsible for unrest among the youth ?
    Arguments : I. Yes. There is no discipline in educational institutions.
    II. No. There are no disciplinary problems in educational institutions.

40. **Statement** : Should the political parties be banned ?
    Arguments : I. Yes. It is necessary to teach a lesson to the politicians.
    II. No. It will lead to an end of democracy.

41. **Statement** : Should jobs be linked with academic degrees and diplomas ?
    Arguments : I. No. A very large number of persons with meagre academic qualifications will apply.
    II. No. Importance of higher education will be diminished.

42. **Statement** : Should we scrap the system of formal education beyond graduation ?

Arguments : I. Yes. It will mean taking employment at an early date.

II. No. It will mean lack of depth of knowledge. **(M.B.A. 1997)**

43. Statement : Is Governorship better than Chief Ministership ?

Arguments : I. Yes. It is the highest post in a state.

II. No. The Chief Minister commands more power.

44. Statement : Should all news be controlled by Govenment in a democracy ?

Arguments : I. Yes. Variety of news only confuses people.

II. No. Controlled news loses credibility.

45. Statement : Should there be no place of interview in selection ?

Arguments : I. Yes. It is very subjective in assessment.

II. No. It is the only instrument to judge candidates' motives and personality.

46. Statement : Should higher education be completely stopped for sometime ?

Arguments : I. No. It will hamper the country's future progress.

II. Yes. It will reduce the educated unemployment.

47. Statement : Should mercy death be legalized ?

Arguments : I. Yes. Patients undergoing terrible suffering and having absolutely no chance of recovery should be liberated from suffering through mercy death.

II. No. Even mercy death is a sort of killing and killing can never be legalized.

48. Statement : Should the institution of marriages be abolished ?

Arguments : I. Yes. It is already showing cracks.

II. No. It is necessary for the survival of the society.

49. Statement : Should non-vegetarian food be totally banned in our country ?

Arguments : I. Yes. It is expensive and therefore it is beyond the means of most people in our country.

II. No. Nothing should be banned in a democratic country like ours.

50. Statement : Should election expenses to Central and State Legislatures be met by the government ?

Arguments : I. Yes. It will put an end to political corruption.

II. No. It is not good in any country.

ANSWERS

1. (e) : Clearly, it is the advertisement which makes the customer aware of the qualities of the product and leads him to buy it. So. argument I is valid. But at the same time, advertising nowadays has become a costly affair and the expenses on it add to the price of the product. So, argument II also holds strong.

2. (d) : Clearly, ban is necessary to protect our natural environment. So, none of the arguments is strong enough.

3. (d) : The argument I in support is not valid because films also educate masses. Similarly, argument II against the statement is weak because it is not the only way to educate the masses, there are other ways as well.

4. (b) : Making education free for all only cannot ensure full literacy. An awareness needs to be aroused for this. So, argument I is vague. Also, such a step would require immense funds for providing the necessary facilities to all institutions and lead to financial drain. So, argument II is valid.

5. (e) : Clearly, both the arguments in for and against are strong and enough. The conditions have to be agreed to, in order to save the life of the victims, though actually they ought not to be agreed to, as they encourage the sinister activities of the kidnappers.

6. (a) : Clearly, government jobs in rural areas are underlined with several difficulties. In lieu of these, extra incentives are needed. So, only argument I holds strong.

7. (b) : Clearly, the pursuance of a policy in India cannot be based on the pretext that an advanced country like USA desires so. So. argument I does not hold. However, it is always necessary for a nation to be equipped with the latest sophisticated defence strategies and equipments so as to be safe. So, argument II is valid.

8. (d) : The Public Distribution System is indeed necessary to provide basic amenities to the economically backward sections of population. So, argument I is vague. Also, if the objectives of a system are not fulfilled because of corruption, then getting rid of the system is no solution. Instead, efforts should be made to end corruption and extend its benefits to the people for which it is meant. So, argument II is also not valid.

9. (d) : Clearly, development in a new field is not a matter of merely following up other countries. So, argument II is not valid. Also, computerisation is a much beneficial project and investment in it is not at all a waste. So, argument I is also not strong enough.

10. (e) : Citizens, who do not get employment due to the large number of applicants in all fields, must surely be given allowance so that they can support themselves. So, argument I is valid. However, such allowances would mar the spirit to work in there and make them idle. So, argument II also holds.

11. (d) : In buying things on instalments, a customer has to pay more as the interest is also included. So, argument I does not hold. Moreover, one who buys an item on instalments maintains his future budget accordingly as he is well acquainted with when and how much he has to pay before hand. So, argument II is also not valid.

12. (b) : An organisation like UNO is meant to maintain peace all over and will always serve to prevent conflicts between countries. So, its role never ends. So, argument I does not hold. Also, lack of such an organisation may in future lead to increased mutual conflicts and international wars. So, argument II is valid.

13. (d) : Clearly, the success of a government does not rest on the firmness of its claim to the chair but depends on its outlooks and policies. So, argument I is not strong enough. Argument II is also vague because a democracy is coveted for the reason that in it, the voice of the people is above all.

14. (a) : Clearly, the autonomous status of the Doordarshan will be a step towards giving it independence for an impartial coverage. Autonomous status does not mean that the coverage will be decided by a few. So, only argument I holds.

15. (b) : Clearly, strike is not a means of indiscipline but only a practice in which the citizens exercise their fundamental right. So, argument I is vague and II alone holds.

16. (a) : Clearly, mechanisation would speed up the work and increase the production. So, argument I is strong enough. Argument II is vague because mechanisation will only eliminate wasteful employment, not create unemployment.

17. (b) : Clearly, the argument I is not strong enough because no one can be debarred from his constitutional right even if he cannot practise it to his benefit. In the same context, argument II is strong.

18. (b) : Clearly, the luxury hotels are a mark of country's standard and a place for staying for the affluent foreign tourists. So, argument II holds. Argument I is not a strong reason because ban on hotels is not a way to end the success of international criminals.

19. *(e)* : The Students' Union formation shall be a step towards giving to students the basic education in the field of politics. However, it shall create the same political atmosphere in the campus. Thus, both the arguments hold strong.

20. *(e)* : With big industries, pollution is always a big problem. However, they are also advantageous in opening fields of more employment. So, both the arguments hold strong.

21. *(a)* : Abolishing the internal assessment would surely reduce favouritism on personal grounds because the teachers would not be involved in examination system so that they cannot extend personal benefits to anyone. So, argument I holds strong. But, it will not affect the control of teaching faculty on students because still the teachers would be teaching them. So, argument II is vague.

22. *(c)* : The control of population, on one hand, seems to be impossible because of the ever growing needs and the disconcern of the people but, on the other hand, the control is possible by a joint effort. So, either of the arguments will hold strong.

23. *(b)* : Clearly, military service is not meant to create violence but to defend against violence. So, argument I is vague. Since every citizen must have a share in the service towards the country, so argument II holds strong.

24. *(b)* : Connecting remote parts by roads will only help the people there. So, argument II alone holds strong.

25. *(b)* : Clearly, the pursuance of a policy in India cannot be based on the pretext that it is followed in other countries because every country has its own environment and situations. So, argument I is vague. Also, imparting sex education in co-educational schools where boys and girls study together, would spoil the atmosphere there and hinder the studies. So, argument II is strong.

26. *(d)* : Clearly, at the college level, all the students are assessed according to their performance in the University Exams and not on the basis of any criteria of a more intimate dealing with the students. So, argument I is vague. Also, at this level the awarding of degrees is impartial and simply based on his performance. So, argument II also does not hold.

27. *(b)* : Clearly, argument I gives a reason in support of the statement and so it does not hold strong against it. The adult education programme needs to be given priority because it shall eliminate adult illiteracy and thus help in further spread of education. So, only argument II is strong enough.

28. *(d)* : Clearly, going in for something just because others have done it, is not a strong argument. Also, on the other hand, nationalisation of health care service will only promote the service and not deteriorate it. So, none of the arguments holds strong.

29. *(b)* : Clearly, imposing ban on fashionable dresses will be a restriction on the personal choice and hence the right to freedom of an individual. So, only argument II is strong.

30. *(a)* : The legislators should surely not be engaged in any other profession because only then will they be able to work with devotion. So, argument I is valid. Also, if such a law is enforced, only those people will contest elections who are really prepared to work for the country. So, argument II is vague.

31. *(e)* : Clearly, sensible ragging makes students broad-minded and well- acquainted with each other. So, argument I is valid. However, sometimes, these young boys and girls are tortured and humiliated too much in the name of ragging, which makes it an unhealthy practice. So, argument II also holds strong.

32. *(a)* : Clearly, in the blind chase for attaining nuclear powers, manufacture of atom bombs is an inevitability to protect the country from the threat of nuclear powers. So, argument I holds strong. However, argument II against the statement is weak.

33. *(a)* : Clearly, the need of today is to put to better use the underutilised human resources. Computers with better and speedy efficiency can accomplish this. So, only argument I holds strong.

34. (*e*) : Family planning is an essential step to curb population growth. So, argument I holds strong. Also, family planning being against the tenets of some of the Indian religions, it is not necessary to make it compulsory. Instead, it can be enforced by creating public awareness of the benefits of family planning. So, argument II is also valid.

35. (*a*) : If films are included in concurrent list instead of the union list, the views of the states will be considered and respected. There is however, no reason why it shall deteriorate the standards. So, only argument I holds strong.

36. (*b*) : Clearly, to bring uniformity in educational standards, we can have many universities all following same curricular and policies under one Board. But having one university will make the management of education throughout the country almost impossible. So, only argument II holds.

37. (*b*) : Clearly, a world government cannot eliminate tensions among nations because it will also have the ruling group and the opposition group. Further, the more powerful and diplomatic shall rule the world to their interests. So, only argument II holds.

38. (*b*) : The argument I in support does not provide a valid reason for the pursuance of the policy. So, it is vague. The argument II provides a valid reason that illiterate workers will create wastefulness in management. So, only argument II follows.

39. (*d*) : Clearly, both the arguments do not provide strong reasons in support or against the statement.

40. (*d*) : Clearly, with the ban on political parties, candidates can independently contest elections. So, it will not end democracy. Thus, argument II is wrong. Argument I does not give a strong reason.

41. (*b*) : Clearly, delinking jobs with degrees will diminish the need for higher education as many of them pursue such education for jobs. So, only argument II is strong.

42. (*b*) : Clearly, argument I is vague because at present too, many fields are open to all after graduation. However, eliminating the post-graduate courses would abolish higher and specialised studies which lead to understanding things better and deeply. So, argument II is valid.

43. (*e*) : In one place, Governorship is the highest post in name in a state but actually the powers of the Chief Minister are more. So. both the arguments hold strong.

44. (*b*) : Clearly, the variety of news helps people to develop their own views. So, argument I is vague. Also, controlled news shall be a partial produce. So, it loses credibility. Thus, argument II holds.

45. (*a*) : Clearly, besides interview, there can be other modes of written examination to judge candidate's motives. So, second argument is not strong enough. However, the interview is a subjective assessment without doubt. So, argument I holds.

46. (*a*) : Clearly, higher education is not the cause of unemployment. In fact, it has created greater job opportunities. So, argument II is vague. Also, higher education promotes the country's development. So, argument I holds.

47. (*e*) : Clearly, mercy death will serve as a liberation to those to whom living is more difficult. But then, it is an inhuman act and does not appeal. So, both the arguments hold strong.

48. (*b*) : There may be cracks in the institution of marriages but this alone cannot be the reason for abolishing the system as it is inevitable for the survival of the society. So, only argument II holds.

49. (*b*) : Clearly, restriction on the diet of people will be denying them their basic human right. So, only argument II holds.

50. (*a*) : Clearly, the policy will end political corruption that is unleashed to extract these amounts. The second argument is vague. So, only argument I holds.

EXERCISE 2 B

Directions : *Each question below consists of a statement followed by two arguments numbered I and II. You have to decide which of the arguments is a 'strong' argument and which is a 'weak' argument.*

Give answer (a) if only argument I is strong; (b) if only argument II is strong; (c) if either I or II is strong; (d) if neither I nor II is strong and (e) if both I and II are strong.

1. **Statement** : Should Central Government open well-equipped hospital for every sub-division of every district ?   **(Bank P.O. 1998)**

   Arguments : I. Yes. Health and well-being of every citizen is the primary responsibility of the government.

   II. No. It is not possible. Society must come forward to help government.

2. **Statement** : Should students take part in politics ?

   Arguments : I. Yes. It inculcates in them qualities of leadership.

   II. No. They should study and build up their career.

3. **Statement** : Should girls learn arts like judo and karate ?

   Arguments : I. Yes. It will enable them to defend themselves from rogues and ruffians.

   II. No. They will lose their feminine grace.

4. **Statement** : Should articles of only deserving authors be allowed to be published ?

   Arguments : I. Yes. It will save a lot of paper which is in short supply.

   II. No. It is not possible to draw a line between the deserving and the undeserving.

5. **Statement** : Should religion be banned ?

   Arguments : I. Yes. It develops fanaticism in people.

   II. No. Religion binds people together.

6. **Statement** : Should the age of retirement in government service be increased in view of longer life span in India ?   **(Bank P.O. 1996)**

   Arguments : I. Yes. Other countries have already taken such decision.

   II. Yes. It is a genuine demand of lakhs of employees.

7. **Statement** : Should shifting agriculture be practised ?

   Arguments : I. No. It is a wasteful practice.

   II. Yes. Modern methods of farming are too expensive.

8. **Statement** : Does India need so many plans for development ?

   Arguments : I. Yes. Nothing can be achieved without proper planning.

   II. No. Too much time, money and energy is wasted on planning.

9. **Statement** : Should India encourage exports, when most things are insufficient for internal use itself ?

   Arguments : I. Yes. We have to earn foreign exchange to pay for our imports.

   II. No. Even selective encouragement would lead to shortages.

10. **Statement** : Should India make efforts to harness solar energy to fulfil its energy requirements ?

Arguments :   I. Yes. Most of the energy sources used at present are exhaustible.

II. No. Harnessing solar energy requires a lot of capital, which India lacks in.

11. **Statement** : Should public holidays be declared on demise of important national leaders ?   **(S.B.I.P.O. 1995)**

Arguments :   I. No. Such unscheduled holidays hamper national progress.

II. Yes. People would like to pay their homage to the departed soul.

12. **Statement** : Should cutting of trees be banned altogether ?

Arguments :   I. Yes. It is very much necessary to do so to restore ecological balance.

II. No. A total ban would harm timber based industries.

13. **Statement** : Is the Government justified in spending so much on defence ?

Arguments :   I. Yes. Safety of the country is of prime importance.

II. No. During peace, this money could be used for the development of the country.

14. **Statement** : Should judiciary be independent of the executive ?

Arguments :   I. Yes. This would help curb the unlawful activities of the executive.

II. No. The executive would not be able to take bold measures.

15. **Statement** : Should so much money be spent on advertisements ?

Arguments :   I. Yes. It is an essential concomitent in a capitalist economy.

II. No. It leads to wastage of resources.

16. **Statement** : Should all the transport corporations be handed over to the private organisations ?

Arguments :   I. Yes. There will be a significant change in the quality and punctuality of services.

II. No. There would not be job security for the employees at all the levels.   **(Bank P.O. 1996)**

17. **Statement** : Should loyalty be the only criterion for promotion in any organisation ?

Arguments :   I. Yes. Without loyal men, no organisation can function.

II. No. It leads to hypocrisy and partiality.

18. **Statement** : Should untouchability be banned in India ?

Arguments :   I. No. Menial people deteriorate the living standard of society.

II. Yes. All people should be equally treated in a democratic country like India.

19. **Statement** : Should there be a complete ban on manufacture of firecrackers in India ?   **(S.B.I.P.O. 1997)**

Arguments :   I. No. This will render thousands of workers jobless.

II. Yes. The firecracker manufacturers use child labour to a large extent.

20. **Statement** : Is caste based reservation policy justified ?

Arguments :   I. Yes. The step is a must to bring the underprivileged at par with the privileged ones.

II. No. It obstructs the establishment of a classless society.

21. **Statement** : Should cottage industries be encouraged in rural areas ?
    Arguments : I. Yes. Rural people are creative.
    II. Yes. This would help to solve the problem of unemployment to some extent.

22. **Statement** : Should income tax be evaded by people ?
    Arguments : I. Yes. Taxes are excessively high.
    II. No. It is anti-national to do so.

23. **Statement** : Should correspondence courses at the university level be discontinued in India ?   **(Hotel Management, 1992)**
    Arguments : I. Yes. Only interaction between teachers and students at the college helps total development of personality.
    II. No. The demand for discontinuance comes only from the elite who have no knowledge of what is meant by poverty.

24. **Statement** : Should state lotteries be stopped ?
    Arguments : I. Yes. Government should not promote gambling habits.
    II. No. Government will lose a large amount of revenue.

25. **Statement** : Should new universities be established in India ?
    Arguments : I. No. We have still not achieved the target for literacy.
    II. No. We will have to face the problem of unemployed but highly qualified people.   **(Bank P.O. 1996)**

26. **Statement** : Should dams be built on rivers ?
    Arguments : I. No. Some dam projects have proved to be unsuccessful in recent years.
    II. Yes. They are beneficial in checking floods and conserving soil.

27. **Statement** : Should all Government-owned educational institutions be handed over to private institutions ?   **(Bank P.O. 1996)**
    Arguments : I. Yes. Standard of education of these institutions will improve.
    II. No. Standard of education of these institutions will fall.

28. **Statement** : Should administrative officers be transferred after one or two years ?
    Arguments : I. Yes. They get friendly with local people and are manipulated by them.
    II. No. By the time their policies and schemes start taking shape, they have to leave.

29. **Statement** : Should words like 'Smoking is injurious to heath' essentially appear on cigarette packs ?
    Arguments : I. Yes. It is a sort of brain-wash to make the smokers realise that they are inhaling poisonous stuff.
    II. No. It hampers the enjoyment of smoking.

30. **Statement** : Should high chimneys be installed in industries ?
    Arguments : I. Yes. It reduces pollution at ground level.
    II. No. It increases pollution in upper atmosphere.

31. **Statement** : Should we take care of the ozone layer ?
    Arguments : I. Yes. It protects us from the harmful ultraviolet rays.
    II. No. There is no harm to it.

32. Statement : Should the government levy tax on agricultural income also ?

Arguments : I. Yes. That is the only way to fill government coffers.

II. No. Eighty percent of our population live in rural areas.

(S.B.I.P.O. 1995)

33. Statement : Should coal engines be replaced by electric engines in trains ?

Arguments : I. Yes. Coal engines cause a lot of pollution.

II. No. India does not produce enough electricity to fulfil its domestic needs also.

34. Statement : Should women be provided more job opportunities ?

Arguments : I. No. They are entrusted with household jobs.

II. Yes. They should also go into the outside world.

35. Statement : Should personal tax be abolished in India ?

Arguments : I. Yes. It will motivate people to earn more.

II. No. Individuals must learn to share their wealth with other people.

36. Statement : Should judicial activism be discouraged ?   **(Bank P.O. 1998)**

Arguments : I. No. If we leave everything in the hands of executive, justice may be a distant dream.

II. Yes. Judiciary should mind its own business. Executive will take its own course.

37. Statement : Should officers accepting bribe be punished ?

Arguments : I. No. Certain circumstances may have compelled them to take bribe.

II. Yes. They should do the job they are entrusted with, honestly.

38. Statement : Are nuclear families better than joint families ?

Arguments : I. No. Joint families ensure security and also reduce the burden of work.

II. Yes. Nuclear families ensure greater freedom

39. Statement : Should India give away Kashmir to Pakistan ?

Arguments : I. No. Kashmir is a beautiful state. It earns a lot of foreign exchange for India.

II. Yes. This would help settle conflicts.

40. Statement : Should India have no military force at all ?

Arguments : I. No. Other countries in the world do not believe in non-violence.

II. Yes. Many Indians believe in non-violence.

41. Statement : Should students' union in universities be abolished ?

Arguments : I. Yes. Students can pay full attention to their career development.

II. No. All the great leaders had been students' union leaders.

(Bank P.O. 1996)

42. Statement : Should higher education be reserved for deserving few ?

Arguments : I. No. It will increase unemployment.

II. Yes. It will minimise wastage in higher education.

43. Statement : Should those who receive dowry, despite the law prohibiting it, be punished ?

    Arguments : I. Yes. Those who violate the law, must be punished.

           II. No. Dowry system is firmly rooted in the society since time immemorial.

44. Statement : Should all refugees, who make unauthorised entry into a country, be forced to go back to their homeland ?

    Arguments : I. Yes. They make their colonies and occupy a lot of land.

           II. No. They leave their homes because of hunger or some terror and on human grounds, should not be forced to go back.

45. Statement : Should the system of Lok Adalats and mobile courts be encouraged in India ?

    Arguments : I. Yes. It helps to grant speedy justice to the masses.

           II. No. These courts are usually partial in granting justice.

46. Statement : Should the tuition fees in all post-graduate courses be hiked considerably ? **(S.B.I.P.O. 1997)**

    Arguments : I. Yes. This will bring in some sense of seriousness among the students and will improve the quality.

           II. No. This will force the meritorious poor students to stay away from post-graduate courses.

47. Statement : Should smoking be prohibited ?

    Arguments : I. Yes. It is wrong to smoke away millions of money.

           II. No. It will throw thousands of workers in the tobacco industry out of employment.

48. Statement : Should selection tests be of the objective rather than of the descriptive type ?

    Arguments : I. Yes. The assessment of answers to objective type questions is fair and impartial.

           II. No. The descriptive type test is certainly a better tool than the objective type test.

49. Statement : Should education be made compulsory for all children upto the age of 14 ? **(M.A.T. 1997)**

    Arguments : I. Yes. This will help to eradicate the system of forced employment of these children.

           II. Yes. This would increase the standard of living.

50. Statement : Should religion be taught in our schools ?

    Arguments : I. No. Ours is a secular state.

           II. Yes. Teaching religion helps inculcate moral values among children.

ANSWERS

1. (*a*) : Clearly, health care services must be looked after by the Government and opening well-equipped hospitals in every area would surely provide better health services to the citizens. So, argument I is valid. Also, it is not an impractical task and can be achieved by the Government. So, argument II is vague.

2. (*c*) : Clearly, indulgement in politics trains the students for future leadership but its ways them from the studies. So, either of the arguments I or II can hold.

3. (a) : Learning martial arts is necessary for girls for self-defence. So, argument I holds. However, argument II is vague since a training in these arts has nothing to do with their feminine grace.

4. (b) : Clearly, the first argument is not a strong reason in support of the statement. Also, it is not possible to analyse the really deserving and not deserving. So, argument II holds strong.

5. (c) : Religion binds people together through the name of God and human values. But it may also develop fanaticism and ill-will among people. So, both the arguments hold strong.

6. (b) : Clearly, the pursuance of a policy in India cannot be based on the pretext that it is followed in other countries because every country has its own environment and situations. So, argument I is vague. But increasing the age of retirement is indeed a genuine demand of most of the employees to be self-dependent throughout. So, argument II holds.

7. (a) : Clearly, shifting agriculture is a practice in which a certain crop is grown on a land and when it becomes infertile it is left bare and another piece of land is chosen. Clearly, it is a wasteful practice. So, only argument I holds.

8. (a) : Before indulging in new development programme it is much necessary to plan the exact target, policies and their implementation and the allocation of funds which shows the right direction to work. So, argument I holds strong. Also, planning ensures full utilisation of available resources and funds and a stepwise approach towards the target. So, spending a part of money on it is no wastage. Thus, argument II is not valid.

9. (a) : Clearly, India can export only the surplus and those which can be saved from the luxury needs to pay for its import. Encouragement to export cannot lead to shortages as it shall provide the resources for imports. So, only argument I holds.

10. (a) : Clearly, harnessing solar energy will be helpful as it is an inexhaustible resource unlike other resources. So, argument I holds. But argument II is vague as solar energy is the cheapest form of energy.

11. (a) : Clearly, unscheduled and untimely holidays would naturally cause the work to suffer. So, argument I holds strong. Also, a holiday is not necessary to pay homage to someone. So, argument II is vague.

12. (e) : Clearly, trees play a vital role in maintaining ecological balance and so must be preserved. So, argument I holds. Also, trees form the basic source of timber and a complete ban on cutting of trees would harm timber based industries. So, only a controlled cutting of trees should be allowed and the loss replenished by planting more trees. So, argument II is also valid.

13. (a) : Clearly, defence is necessary for the safety of the country, which is of prime importance. So, argument I holds. Also, a country can concentrate on internal progress and development only when it is safe from external aggressions. So, argument II is not valid.

14. (a) : Clearly, independent judiciary is necessary for impartial judgement so that the Executive does not take wrong measures. So, only argument I holds.

15. (a) : Clearly, the advertisements are the means to introduce people with the product and its advantages. So, argument I holds strong. But argument II is vague because advertisements are an investment for better gain and not a wastage.

16. (e) : Since both the arguments contain a strong reason in explanation of the statement, so both I and II hold.

17. (d) : Clearly, the argument in support of the statement is quite vague. Also, when loyalty is considered, hypocrisy does not matter much as the fact that efficiency is neglected. So, the arguments are not strong enough.

18. (b) : Clearly, there is no question of 'menial' when all the persons are born equal. So, only argument II holds.

19. (*a*) : Clearly, banning a product would surely render jobless the large number of workers involved in manufacturing it. So, argument I holds. However, to stop child labour, it is not necessary to close down the industry but strict laws against child abuse should be enforced and legal actions taken. So, argument II is vague.

20. (*b*) : Clearly, capability is an essential criteria for a post and reservation cannot ensure capable workers. So, argument I does not hold strong. Also, making one caste more privileged than the other through reservations would hinder the objectives of a caste-less society. So, argument II is valid.

21. (*b*) : Clearly, cottage industries need to be promoted to create more job opportunities for rural people in the villages themselves. The reason that rural people are creative is vague. So, only argument II holds.

22. (*b*) : Clearly, the income tax taken from the people is utilised for welfare activities. So, it will be anti-national on their part to evade taxes. Thus, only argument II holds strong.

23. (*a*) : Correspondence courses are absolutely essential for students who are incapable of attending colleges regularly. So, only argument I holds strong.

24. (*d*) : Clearly, none of the reasons is strong enough in favour of or against the statement. So, none of them holds.

25. (*e*) : Clearly, instead of improving upon higher education, increasing the literacy rate should be heeded first. So, argument I holds. Also, more number of universities will produce more degree-holders with the number of jobs remaining the same, thus increasing unemployment. So, argument II also holds strong.

26. (*b*) : Clearly, success and failure are two aspects of any work. Though some dam projects have been unsuccessful but most of them are beneficial in checking floods and conserving soil.

27. (*d*) : It is not that the Government or the private institutions can provide higher standards of learning. So, both arguments I and II are not valid.

28. (*b*) : Clearly, the acquaintance of administrative officers with the local people poses no harm. So, argument I is vague. However, argument II holds strong, because making transfers too often would not enable them to formulate their policies in toto.

29. (*a*) : Clearly, such words on cigarette packs would warn the smokers beforehand of its adverse effects. So, argument I holds strong. However, smoking is a bad habit with long-term health hazards and is no means of enjoyment. So, argument II is vague.

30. (*a*) : Pollution at ground level is the most hazardous in the way of being injurious to human and animal life. So, argument I alone holds valid.

31. (*a*) : Clearly, any damage to ozone layer will cause the sun's ultraviolet rays to reach the earth and affect life adversely. So, argument I holds. Argument II is vague because ozone layer is being damaged by the increasing pollution.

32. (*d*) : Clearly, earning revenue is not the only criteria on which tax is imposed and also, there are several other ways to add to government treasury. So, argument I is vague. Moreover, a tax cannot be curtailed just because a greater part of the population has to pay it. So, argument II is also not valid.

33. (*a*) : Clearly, use of electricity in trains shall avoid the pollution caused by the coal engines. So, argument I holds. Clearly, the second reason is vague and does not hold.

34. (*b*) : Clearly, in present times, women are looking to outside jobs with the household jobs. So, argument I is vague. But clearly, offering them greater job opportunities shall cause them to come more into the contact of the outside world. So, argument II holds.

35. (*d*) : Abolishing the tax will increase the people's income and make them passive. So, argument I is vague. The personal tax is no way of sharing wealth with other people. So, argument II also does not hold.

36. (*d*) : Clearly, none of them should be made more powerful than the other. Instead, a balance should be created between the Executive and the Judiciary so that each can exercise its influence over the other and prevent its malfunctioning. So, both I and II do not hold strong.

37. (*b*) : Clearly, officers are paid duly for the jobs they do. So, they must do it honestly. Thus, argument II alone holds.

38. (*e*) : Clearly, with so many people around in a joint family, there is more security. Also, work is shared. So, argument I holds. In nuclear families, there are lesser number of people and so lesser responsibilities and more freedom.

39. (*a*) : Clearly, India cannot part with its state that is a major foreign exchange earner to it. So, argument I holds strong. Further, giving away a piece of land unconditionally and unreasonably is no solution to settle disputes. So, argument II is vague.

40. (*d*) : Clearly, India needs to have military force to defend itself against the threat of other military powers in the world. So, both the arguments do not hold strong.

41. (*a*) : Clearly, abolishing students' union would relieve the students of the unnecessary activities and enable them to concentrate well on studies. So, argument I holds. However, it is not that participation in students' unions only can make one a great leader. So, argument II is vague.

42. (*b*) : Clearly, higher education in no way reduces unemployment. So, argument I is vague. If higher education is imparted to only those who are worth it, the wasteful expenditures on undeserving shall be reduced. So, argument II also holds.

43. (*a*) : Clearly, laws are made to ensure that no person pursues the practice. So, persons who violate the laws need to be punished. Thus, argument I holds. A wrong practice, no matter how firmly rooted, needs to be ended. So, argument II is vague.

44. (*b*) : Clearly, refugees are people forced out of their homeland by some misery and need shelter desperately. So, argument II holds. Argument I against the statement, is vague.

45. (*a*) : Courts are meant to judge impartially. So, argument II is vague. The system of local courts shall speed up the justice. So, argument I holds.

46. (*b*) : A hike in fees is no means to make the students more serious in studies. So, argument I is vague. However, with the increase in fees, poor meritorious students would not be able to afford post-graduate studies. So, argument II holds.

47. (*d*) : Clearly, smoking needs to be abolished because it is injurious to health and not only to save money. So, argument I is vague. Clearly, to provide employment one cannot continue a hazardous task. So, argument II is also vague.

48. (*a*) : Clearly, judgement in subjective tests depends upon the individual who judges while that in objective tests is fair and impartial. So, argument I alone holds and argument II is vague.

49. (*d*) : Clearly, education is necessary to make the children better citizens. So, none of the arguments is strong enough.

50. (*b*) : Ours is a secular state does not mean that religion and religious values should be eradicated. In fact, these inculcate moral values. So, argument I is vague and only argument II is strong.

3. STATEMENT — ASSUMPTIONS

An **assumption** is something taken for granted *i.e.*, a fact that can be supposed on considering the contents of the given statement.

TYPE 1

In this type of questions, a statement is given, followed by two assumptions. The candidate is required to assess the given statement and then decide which of the given assumptions is implicit in the statement and choose the same from the alternatives provided.

ILLUSTRATIVE EXAMPLES

Directions : *In each question below is given a statement followed by two assumptions numbered I and II. Consider the statement and decide which of the given assumptions is implicit.*

Give answer (a) if only assumption I is implicit; (b) if only assumption II is implicit; (c) if either I or II is implicit; (d) if neither I nor II is implicit and (e) if both I and II are implicit.

Ex. 1. Statement : It is desirable to put the child in school at the age of 5 or so.

    Assumptions : I. At that age the child reaches appropriate level of development and is ready to learn.

                  II. The schools do not admit children after six years of age.

                                            (Bank P.O. 1997)

Sol. Since the statement talks of putting the child in school at the age of 5, it means that the child is mentally prepared for the same at this age. So, I is implicit. But, nothing about admission after six years of age is mentioned in the statement. So, II is not implicit.

    Hence, the answer is (*a*).

Ex. 2. Statement : "You must learn to refer to dictionary if you want to become a good writer." — A advises B.

    Assumptions : I. Only writers refer to the dictionary.

                  II. All writers good or bad refer to the dictionary.

Sol. It does not follow from the statement that only writers and nobody else refers to the dictionary. Also, nothing is mentioned about bad writers. So, both the assumptions I and II are not implicit.

    Hence, the answer is (*d*).

Ex. 3. Statement : The chairman and secretary of the housing society have requested society members to use water economically to help society to save on water tax.   **(Bank P.O. 1998)**

    Assumptions : I. Majority of members of society are likely to follow the request.

                  II. It is desirable to reduce expenditure wherever possible.

Sol. Clearly, nothing about the response of society members to the society's request can be deduced from the statement. So, I is not implicit. Also, the society requests the members to save the money on tax. So, II is implicit.

Hence, the answer is (*b*).

Ex. 4. Statement : "If you want to give any advertisement, give it in the newspaper X." — A tells B.

Assumptions : I. B wants to publicise his products.

II. Newspaper X has a wide circulation.

Sol. The word 'If' in the statement shows that B may or may not want to publicise his products. So, I is not implicit. It is advised that advertisements be given in newspaper X. This means that X will help advertise better *i.e.*, it has wider circulation. So, II is implicit.

Hence, the answer is (*b*).

Ex. 5. Statement : We must settle all the payment due to our suppliers within three working days.   **(S.B.I.P.O. 1997)**

Assumptions : I. We will always have necessary funds in our account to settle the bills.

II. We are capable of verifying and clearing the bills in less than three working days.

Sol. Since the statement talks of making all payments within three days, it is evident that the company has the necessary funds and the bills can be verified and cleared within the stipulated time. So, both I and II are implicit.

Hence, the answer is (*e*).

Ex. 6. Statement : A good book, even if costly, is sold.

Assumptions : I. Some books are better than others.

II. Most of the books are costly.

Sol. The statement mentions about a 'good' book. This means some books may not be good. So, I is implicit. The words 'if costly' show that most books are not costly. So, II is not implicit.

Hence, the answer is (*a*).

EXERCISE 3A

Directions : *In each question below is given a statement followed by two assumptions numbered I and II. You have to consider the statement and the following assumptions and decide which of the assumptions is implicit in the statement.*

Give answer (a) if only assumption I is implicit; (b) if only assumption II is implicit; (c) if either I or II is implicit; (d) if neither I nor II is implicit and (e) if both I and II are implicit.

1. **Statement**   : The patient's condition would improve after operation.

Assumptions : I. The patient can be operated upon in this condition.

II. The patient cannot be operated upon in this condition.

2. **Statement**   : A's advice to B — "Go to Jammu via Amritsar — the shortest route."

Assumptions : I. B wishes to go to Jammu.

II. A gives advice to everybody.

3. **Statement** : Savita made an application to the bank for a loan of Rs 1,80,000 by mortgaging his house to the bank and promised to repay it within five years. **(Bank P.O. 1997)**

   Assumptions : I. The bank has a practice of granting loans for Rs. 1,00,000/- and above.

   II. The bank accepts house as collateral security against such loans.

4. **Statement** : Detergents should be used to clean clothes.

   Assumptions : I. Detergents form more lather.

   II. Detergents help to dislodge grease and dirt.

5. **Statement** : "As there is a great demand, every person seeking tickets of the programme will be given only five tickets."

   Assumptions : I. The organisers are not keen on selling the tickets.

   II. No one is interested in getting more than five tickets.

   (S.B.I.P.O. 1997)

6. **Statement** : "If you trouble me, I will slap you." — A mother warns her child.

   Assumptions : I. With the warning, the child may stop troubling her.

   II. All children are basically naughty.

7. **Statement** : Double your money in five months — An advertisement.

   Assumptions : I. The assurance is not genuine.

   II. People want their money to grow. **(Bank P.O. 1998)**

8. **Statement** : Of all the radio sets manufactured in India, the 'X' brand has the largest sale.

   Assumptions : I. The sale of all the radio sets manufactured in India is known.

   II. The manufacturing of no other radio set in India is as large as 'X' brand radio.

9. **Statement** : The first step in treating addicts is to re-establish their lost ties, for which a continuous personal attention should be paid to the addicts under treatment. **(Central Excise, 1996)**

   Assumptions : I. Addicts under treatment respond better when shown personal interest.

   II. Addiction and strained relationships are intimately connected.

10. **Statement** : Films have become indispensable for the entertainment of people.

    Assumptions : I. Films are the only media of entertainment.

    II. People enjoy films.

11. **Statement** : "To keep myself up-to-date, I always listen to 9.00 p.m. news on radio." — A candidate tells the interview board.

    Assumptions : I. The candidate does not read newspaper.

    II. Recent news are broadcast only on radio.

12. **Statement** : Never before such a lucid book was available on the topic.

    Assumptions : I. Some other books were available on this topic.

    II. You can write lucid books on very few topics.

    (Bank P.O. 1996)

13. Statement : A line in an advertisement in a newspaper — "You really get your money's worth when you buy from our shop."

Assumptions : I. Other shops price goods above their worth.

II. People want full value for their money.

14. Statement : The private bus services in the city has virtually collapsed because of the ongoing strike of its employees.

Assumptions : I. Going on strikes has become the right of every employee.

II. People no more require the services of private bus operators.
                                                                      (Bank P.O. 1998)

15. Statement : In Bombay, railway trains are indispensable for people in the suburbs to reach their places of work on time.

Assumptions : I. Railway trains are the only mode of transport available in the suburbs of Bombay.

II. Only railway trains run punctually.

16. Statement : "I would like to study the impact of pay revision on job satisfaction of employees." — A tells B.   **(Bank P.O. 1995)**

Assumptions : I. Job satisfaction can be measured.

II. A has necessary competence to undertake such study.

17. Statement : Vitamin E tablets improve circulation, keep your complexion in a glowing condition.

Assumptions : I. People like a glowing complexion.

II. Complexion becomes dull in the absence of circulation.

18. Statement : Try to steal this camera from our store — a display on a departmental store.   **(Bank P.O. 1996)**

Assumptions : I. People want to own a camera.

II. The store has a video monitoring system to detect stealing.

19. Statement : Please consult us before making any decision on investment.

Assumptions : I. You may take a wrong decision if you don't consult us.

II. It is important to take a right decision.

20. Statement : The government has decided to reduce the custom duty on computer peripherals.   **(S.B.I.P.O. 1997)**

Assumptions : I. The domestic market price of computer peripherals may go up in near future.

II. The domestic manufacturers may oppose the decision.

21. Statement : One of the opposition leaders said that the time had come for like-minded opposition parties to unite and dislodge the corrupt government.

Assumptions : I. Like-minded opposition parties should unite only when they have to dislodge a corrupt government.

II. Opposition parties are not corrupted.

22. Statement : The office building needs repairing just as urgently as it needs internal as well as external painting.   **(U.T.I. 1993)**

Assumptions : I. Efficiency of people working in the office cannot be improved unless office building is repaired.

II. Repairing and painting of office building require funds.

23. Statement   : Be humble even after being victorious.
    Assumptions :   I. Many people are humble after being victorious.
                    II. Generally people are not humble.

24. Statement   : I cannot contact you on phone from Karshik.
    Assumptions :   I. Telephone facility is not available at Karshik.
                    II. Nowadays it is difficult to contact on phone.

25. Statement   : Among all the articles, the prices of personal computers show the highest decline from June 1997 to December 1997.
    Assumptions :   I. Comparative prices of all the articles in June and December 1997 were available.
                    II. Prices of personal computers were higher in the first six months than the last six months of 1997.   **(M.B.A. 1998)**

26. Statement   : Today I must satisfy myself only by looking at a pink headed duck in an encyclopaedia.
    Assumptions :   I. Pink headed ducks are as good as extinct now.
                    II. People refer to encyclopaedia to know only about things which do not exist now.

27. Statement   : Read this book to get detailed and most comprehensive information on this issue.   **(Bank P.O. 1997)**
    Assumptions :   I. The person who wants this information can read.
                    II. There are other books available on this issue.

28. Statement   : "If you are a mechanical engineer, we want you as our supervisor." — An advertisement by company X.
    Assumptions :   I. Mechanical engineers are expected to be better performers by company X.
                    II. The company X needs supervisors.

29. Statement   : Even with the increase in the number of sugar factories in India, we still continue to import sugar.   **(Bank P.O. 1997)**
    Assumptions :   I. The consumption of sugar per capita has increased in India.
                    II. Many of the factories are not in a position to produce sugar to their fullest capacity.

30. Statement   : A sentence in the letter to the candidates called for written examination — 'You have to bear your expenses on travel etc.'
    Assumptions :   I. If not clarified all the candidates may claim reimbursement of expenses.
                    II. Many organisations reimburse expenses on travel to candidates called for written examination.

31. Statement   : The party president has directed that no member of the party will give press briefing or interviews to government and private T.V. channels about the discussion in scheduled meeting of the party.   **(S.B.I.P.O. 1997)**
    Assumptions :   I. Party members will observe this directive of the president.
                    II. The general public will not come to know about the happenings in the scheduled meeting of the party.

32. Statement   : Everybody loves reading adventure stories.

Assumptions : I. Adventure stories are the only reading material.
II. Nobody loves reading any other material.

33. Statement : 'Guests should be provided lunch' — A tells B.

Assumptions : I. Unless told, lunch may not be provided.
II. Guests will stay during lunch time. **(Bank P.O. 1998)**

34. Statement : "This drink can be had either as it is, or after adding ice to it." — An advertisement.

Assumptions : I. People differ in their preferences.
II. Some people will get attracted to the drink as it can be had as it is.

35. Statement : "Avon Cycles — Fast, easy to ride, impressive, reliable, crafted and up-to-date automation." — An advertisement.

Assumptions : I. There is no other cycle with any of these features.
II. People do not bother about the cost.

36. Statement : The end of a financial year is the ideal time to take a look at the performance of various companies. **(Bank P.O. 1995)**

Assumptions : I. All the companies take such a review at the end of a financial year.
II. The performance data of various companies is available.

37. Statement : "You are hereby appointed as a programmer with a probation period of one year and your performance will be reviewed at the end of the period for confirmation." — A line in an appointment letter.

Assumptions : I. The performance of an individual generally is not known at the time of appointment offer.
II. Generally an individual tries to prove his worth in the probation period.

38. Statement : In case of any difficulty about this case, you may contact our company's lawyer. **(Bank P.O. 1996)**

Assumptions : I. Each company has a lawyer of its own.
II. The company's lawyer is thoroughly briefed about this case.

39. Statement : The concession in rail fares for the journey to hill stations is cancelled because it is not needed for people who can spend their holidays there.

Assumptions : I. Railways should give concession only to needy persons.
II. Railways should not encourage people to spend their holidays at hill stations.

40. Statement : The campaign of 'Keep your city clean' started by the Civic Council did not evoke any response from the citizens.

Assumptions : I. People do not desire to keep their city clean.
II. The Civic Council has failed in its campaign. **(Bank P.O. 1998)**

41. Statement : If you have any problems, bring them to me.

Assumptions : I. You have some problems.
II. I can solve any problem.

42. Statement : "Computer education should start at schools itself."

Assumptions : I. Learning computers is easy.

II. Computer education fetches jobs easily.

43. Statement : "Though the candidates have been instructed to bring pencils, yet provide some pencils with each invigilator." — An instruction to test administration staff. **(Bank P.O. 1993)**

Assumptions : I. Pencils are in short supply.

II. All the candidates will bring the pencil.

44. Statement : Apart from the entertainment value of television, its educational value cannot be ignored.

Assumptions : I. People take television to be a means of entertainment only.

II. The educational value of television is not realised properly.

45. Statement : The railway authorities have decided to increase the freight charges by 10% in view of the possibility of incurring losses in the current financial year. **(S.B.I.P.O. 1997)**

Assumptions : I. The volume of freight during the remaining period may remain same.

II. The amount so obtained may set off a part or total of the estimated deficit.

46. Statement : "Present day education is in shambles and the country is going to the dogs."

Assumptions : I. A good education system is essential for the well being of a nation.

II. A good education alone is sufficient for the well being of a nation.

47. Statement : If Rajan has finished reading the instructions then let him begin the activities accordingly. **(Bank P.O. 1997)**

Assumptions : I. Rajan would understand the instructions.

II. Rajan is capable of performing the activities.

48. Statement : The next meeting of the Governing Board of the Institute will be held after one year.

Assumptions : I. The Institute will remain in function after one year.

II. The Governing Board will be dissolved after one year.

49. Statement : The U.S.A. re-emerged as India's largest import source in the early nineties. **(Assistant Grade, 1997)**

Assumptions : I. With swift political developments in the Soviet Union, India began to rely on U.S.A.

II. U.S.A. was the only country which wanted to meet the requirements of India.

50. Statement : Children are influenced more by their teachers nowadays.

Assumptions : I. The children consider teachers as their models.

II. A large amount of children's time is spent in school.

51. Statement : The two countries have signed a fragile pact, but the vital sovereignty issue remains unresolved. **(Bank P.O. 1996)**

Assumptions : I. The two countries cannot have permanent peace pact.

        II. The two countries may become hostile again after a short spell of time.

52. Statement : A's advice to B — "If you want to study Accounts, join institute Y."

Assumptions : I. Institute Y provides good Accounts education.

        II. B listens to A's advice.

53. Statement : Read this notice before entering the club.

Assumptions : I. People are literate.

        II. No blind person comes to the club.

54. Statement : The civic authority appealed to the people for reduction in usage of water as there may be an acute shortage during the coming weeks. **(Bank P.O. 1994)**

Assumptions : I. There will be no rain in recent future.

        II. The people are ready to follow the advice of the civic authority.

55. Statement : Equality of income throughout a community is the essential condition for maximising the total utility which the total income available could confer on the members of that community.

Assumptions : I. If extra income were taken from the rich and given to the poor, the total utility experienced by the community would increase.

        II. Equal pay for equal work.

56. Statement : Many historians have done more harm than good by distorting truth.

Assumptions : I. People believe what is reported by the historians.

        II. Historians are seldom expected to depict the truth.

57. Statement : How is it that the village is not shown in this so-called official map of this district ? **(Bank P.O. 1996)**

Assumptions : I. The official district map is expected to show all the villages of that district.

        II. This is not an authentic and official map.

58. Statement : The integrated steel plants in India would no longer have to depend on imports for continuous casting refractories.

Assumptions : I. Continuous casting refractories are needed by India.

        II. Continuous casting refractories are in demand.

59. Statement : "The programme will start at 6 p.m. but you can come there upto 7 p.m. or so and still there is no problem."

Assumptions : I. The programme will continue even after 7 p.m.

        II. The programme may not even start by that time.

(S.B.I.P.O. 1997)

60. Statement : "Blue tie would help us identify our staff from others." — A suggestion in a company.

Assumptions : I. The company needs to identify its staff.

        II. Blue tie is the latest fashion.

61. Statement : Money is the root cause of all the problems in a family.

56

Reasoning

Assumptions : I. Every problem is caused by something.

II. There are always some problems in a family.

(Bank P.O. 1997)

62. Statement : Ministry has announced an economic package to support the voluntary organisations — An official notice.

Assumptions : I. Voluntary organisations do not need such support.

II. Government was not supporting the voluntary organisations earlier.

63. Statement : "X air-conditioner — the largest selling name with the largest range." — An advertisement.

Assumptions : I. X air-conditioner is the only one with wide variations.

II. There is a demand of air-conditioners in the market.

64. Statement : "Those who are appearing for this examination for the first time, should be helped in filling up the form." — An instruction to invigilating staff. **(Bank P.O. 1993)**

Assumptions : I. The form is somewhat complicated.

II. Candidates can appear more than once for this examination.

65. Statement : "To buy a X-T.V., contact Y — the sole agent of X-T.V." — An advertisement.

Assumptions : I. People generally prefer to buy T.V. through sole agent.

II. The T.V. producing companies do not sell their products directly.

66. Statement : I have written several letters to the branch manager regarding my account in the bank but did not receive any reply so far.

Assumptions : I. Branch manager is expected to read letters received from the customer.

II. Branch manager is expected to reply to the letters received from the customer. **(U.T.I. 1993)**

67. Statement : Government has permitted unaided colleges to increase their fees.

Assumptions : I. Unaided colleges are in financial difficulties.

II. Aided colleges do not need to increase fees.

68. Statement : Of all the newspapers published in Mumbai, readership of the 'Times' is the largest in the Metropolis. **(M.B.A. 1998)**

Assumptions : I. 'Times' is not popular in mofussil areas.

II. 'Times' has the popular feature of cartoons on burning social and political issues.

69. Statement : It is through participative management policy alone that indiscipline in our industries can be contained and a quality of life ensured to the worker.

Assumptions : I. Quality of life in our industry is better.

II. Indiscipline results in poor quality of life.

70. Statement : The government is making efforts to boost tourism in Jammu and Kashmir.

Assumptions :   I. Tourism in Jammu and Kashmir dropped following political unrest.

           II. Special discounts in the air fare have been announced.

ANSWERS

1. (a) : The fact that patient's condition would improve after the operation clearly implies that the patient can be operated upon in this condition. So, I is implicit.

2. (a) : A has advised B the route to Jammu. This means that B wishes to go to Jammu. So, I is implicit. The statement mentions only A's advice to B. So, II is not implicit.

3. (e) : The fact that Savita has applied for a loan of Rs. 1,80,000 implies that the bank can grant a loan above Rs. 1,00,000. So, I is implicit. II also follows directly from the statement and so is implicit.

4. (b) : Nothing is mentioned about lather formation by the detergent. So, I is not implicit. Also, detergents should be used as they clean clothes better and more easily. So, II is implicit.

5. (d) : Clearly, the organisers are adopting this policy not to reduce the sale but to cope up with great demand so that everyone can get the ticket. So, I is not implicit. Also, due to great demand, the maximum number of tickets one person can get has been reduced to five. So, II is also not implicit.

6. (a) : The mother warns her child with the expectation that he would stop troubling her. So, I is implicit. The general nature of children cannot be derived from the statement. So, II is not implicit.

7. (b) : The fact given in I cannot be deduced from the given statement. So, I is not implicit. Since the concerned firm advertises with the assurance that money can be doubled quickly by investing with it, so II is implicit.

8. (a) : Clearly, the comparison could not be made without knowing the sale of all the radio sets. So, I is implicit. The statement mentions only that the sale is largest and nothing is mentioned about the manufacture. So, II is not implicit.

9. (e) : Clearly, treatment of addiction requires personal attention as the first step. So, I is implicit. Also, since intimacy and personal attention are required to treat addicts, it implies that addiction arises out of frustration due to sustained relationships. So, II is also implicit.

10. (b) : 'Films are indispensable' does not mean that they are the only means of entertainment. So, I is not implicit. Clearly, II follows from the statement. So, it is implicit.

11. (d) : The candidate listens to news on the radio does not mean that he does not read newspaper or that radio is the only source of recent news. So, neither I nor II is implicit.

12. (a) : It follows from the statement that books on this topic were available before also but they were not 'lucid'. So, I is implicit. But a general comment as II cannot be made from the given statement. So, II is not implicit.

13. (b) : Clearly, the advertisement mentions nothing about the prices of goods in the various shops. So, I is not implicit. The advertisement is given keeping in mind the desire of the people to get full value of their money. So, II is implicit.

14. (d) : Since both the assumptions do not follow from the given statement, so neither I nor II is implicit.

15. (b) : That the railway trains are indispensable for people to reach the place on time does not mean that there are no other means of transport but shows that trains alone run on time. So, I is not implicit and only II is implicit.

16. (e) : Clearly, A wishes to study the degree of effect of pay revision on job satisfaction of employees. This means that job satisfaction can be measured and A is capable of making such a study. So, both I and II are implicit.

17. (*e*) : The advice is given for people who like glowing complexion. So, I is implicit. Since complexion glows if circulation is improved, so II is also implicit.

18. (*b*) : Clearly, the owners of the store warn that one dare not try to steal the camera. So, only II is implicit while I isn't. So, II is also implicit.

19. (*e*) : Clearly, the statement was spoken for fear that the other person may take a wrong decision. So, I is implicit. Again, the statement confirms that it is important to take the right decision. So, II is also implicit.

20. (*d*) : Since both the assumptions do not follow from the given statement, so neither I nor II is implicit.

21. (*d*) : The call for the like-minded opposition parties to unite is made in a particular situation but they may unite in other situations as well. So, I is not implicit. Clearly, the 'government' mentioned is an opposition party to the 'opposition parties' mentioned in the statement. So, II is also not implicit.

22. (*d*) : Clearly, no deduction can be made regarding the effect of repairs of office building on efficiency of workers, or the requirement of funds for repairs, from the given statement. So, neither I nor II is implicit.

23. (*b*) : Clearly, nothing is mentioned about the nature of the people. So, I is not implicit. Also, the statement gives an advice of being humble even after being victorious. This means that generally people are not humble. So, II is implicit.

24. (*a*) : Clearly, the fact in I may be assumed from the given statement. So, I is implicit. However, II indicates difficulty, not the impossibility of contact as is indicated in the statement. So, II is not implicit.

25. (*e*) : Since prices of personal computers show the highest decline among all the articles, it implies that the comparative prices of all the articles was known. So, I is implicit. Also, it being given that prices of computers showed decline during the last six months, it means that they were higher in the first six months. So, II is implicit.

26. (*a*) : Since the narrator talks of satisfying himself by just looking at a picture in encyclopaedia, it means that pink headed ducks are not to be seen alive. So, I is implicit. But II does not follow from the statement and is not implicit.

27. (*e*) : Clearly, I directly follows from the statement. So, I is implicit. Also, according to the statement, this particular book gives 'most comprehensive' information on the issue. So, it can be assumed that other books are also available on this topic.

28. (*e*) : Clearly, the company lends more importance to mechanical engineers. This shows that they are believed to perform better. So, I is implicit. Also, the advertisement is given because the company needs supervisors. So, II is also implicit.

29. (*c*) : Clearly, the need to import sugar could be either due to increase in consumption or the inefficiency of the factories to produce sugar to their fullest capacity. So, either I or II is implicit.

30. (*e*) : Clearly, not mentioning the condition may provoke all the candidates to demand their claim. So, I is implicit. The condition is mentioned because some companies do reimburse the travel expenses. So, II is also implicit.

31. (*e*) : Clearly, the party president lays down the policies for its members. So, I is implicit. Also, when no party member would publicly reveal the happenings in the meeting, nobody will come to know. So, II is also implicit.

32. (*d*) : The statement mentions that adventure stories are liked by everybody. This does not mean that there is no other reading material or nobody loves reading any other material. So, neither I nor II is implicit.

33. (*e*) : Since both I and I follow from the statement, so both are implicit.

34. (*e*) : The advertisement tells the different ways in which the drink can be had. This means that different people prefer to have it in a different way and that some people would prefer it only because it can be taken in a particular manner. So, both I and II are implicit.

35. (*d*) : The advertisement is for Avon cycles and nothing about the cost or the features of other brands of cycles, is mentioned. So, neither I nor II is implicit.

36. (*e*) : Since both I and II follow from the given statement, so both are implicit.

37. (*e*) : The performance of the individual has to be tested over a span of time as the statement mentions. So, I is implicit. The statement mentions that the individual's worth shall be reviewed before confirmation. So, II is also implicit.

38. (*b*) : No deduction can be made regarding other companies. So, I is not implicit. Since one is advised to contact the company's lawyer in case of any problem, it means that the lawyer is fully acquainted with the case. So, II is implicit.

39. (*a*) : The statement mentions that concessions should not be given to people who can afford to spend holidays in hill stations. This means that they should be given only to needy persons. So, I is implicit. But, II does not follow from the statement and is not implicit.

40. (*e*) : According to the statement, the campaign did not get any response from citizens. This means that people are not interested in keeping the city clean and the campaign has failed. So, both I and II are implicit.

41. (*b*) : The word 'If' shows that 'you' do not necessarily have problems. So, I is not implicit. Also, the statement states that problems will be solved by 'me'. So, II is implicit.

42. (*a*) : Clearly, the computer education can be started at the school level only if it is easy. So, I is implicit. In the statement, nothing is mentioned about the link between jobs and computer education. So, II is not implicit.

43. (*d*) : Nothing about the availability of pencils is mentioned in the statement. So, I is not implicit. Also, in the statement, the staff has been instructed to provide pencils with each invigilator. This means that despite being instructed, all the candidates might not bring the pencil. So, II is also not implicit.

44. (*e*) : The statement makes the first assumption clear though educational value is not to be ignored. So, I is implicit. That the educational value must not be ignored also shows that educational value is not realised properly. So, II is also implicit.

45. (*b*) : Nothing about the volume of freight is mentioned in the statement. So, I is not implicit. According to the statement, the freight charges are being increased to cover up the possible losses. So, II is implicit.

46. (*a*) : Clearly, the statement mentions the degradation of the country with the disruption of the education system. So, I is implicit. However, it does not mean that education alone is sufficient and no other factor is responsible for the well being of the nation. So, II is not implicit.

47. (*e*) : According to the statement, Rajan can begin the activities according to the instructions. So, both I and II are implicit.

48. (*a*) : That the meeting of the Governing Board will be held after one year means the Institute will be functioning at that time. So, I is implicit. The Board cannot be dissolved at the time when its meeting starts. So, II is not implicit.

49. (*d*) : Nothing about India's trade relations with Soviet Union is mentioned in the statement. So, I is not implicit. Also, II does not follow from the statement and so is not implicit.

50. (*a*) : Clearly, it is because children consider teachers as their model that they are more influenced by them. So, I is implicit. It is not necessary that the children are influenced by teachers because they spend much time in school. So, II is not implicit.

51. (*b*) : From the fact that the present pact is not a lasting one, the possibility of a permanent pact cannot be ruled out. So, I is not implicit. The statement mentions that the present pact is a 'fragile' one and the vital sovereignty issue still remains unresolved. So the same issue may rise again in the future. Thus, II is implicit.

52. (*a*) . Clearly, A advises B to join Y because it provides good Accounts education. So, I is implicit. It is not mentioned whether B listens to A's advice or not. So, II is not implicit.

53. (*e*) : The notice is meant for the people to read. So, it is assumed that the people are literate and I is implicit. Since the notice is to be read by everyone entering the club, so it is assumed that no blind person comes to the club. Thus, II is implicit.

54. (*b*) : Clearly, I is not directly related to the issue in the given statement and so is not implicit. The civic authority makes an appeal to the people with the hope that it would surely be attended to by the people. So, II is implicit.

55. (*a*) : The total utility can be maximised by equality of income throughout the community *i.e.*, by giving extra income from the rich to the poor. So, I is implicit. Also, II pertains to economic right and is not concerned with equality of income throughout the community. So, it is not implicit.

56. (*a*) : The fact that historians have done harm by distorting truth, means that people believe what is reported by the historians. So, I is implicit. II does not follow from the statement and so is not implicit.

57. (*e*) : The statement expresses a doubt at the non-depiction of the village in a map which was said to be an 'official' one. So, both I and II are implicit.

58. (*e*) : The statement mentions the self-sufficiency of India in continuous casting refractories. This means that they are needed in the country. So, I is implicit. Since continuous casting refractories are needed in integrated steel plants it means that they are in demand. So, II is implicit.

59. (*a*) : The statement mentions that there is no problem if one comes upto 7 p.m. also. This means that the programme will continue even after 7 p.m. So, I is implicit. Also, it is clearly mentioned that the programme will start at 6 p.m. So, II is not implicit.

60. (*a*) : Clearly, the suggestion is given for providing a method of identification. This means that the staff needs to be identified. So, I is implicit. The statement does not mention anything about the fashion. So, II is not implicit.

61. (*d*) : The statement mentions the cause of family problems and does not deal with all the problems. So, I is not implicit. Also, it is mentioned that money is the cause of family problems. But this does not mean that problems always exist in a family. So, II is also not implicit.

62. (*b*) : Since the Ministry has decided to support the voluntary organisations, it is quite probable that they are in need of it. So, I is not implicit. Further, since the economic package for the voluntary organisations has been announced recently, it can be assumed that no such support was being given to them earlier. So, II is implicit.

63. (*b*) : Clearly, the advertisement does not mention the word 'only' *i.e.*, other air-conditioners may also have wide variations. So, I is not implicit. Clearly, the advertisement is given so that the people know about that which they demand. So, II is implicit.

64. (*b*) : The statement mentions that only those students are to be helped who are filling up the form for the first time. This does not mean that the form is complicated. So, I is not implicit. However, II follows from the statement and so is implicit.

65. (*d*) : The advertisement persuades the people to meet the sole agent Y to buy T.V. but does not mean that the people prefer to buy T.V. through the sole agent or that the T.V. companies only sell their products through the sole agents. So, both I and II are not implicit.

66. (*e*) : Since both I and II follow from the given statement, so both are implicit.

67. (*a*) : Unaided colleges have been allowed to increase their fees. This means that they are in financial difficulties. So, I is implicit. Nothing is mentioned about the aided colleges. So, II is not implicit.

68. (*d*) : Neither the volume of readership of the 'Times' in areas other than the Metropolis nor the reason for its huge acclamation is evident from the statement. So, neither I nor II is implicit.

69. (*b*) : The statement mentions that participative management policy 'will' provide quality life to the workers. So, I is not implicit. Clearly, the statement mentions that participative management will contain the indiscipline and ensure quality life to workers. So, II is implicit.

70. (d) : Efforts are being made to boost tourism does not mean that tourism has dropped. So, I is not implicit. Also, the statement mentions nothing about discounts in air fare. So, II is also not implicit.

EXERCISE 3B

Directions : *In each question below is given a statement followed by two assumptions numbered I and II. You have to consider the statement and the following assumptions and decide which of the assumptions is implicit in the statement.*

Give answer (a) if only assumption I is implicit; (b) if only assumption II is implicit; (c) if either I or II is implicit; (d) if neither I nor II is implicit and (e) if both I and II are implicit.

1. **Statement** : Unemployment allowance should be given to all unemployed Indian youth above 18 years of age. **(Bank P.O. 1996)**

   Assumptions : I. There are unemployed youth in India who need monetary support.

   II. The government has sufficient funds to provide allowance to all unemployed youth.

2. **Statement** : "If I am not well you will have to go for the meeting." — A manager tells his subordinate.

   Assumptions : I. It is not necessary that only manager level personnel attend the meeting.

   II. If the manager is well, he would himself like to go for the meeting.

3. **Statement** : The electric supply corporation has decided to open a few more collection centres in the business district area.

   Assumptions : I. The people in the area may welcome the decision.

   II. Henceforth, there may be less time required by the customers for paying electricity bill. **(S.B.I.P.O. 1997)**

4. **Statement** : Like a mad man, I decided to follow him.

   Assumptions : I. I am not a mad man.

   II. I am a mad man.

5. **Statement** : What a fool I am to rely on trickster like Shaleen !

   Assumptions : I. Shaleen is unreliable.

   II. I am a fool.

6. **Statement** : "If you want timely completion of work, provide independent cabins." — An employee tells the Director of a company.

   Assumptions : I. There are not enough cabins.

   II. Others' presence hinders timely completion of work.

7. **Statement** : If it is easy to become an engineer, I don't want to be an engineer.

   Assumptions : I. An individual aspires to be professional.

   II. One desires to achieve a thing which is hard earned.

8. **Statement** : Interview conducted for selecting people for jobs should measure personality characteristics of candidates.   **(U.T.I. 1993)**
   Assumptions : I. Performance on job depends on personality characteristics.
   II. Personality characteristics can be measured in interview.

9. **Statement** : All the employees are notified that the organisation will provide transport facilities at half cost from the nearby railway station to the office except those who have been provided with travelling allowance.
   Assumptions : I. Most of the employees will travel by the office transport.
   II. Those who are provided with travelling allowance will not read such notice.

10. **Statement** : An advertisement of a Bank "Want to open a bank account ! Just dial our 'room service' and we will come at your doorsteps".
    Assumptions : I. There is a section of people who require such service at their home.
    II. Nowadays banking has become very competitive.
    (Bank P.O. 1998)

11. **Statement** : Who rises from the prayer a better man, his prayer is answered.
    Assumptions : I. Prayer makes a man more humane.
    II. Prayer atones all of our misdeeds.

12. **Statement** : I can take you quickly from Kanpur to Lucknow by my cab but then you must pay me double the normal charges.
    Assumptions : I. Normally, it will take more time to reach Lucknow from Kanpur.
    II. People want to reach quickly but they will not pay extra money for it.   **(Bank P.O. 1996)**

13. **Statement** : The present examination system needs overhauling thoroughly.
    Assumptions : I. The present examination system is obsolete.
    II. Overhauling results in improvement.

14. **Statement** : The economic condition of the country has gone from bad to worse.
    Assumptions : I. The government has failed to tackle economic problems.
    II. People are not cooperating with the government.

15. **Statement** : The entire north India, including Delhi and the neighbouring states remained 'powerless' the whole day of 19th December 97 as the northern grid supplying electricity to the seven states collapsed yet again.   **(M.B.A. 1998)**
    Assumptions : I. The northern grid had collapsed earlier.
    II. The grid system of providing electricity to a group of states is an ineffective type of power supply system.

16. **Statement** : The improvement in the quality of T.V. programmes will lead to increase in the sales of T.V.
    Assumptions : I. T.V. is a good entertainment medium.
    II. The quality of T.V. programmes has improved recently.

17. **Statement** : Inspite of poor services, the commutators have not complained against it.

Assumptions : I. Generally people do not tolerate poor services.

II. Complaints sometimes improve services.

18. **Statement** : Children, who get encouragement, usually perform better — a note by the Principal to the parents. **(Bank P.O. 1993)**

Assumptions : I. Some parents do not encourage children.

II. Parents may follow Principal's advice.

19. **Statement** : "Banking services are fine tuned to meet growing business needs." — An advertisement.

Assumptions : I. Banking is a part of business activity.

II. Industrialists prefer better banking services.

20. **Statement** : Whenever you have any doubt on this subject, you may refer to the book by Enn & Enn. **(Bank P.O. 1998)**

Assumptions : I. The book by Enn & Enn is available.

II. There is no other book on this subject.

21. **Statement** : "According to me, you should get your child examined by a specialist doctor." — A tells B.

Assumptions : I. Specialist doctors are able to diagnose better than ordinary doctors.

II. B will certainly not agree with A's advice.

22. **Statement** : A Notice Board at a ticket window : 'Please come in queue.'

Assumptions : I. Unless instructed people will not form queue.

II. People any way want to purchase tickets. **(S.B.I.P.O. 1997)**

23. **Statement** : "In case you cannot return from the office by 8 P.M., inform us on phone at home." — The parents tell their son.

Assumptions : I. The son never informs about his late coming.

II. Unless specified, the son may not inform his parents.

24. **Statement** : Retired persons should not be appointed for executive posts in other organisations. **(Bank P.O. 1997)**

Assumptions : I. Retired persons may lack the zeal and commitment to carry out executive's work.

II. Retired persons do not take interest in the work and welfare of the new organisation.

25. **Statement** : Lack of stimulation in the first four or five years of life can have adverse consequences.

Assumptions : I. A great part of the development of observed intelligence occurs in the earliest years of life.

II. 50 per cent of the measurable intelligence at age of 17 is already predictable by the age of four.

26. **Statement** : "In my absence, I request you to look after the affairs of our company." — B tells C. **(Bank P.O. 1995)**

Assumptions : I. C may not accept the request of B.

II. C has the expertise to handle the affairs of the company.

27. **Statement** : Lock your valuables in a cupboard and call everybody gentleman.

Assumptions : I. Valuables locked in cupboard cannot be stolen.

II. Stealing is a crime.

28. Statement : The President assured the people that elections will be held here after every five years.

    Assumptions : I. People are afraid that the elections may not be held at all.

                   II. People are afraid that the elections may not be held after five years.

29. Statement : Use PVC pipes which have 10 years longer life to any other.

    Assumptions : I. People prefer only those pipes which are durable.

                   II. Other pipes are not durable. **(L.I.C.A.A.O. 1995)**

30. Statement : "Ensure a good night's sleep for your family with safe and effective X mosquito coil." — An advertisement.

    Assumptions : I. X mosquito coil is better than any other mosquito coil.

                   II. A good night's sleep is desirable.

31. Statement : There is no reason to rule out the possibility of life on Mars. Therefore, the exploration of that planet has to be undertaken.

    Assumptions : I. There is life on Mars.

                   II. The search for life is the sufficient reason for space exploration. **(C.B.I. 1995)**

32. Statement : An advertisement in a newspaper — "Wanted unmarried, presentable matriculate girls between 18 and 21, able to speak fluently in English to be taken as models."

    Assumptions : I. Fluency in English is a pre-requisite for good performance as a model.

                   II. Height does not matter in performing as a model.

33. Statement : Government aided schools should have uniformity in charging various fees. **(Bank P.O. 1996)**

    Assumptions : I. The Government's subsidy comes from the money collected by way of taxes from people.

                   II. The Government while giving subsidy may have stipulated certain uniform conditions regarding fees.

34. Statement : "The function will start at 3 P.M. You are requested to take your seats before 3 P.M." — Last sentence in an invitation card.

    Assumptions : I. If the invitee is not in his seat before 3 P.M., the function will not start.

                   II. Function will start as scheduled.

35. Statement : "A visit of school children to forest to widen their knowledge of natural resources has been arranged." — A notice in the school.

    Assumptions : I. Forests are full of natural resources.

                   II. Children are likely to learn from their interaction with the new environment.

36. Statement : Sachin wrote to his brother at Bangalore to collect personally the application form from the University for the post-graduation course in Mathematics. **(S.B.I.P.O. 1997)**

    Assumptions : I. The University may issue application forms to a person other than the prospective student.

                   II. Sachin's brother may receive the letter well before the last date of collecting application forms.

37. Statement : Neither fascism nor communism has any chance of succeeding in America.

    Assumptions : I. American people are strongly in favour of preserving the rights of the individual.

               II. Americans have so far not suffered any pangs of poverty or deprivation.

38. Statement : "Best way to solve this problem of workers' dissatisfaction is to offer them cash rewards. If this type of incentive can solve the problem in CIDCO company then why not here." — A Personnel Manager tells the Chairman of a company.

    Assumptions : I. The reason for workers' dissatisfaction in both the companies was similar.

               II. Monetary incentives have universal appeal. **(Bank P.O. 1993)**

39. Statement : The taste of food contributes to the intake of nourishment which is essential for the survival of human beings.

    Assumptions : I. Human beings take food for the enjoyment of its taste.

               II. Human beings experience the taste of food.

40. Statement : The economic prosperity of any nation is dependent on the quality of its human resources. **(Bank P.O. 1998)**

    Assumptions : I. It is possible to measure the quality of human resources of a nation.

               II. Achieving economic prosperity is a cherished goal of every nation.

41. Statement : "We offer the best training in the field of computers." — An advertisement.

    Assumptions : I. People are interested in getting training in computers.

               II. People want best training.

42. Statement : The coffee powder of company X is quite better in taste than the much advertised coffee of company Y. **(Bank P.O. 1996)**

    Assumptions : I. If your product is not good, you spend more on advertisement.

               II. Some people are tempted to buy a product by the advertisement.

43. Statement : "Please put more people on the job but make up for the delay".

    Assumptions : I. Delay is inevitable in most jobs.

               II. Output will increase with more number of people on the job.

44. Statement : Amongst newspapers, I always read the National Times.

    Assumptions : I. The National Times gives very comprehensive news.

               II. Some people prefer other newspapers.

45. Statement : Do not copy our software without our permission — A notice.

    Assumptions : I. It is possible to copy the software.

               II. Such warning will have some effect. **(Bank P.O. 1998)**

46. Statement : A warning in a train compartment — "To stop train, pull chain. Penalty for improper use Rs. 500."

    Assumptions : I. Some people misuse the alarm chain.

               II. On certain occasions, people may want to stop a running train.

47. Statement : Over 1-4 lakh quintals of cotton has been procured in the state under Cotton Procurement Scheme, a press note said.

Assumptions : I. Cotton procurement scheme is successful.

II. No cotton procurement should be done now.

48. Statement : Most people who stop smoking gain weight. **(C.B.I. 1995)**

Assumptions : I. If one stops smoking one will gain weight.

II. If one does not stop smoking one will not gain weight.

49. Statement : "If it does not rain throughout this month, most farmers would be in trouble this year."

Assumptions : I. Timely rain is essential for farming.

II. Most farmers are generally dependent on rains.

50. Statement : No budgetary provision for the purpose of appointing additional faculty would be made in the context of institute's changed financial priorities. **(U.T.I. 1993)**

Assumptions : I. Appointment of faculty requires funds.

II. There are areas other than appointment of faculty which require more financial attention.

51. Statement : The new education policy envisages major modifications in the education system.

Assumptions : I. Present education system is inconsistent with national needs.

II. Present education system needs change.

52. Statement : Many people have expressed surprise as the princess has broken the royal tradition of marriage by choosing a commoner as her life partner. **(Bank P.O. 1998)**

Assumptions : I. People expect royal families to observe customs and traditions.

II. People still value 'purity of royal blood' and 'status' when it comes to a marriage of members of royal family.

53. Statement : "In order to bring punctuality in our office, we must provide conveyance allowance to our employees." — Incharge of a company tells Personnel Manager. **(Bank P.O. 1993)**

Assumptions : I. Conveyance allowance will not help in bringing punctuality.

II. Discipline and reward should always go hand in hand.

54. Statement : If you are an engineer, we have a challenging job for you.

Assumptions : I. We need an engineer.

II. You are an engineer.

55. Statement : You know that your suit is excellent when people ask about your tailor who tailored the suit. **(L.I.C.A.A.O. 1995)**

Assumptions : I. People do not ask about your tailor if your suit is not good.

II. The people want to know the criterion of an excellent suit.

56. Statement : All existing inequalities can be reduced, if not utterly eradicated, by action of governments or by revolutionary change of government.

Assumptions : I. Inequality is a man-made phenomenon.

II. No person would voluntarily part with what he possesses.

57. Statement : Why don't you invite Anthony for the Christmas party this year ? **(Bank P.O. 1997)**

    Assumptions : I. Anthony is not from the same city.

                 II. Unless invited Anthony will not attend the party.

58. Statement : "You should not grant him leave in this week due to exigency of work." — A supervisor advises the administrative officer.

    Assumptions : I. Request for leave can be turned down also.

                 II. The supervisor has reviewed the work required to be done during the said period.

ANSWERS

1. (*a*) : I directly follows from the statement and so is implicit. Also, the statement is a suggestion and does not tell about a government policy or its position of funds. So, II is not implicit.

2. (*e*) : Clearly, the subordinate can attend the meeting as told by the Manager only when there is no inhibition. So, I is implicit. The subordinate is told to go only in case when the Manager is not well. This also shows the urgency to attend the meeting. So, II is also implicit.

3. (*e*) : Clearly, more collection centres would enable the common people to pay their bills easily, conveniently and quickly and this would cause them to welcome the idea. So, both I and II are implicit.

4. (*c*) : The words 'Like a mad man' show that either a person is really mad or he is not mad but acted like mad. So, either I or II is implicit.

5. (*e*) : Since one condemns oneself to rely on Shaleen, so I is implicit. The statement mentions that it was foolish to rely on Shaleen. So, the person is a fool. Thus, II is implicit.

6. (*e*) : The statement clearly hints at the need for cabins. So, I is implicit. Since independent cabins are expected to improve efficiency, it means that others' presence hinders work. So, II is also implicit.

7. (*b*) : Clearly, nothing is mentioned about the professional nature of the job. So, I is not implicit. The statement hints that one rejects a thing that is easy to achieve. So, II is implicit.

8. (*e*) : According to the statement, the personality characteristics of candidates should be essentially measured in interviews before selection for jobs. So, both I and II are implicit.

9. (*d*) : The response of the employees towards the policy cannot be deduced. So, I is not implicit. Also, the statement 'All the employees are notified....' implies that the notice is for all the employees. So, II is also not implicit.

10. (*b*) : The requirement for such a service is not mentioned in the statement. So, I is not implicit. Further, providing banking services at home means that banking has become so competitive that door-to-door service is being provided by the Bank to attract people. So, II is implicit.

11. (*d*) : The fact that only persons who become better by saying prayer are responded to, shows that prayer does not necessarily make man humane. So, I is not implicit. Nothing is mentioned as regards the fruitfulness of prayer. So, II is also not implicit.

12. (*a*) : Since the narrator asks for double charges to take the person quickly to Lucknow, it implies that normally it takes more time to reach Lucknow. So, I is implicit. Since one demands extra charges to reach the destination earlier than usual, the person in need would have to pay accordingly. So, II is not implicit.

13. (*e*) : The 'thorough' overhauling is needed only in case of an obsolete system. So, I is implicit. Overhauling is done for improvement. So, II is also implicit.

14. (*a*) : The statement implies that the existing economic problems have worsened. So, I is implicit. Nothing about the people's attitude is mentioned. So, II is not implicit.

15. (*a*) : The statement mentions that the northern grid collapsed 'yet again'. This means that it had collapsed earlier also. So, I is implicit. Also, the statement talks of a particular fault in the system but does not condemn the grid system. So, II is not implicit.

16. (*a*) : The improvement in quality of programmes will increase the sale shows that it is in great use. So, I is implicit. Nothing is mentioned of recent changes. So, II is not implicit.

17. (*a*) : The statement expresses an expectation of complaints from the people against poor services. So, I is implicit. But the effect of complaints cannot be deduced. So, II is not implicit.

18. (*e*) : The statement talks of the performance of children who get encouragement. It means that there are some children who are not encouraged. So, I is implicit. Also, the Principal notifies to the parents that encouragement helps children improve their performance, with the hope that they too would encourage their children. So, II is also implicit.

19. (*e*) : According to the statement, banking is connected to business activity. So, I is implicit. Banking is adjusted in a way to promote business needs. This means that business is promoted by better banking. So, II is also implicit.

20. (*a*) : The recommendation of the book by Enn and Enn implies that it is available. So, I is implicit. Also, the book has been referred to as a good one, but this does not mean that no other books are available on the subject. So, II is not implicit.

21. (*a*) : The advice particularly mentions 'a specialist doctor' and not simply 'doctor'. So, I is implicit. B's response to A's advice cannot be deduced from the given statement. So, II is not implicit.

22. (*e*) : The instructions have been given so that people willing to buy tickets may not form a crowd. So, I is implicit. Also, it is clear that people would purchase the tickets even after following the given instructions. So, II is also implicit.

23. (*b*) : Clearly, the statement is merely a reminder. So, I is not implicit. There is a possibility that if not specified, the son may not inform. So, II is implicit.

24. (*d*) : Since both I and II do not follow from the statement, so neither of them is implicit.

25. (*a*) : The lacking in first four or five years can be adverse because it is the main period of development. So, I is implicit. Since nothing is mentioned about the predictability of intelligence, II is not implicit.

26. (*b*) : C's response to B's request cannot be deduced from the statement. So, I is not implicit. Also, B wishes to authorise C to look after the company in his absence. This means that C is capable of handling the affairs. So, II is implicit.

27. (*a*) : The statement points out that a person who keeps his things locked away shall feel that every person is good because he has no danger for his things. So, I is implicit. The statement mentions nothing about the lawful nature of the act of stealing. So, II is not implicit.

28. (*c*) : Clearly, the statement is made to eliminate the fear of the people that the elections may not be held at all or they may not be held after five years. So, either I or II is implicit.

29. (*b*) : Clearly, nothing is mentioned about the choice of the people. It is simply an advice. So, I is not implicit. Clearly, the other pipes are not as durable as the PVC pipes. So, II is implicit.

30. (*b*) : The statement mentions the good qualities of X coil but this does not mean it is the best. So, I is not implicit. The advertisement is meant to enable people to have a good night's sleep. So, II is implicit.

31. (*e*) : According to the statement, the possibility of life on Mars cannot be ruled out. So, I is implicit. Also, the statement mentions that the planet should be explored to probe for any life present. So, II is also implicit.

32. (*a*) : 'Fluency in English' is a condition mentioned for girls to be taken as model. So, I is implicit. Since nothing is mentioned about the height, so II is not implicit.

33. (*b*) : Nothing about the source of Government's subsidy can be deduced from the statement. So, I is not implicit. However, II follows from the statement and so it is implicit.

34. (*b*) : It is mentioned that the function will start at 3 P.M. and not that the invitees will be waited for. So, I is not implicit and only II is implicit.

35. (*e*) : The forests shall be visited to increase the knowledge of natural resources. This means that forests abound in natural resources. So, I is implicit. The children are being taken to forests to help them learn more. So, II is also implicit.

36. (*e*) : Since Sachin has asked his brother to collect the form, it is evident that the University may issue the form to anybody and that Sachin's brother would receive the letter before the last date of collecting the forms. So, both I and II are implicit.

37. (*a*) : Clearly, fascism and communism are against the preservation of individual rights. So, I is implicit. Nothing is mentioned about the economic condition of America. So, II is not implicit.

38. (*e*) : Since the policy is expected to work just because it turned out fruitful in another company, it is evident that the problem in both companies was similar and monetary incentives always motivate workers. So, both I and II are implicit.

39. (*b*) : It is mentioned that nourishment is essential for survival. So, this is the basic cause of intake of food. Hence, I is not implicit. Since taste of food affects the intake of nourishment, it means that human beings are affected by taste. So, II is implicit.

40. (*a*) : I follows from the statement and so is implicit. But the status of economic prosperity as a nation's goal is not discussed in the statement. So, II is not implicit.

41. (*e*) : The advertisement is meant to cater to the people's demand of computer training. So, I is implicit. The offer of 'best training' makes II implicit.

42. (*b*) : Since the statement holds the product of company X more superior in quality than that of Y which spends more on advertisement, so I is not implicit. According to the statement, the product of company Y is more known because of more advertisement. So, II is implicit.

43. (*b*) : The advice tells to 'make up for the delay' showing that delay is not to be done. So, I is not implicit. Since increase in number of people will prevent the delay, it means the output will increase with this increase in number. So, II is implicit.

44. (*b*) : The statement does not mention any quality of the National Times. So, I is not implicit. According to the statement, amongst all newspapers, the narrator reads the National Times. This means that some people read other newspapers. So, II is implicit.

45. (*e*) : Since the notice warns one against copying software without permission, it is evident that software can be copied. So, I is implicit. Also, the warning is given with the motive that no one dares to copy the software. So, II is also implicit.

46. (*e*) : Clearly, the penalty is imposed to prevent people from misusing the alarm chain. This means that some people misuse it. So, I is implicit. The alarm chain is provided to stop the running train in times of urgency. So, II is also implicit.

47. (*d*) : The statement mentions only the quantity procured and not the success or failure of the scheme. So, I is not implicit. Since the statement does not mention whether the requirements are fully satisfied, so II is also not implicit.

48. (*d*) : The statement talks of 'most people' and not 'all'. So, I is not necessarily true. Thus, I is not implicit. The condition, if one does not stop smoking, cannot be deduced from the statement. So, II is also not implicit.

49. (*e*) : It is mentioned that farmers will be in trouble without rain. This means that timely rain is essential. Also, it shows that farmers are dependent on rain. So, both I and II are implicit.

50. (*e*) : The phrase 'budgetary provision for the purpose of appointing additional faculty' makes I implicit. Also, since no budgetary provision was provided for appointment of faculty in view of certain changed financial priorities, it means that some other issues require more financial attention. So, II is also implicit.

51. (e) : Clearly, modifications are made in present system finding that it was inconsistent with the needs and required to be changed. So, both I and II are implicit.

52. (b) : The objection has been put to the princess' marrying a commoner and not to non-observance of traditions. So, I is not implicit and only II is implicit.

53. (b) : Assumption I goes against the statement. So, it is not implicit. The allowance will serve as a reward to the employees and shall provoke them to come on time. So, II is implicit.

54. (a) : Clearly, job is offered to an engineer. This means that he is needed. So, I is implicit. The word 'If' in the statement makes II not implicit.

55. (a) : The statement mentions that if the people ask about the tailor, your suit is good. This means that people ask only in the situation when the thing is good. So, I is implicit. The criteria of an excellent suit is not mentioned. So, II is not implicit.

56. (a) : Since inequality can be reduced, it means that it is not natural but created. So, I is implicit. Nothing is mentioned about people's response. So, II is not implicit.

57. (b) : Anthony's place of living is not mentioned in the statement. So, I is not implicit. Assumption II follows from the statement and so it is implicit.

58. (e) : The advice is given to turn down the request for leave. So, I is implicit. The mention of the 'exigency of work' makes II implicit.

TYPE 2

This section also consists of similar type of questions as in Type 1, with the difference that three assumptions are given and the candidate is required to choose that group which is implicit in context of the given statement.

Ex. 1. Statement : The company has recently announced a series of incentives to the employees who are punctual and sincere.

Assumptions : I. Those who are not punctual at present may get motivated by the announcement.

II. The productivity of the company may increase.

III. The profit earned by the company may be more than the amount to be spent for the incentive programmes.

(a) Only I and II are implicit   (b) None is implicit
(c) Only II and III are implicit   (d) All are implicit
(e) None of these   **(Bank P.O. 1997)**

Sol. Announcing incentives for punctual and sincere employees would surely motivate more and more employees to be punctual, and this will surely increase productivity. So, both I and II are implicit. However, the statement does not give any information about the profit earned by the company. So, III is not implicit.

Hence, the answer is (a).

Ex. 2. Statement : Opening a library in Rambli will be a wastage.

Assumptions : I. Inhabitants of Rambli are illiterate.

II. Inhabitants of Rambli are not interested in reading.

III. There is an adequate number of libraries in Rambli already.

(a) Only I and II are implicit   (b) Only III is implicit
(c) Only either I or III is implicit   (d) Only II is implicit
(e) Only either I or II or III is implicit

Sol. Clearly, a library will be a wastage only when either the people of the place cannot read or they are not interested in reading or there are adequate number of libraries there. So, either I or II or III is implicit.

Hence, the answer is (e).

EXERCISE 3C

Directions : *In each question below is given a statement followed by three assumptions numbered I, II and III. You have to consider the statement and the following assumptions, decide which of the assumptions is implicit in the statement and choose your answer accordingly.*

1. **Statement** : "I want to present a book on techniques of yoga to Ajay on his birthday" — A tells B.

   Assumptions : I. A will be invited by Ajay on his birthday.

   II. The person to whom the book is to be presented, is not keeping good health.

   III. Book is an acceptable gift for birthday.

   (a) Only I and II are implicit   (b) Only II and III are implicit

   (c) Only I and III are implicit   (d) None is implicit

   (e) All are implicit

2. **Statement** : "Wanted a two bedroom flat in the court area for immediate possession" — an advertisement.   **(Bank P.O. 1994)**

   Assumptions : I. Flats are available in court area.

   II. Some people will respond to the advertisement.

   III. It is a practice to give such an advertisement.

   (a) All are implicit   (b) Only II is implicit

   (c) None is implicit   (d) Only I and II are implicit

   (e) None of these

3. **Statement** : The situation of this area still continues to be tense and out of control. People are requested to be in their homes only.

   Assumptions : I. There had been some serious incidents.

   II. People will not go to the office.

   III. Normalcy will be restored shortly.   **(Bank P.O. 1996)**

   (a) Only I is implicit   (b) Only I and II are implicit

   (c) None is implicit   (d) Only I and III are implicit

   (e) All are implicit

4. **Statement** : "Buy pure and natural honey of company X" — an advertisement in a newspaper.

   Assumptions : I. Artificial honey can be prepared.

   II. People do not mind paying more for pure and natural honey.

   III. No other company supplies pure honey.

   (a) Only I is implicit   (b) Only I and II are implicit

   (c) Only I and III are implicit   (d) All are implicit

   (e) None of these

5. **Statement** : "Fly with us and experience the pleasure of flying" — an advertisement by an airlines.   **(Bank P.O. 1995)**

   Assumptions : I. More passengers may be attracted to travel by the airline after reading the advertisement.

   II. People generally may prefer an enjoyable flight.

   III. Other airlines may not be offering the same facilities.

   (a) None is implicit   (b) Only I is implicit
   (c) Only II is implicit   (d) Only II and III are implicit
   (e) None of these

6. **Statement** : Unable to manage with the present salary, Arun has decided to join another company.

   Assumptions : I. The new company has better work environment.

   II. The present company offers moderate pay packets.

   III. The new company offers higher salary to all its employees.

   (a) None is implicit   (b) Only II is implicit
   (c) All are implicit   (d) Only II and III are implicit
   (e) None of these

7. **Statement** : "Put a notice on the board that all the employees should come on time to office" — An officer tells his assistant.

   Assumptions : I. All the employees come late.

   II. Employees read such notice on the board.

   III. Employees will follow the instructions.

   (a) Only I and II are implicit   (b) Only III is implicit
   (c) Only II and III are implicit   (d) Only I and III are implicit
   (e) All are implicit   **(S.B.I.P.O. 1994)**

8. **Statement** : "Join X-tuition classes for sure success. Excellent teaching by excellent teachers is our strength" — An advertisement.

   Assumptions : I. Sure success is desirable.

   II. Students expect sure success when they join any tuition class.

   III. Just having excellent teachers does not ensure sure success.

   (a) Only I and II are implicit   (b) Only II and III are implicit
   (c) Only I and III are implicit   (d) Only II is implicit
   (e) All are implicit

9. **Statement** : "Z-T.V., the only T.V. which gives the viewers a chance to watch two programmes simultaneously" — an advertisement.

   Assumptions : I. Sale of Z-T.V. will increase because of the advertisement.

   II. Some people may be influenced by the advertisement and buy Z-T.V.

   III. The sale of Z-T.V. may be on the downward trend.

   (a) None is implicit   (b) All are implicit
   (c) Only I and II are implicit   (d) Only II and III are implicit
   (e) None of these   **(Bank P.O. 1997)**

10. **Statement** : "We do not want you to see our product on newspaper, visit our shop to get a full view" — an advertisement.

Assumptions : I. People generally decide to purchase any product after seeing the name in the advertisement.

II. Uncommon appeal may attract the customers.

III. People may come to see the product.

(a) None is implicit   (b) Only I and II are implicit

(c) Only II and III are implicit   (d) All are implicit

(e) None of these

11. **Statement** : Pramod decided to get the railway reservation in May, for the journey he wants to make in July, to Madras.

Assumptions : I. The railways issues reservations two months in advance.

II. There is more than one trains to Madras.

III. There will be vacancy in the desired class.

(a) Only I is implicit   (b) Only II and III are implicit

(c) Only I and III are implicit   (d) All are implicit

(e) None of these   **(Bank P.O. 1994)**

12. **Statement** : "Work hard to be successful in the examinations" — A advises B.

Assumptions : I. B listens to A's advice.

II. Passing the examination is desirable.

III. Hard practice leads to success.

(a) Only I and II are implicit   (b) Only II and III are implicit

(c) Only I and III are implicit   (d) All are implicit

(e) None of these

13. **Statement** : The residents of the locality wrote a letter to the Corporation requesting to restore normalcy in the supply of drinking water immediately as the supply at present is just not adequate.

Assumptions : I. The Corporation may not take any action on the letter.

II. The municipality has enough water to meet the demand.

III. The water supply to the area was adequate in the past.

(a) Only I and III are implicit   (b) Only II is implicit

(c) Only II and III are implicit   (d) Only III is implicit

(e) None of these   **(Bank P.O. 1994)**

14. **Statement** : "Use Riya cold cream for fair complexion" — an advertisement.

Assumptions : I. People like to use cream for fair complexion.

II. People are easily fooled.

III. People respond to advertisements.

(a) Only I is implicit   (b) Only I and II are implicit

(c) Only II is implicit   (d) Only I and III are implicit

(e) None of these

15. **Statement** : We must be prepared to face any eventuality and all the assignments must be completed as per their schedule — Director tells the Faculty members.   **(Bank P.O. 1996)**

Assumptions : I. There is possibility of any serious eventuality.

II. Dates are fixed for all the assignments.

III. Faculty members are supposed to complete all the assignments.

(a) Only I is implicit   (b) None is implicit
(c) Only III is implicit   (d) Only II and III are implicit
(e) All are implicit

16. **Statement**   : The successful man has the ability to judge himself correctly.

    Assumptions :   I. Inability to judge correctly cause failure.

    II. To judge others is of no use to a successful man.

    III. The successful man cannot make a wrong judgement.

    (a) None is implicit   (b) All are implicit
    (c) Only I and II are implicit   (d) Only II and III are implicit
    (e) Only I and III are implicit

17. **Statement**   : The professor announced in the class that the next periodical examination will be held on 15th of the next month.

    Assumptions :   I. All the students may appear in the examination.

    II. The college will remain open on 15th of the next month.

    III. The students can study till 15th of the next month to pass the examination.

    (a) Only I and II are implicit   (b) Only II is implicit
    (c) Only II and III are implicit   (d) Only III is implicit
    (e) None of these   **(Bank P.O. 1995)**

18. **Statement**   : The telephone company informed the subscribers through a notification that those who do not pay their bills by the due date will be charged penalty for every defaulting day.

    Assumptions :   I. Majority of the people may pay their bills by the due date to avoid penalty.

    II. The money collected as penalty may set off the losses due to delayed payment.

    III. People generally pay heed to such notices.

    (a) All are implicit   (b) Only II and III are implicit
    (c) Only I and II are implicit   (d) None is implicit
    (e) None of these

19. **Statement**   : "As our business is expanding, we need to appoint more staff" — Owner of a company informs his staff.

    Assumptions :   I. The present staff is not competent.

    II. More staff will further expand the business.

    III. Suitable persons to be taken as staff will be available.

    (a) None is implicit   (b) Only I is implicit
    (c) Only II is implicit   (d) Only III is implicit
    (e) All are implicit   **(S.B.I.P.O. 1994)**

20. **Statement**   : Delink degrees with jobs. Then, boys will think twice before joining colleges.

    Assumptions :   I. Boys join college education for getting jobs.

    II. A degree is of no use for getting a job.

    III. Girls do not try for jobs.

    (a) Only I is implicit   (b) Only I and II are implicit
    (c) Only II and III are implicit   (d) Only I and III are implicit
    (e) All are implicit

21. **Statement** : Ravi decided to leave office at 4.00 p.m. to catch a flight to Bangalore departing at 6.00 p.m. **(Bank P.O. 1997)**

   Assumptions : I. The flight to Bangalore may be delayed.

   II. He may be able to reach airport well before 6.00 p.m.

   III. He may get adequate time to search for a vehicle to go to the airport.

   (a) None is implicit   (b) Only II is implicit
   (c) Only II and III are implicit   (d) All are implicit
   (e) None of these

22. **Statement** : During pre-harvest kharif season, the government has decided to release vast quantity of foodgrains from FCI.

   Assumptions : I. There may be a shortage of foodgrains in the market during this season.

   II. The kharif crop may be able to replenish the stock of FCI.

   III. There may be a demand from the farmers to procure kharif crop immediately after harvest.

   (a) All are implicit   (b) Only II and III are implicit
   (c) Only I and II are implicit   (d) None is implicit
   (e) None of these   **(Bank P.O. 1995)**

23. **Statement** : 'Smoking is injurious to health' — a warning printed on the cigarette packets.

   Assumptions : I. People read printed matter on a cigarette packet.

   II. People take careful note of a warning.

   III. Non-smoking promotes health.

   (a) Only I is implicit   (b) Only I and II are implicit
   (c) Only II is implicit   (d) All are implicit
   (e) None of these

24. **Statement** : In view of the recent spurt in sugar prices in the open market, the government has asked the dealers to release a vast quantity of imported sugar in the open market.

   Assumptions : I. The dealers will follow the government directive.

   II. The sugar prices will come down.

   III. The price of indigenous sugar will remain unchanged.

   (a) Only I and II are implicit   (b) Only II and III are implicit
   (c) Only I and III are implicit   (d) None is implicit
   (e) All are implicit   **(Bank P.O. 1994)**

25. **Statement** : "We must introduce objective type tests to improve our examinations for admission to MBA" — The Chairman of the Admission Committee tells the Committee.

   Assumptions : I. The admission at present is directly through the interview.

   II. The Admission Committee is desirous of improving the admission examinations.

   III. The Chairman himself is an MBA.

   (a) Only I and III are implicit   (b) Only II is implicit
   (c) Only I and II are implicit   (d) Only I is implicit
   (e) None is implicit

26. Statement : "To make the company commercially viable, there is an urgent need to prune the staff strength and borrow money from the financial institutions" — opinion of a consultant.

Assumptions : I. The financial institutions lend money for such proposals.
II. The product of the company has a potential market.
III. The employees of the company are inefficient.

(*a*) None is implicit   (*b*) All are implicit
(*c*) Only I and II are implicit   (*d*) Only II and III are implicit
(*e*) Only I and III are implicit   **(Bank P.O. 1994)**

27. Statement : In the recently held All Indian Commerce Conference the session on 'Management of Service Sector in India' surprisingly attracted large number of participants and also received a very good media coverage in the leading newspapers.

Assumptions : I. People were not expecting such an encouraging response for service sector.
II. Service sector is not managed properly in India.
III. Media is always very positive towards service sector.

(*a*) Only I is implicit   (*b*) Only II and III are implicit
(*c*) None is implicit   (*d*) All are implicit
(*e*) Only either I or III is implicit   **(Bank P.O. 1996)**

28. Statement : Let us increase the taxes to cover the deficit.

Assumptions : I. The present taxes are very low.
II. Deficit in a budget is not desirable.
III. If the taxes are not increased, the deficit cannot be met.

(*a*) Only I and II are implicit   (*b*) Only II and III are implicit
(*c*) Only I and III are implicit   (*d*) All are implicit
(*e*) None of these

29. Statement : In order to reduce the gap between income and expenditure, the company has decided to increase the price of its product from next month.   **(Bank P.O. 1995)**

Assumptions : I. The rate will remain more or less same after the increase.
II. The expenditure will more or less remain the same in near future.
III. The rival companies will also increase the price of the similar product.

(*a*) Only I and II are implicit   (*b*) Only II and III are implicit
(*c*) Only III is implicit   (*d*) All are implicit
(*e*) None of these

30. Statement : The national air carrier has decided to start a weekly air service from town A to town B.

Assumptions : I. There will be enough passengers to make the operation economically viable.
II. Other carriers may not start such service.
III. The people staying around these towns can afford the cost of air travel.

(a) Only I is implicit   (b) Only I and II are implicit
(c) Only II and III are implicit   (d) All are implicit
(e) None of these

31. **Statement** : Quality of life of a person is not dependent only on his wealth.

    Assumptions : I. The aim of most people is just to acquire more wealth.

    II. There are some factors other than wealth which contribute to the quality of life.

    III. Wealth does not contribute to the quality of life at all.

(a) Only I is implicit   (b) Only II is implicit
(c) Only I and II are implicit   (d) Only II and III are implicit
(e) Only I and III are implicit

32. **Statement** : The State Government has unilaterally increased by five per cent octroi on all commodities entering into the state without seeking approval of the Central Government.

    Assumptions : I. The State Government may be able to implement its decision.

    II. The Central Government may agree to support the State Government's decision.

    III. The State Government may be able to earn considerable amount through the additional octroi.

(a) Only I and II are implicit   (b) None is implicit
(c) Only II and III are implicit   (d) All are implicit
(e) None of these   **(Bank P.O. 1997)**

33. **Statement** : The Reserve Bank of India has directed the banks to refuse fresh loans to major defaulters.   **(Bank P.O. 1995)**

    Assumptions : I. The banks may still give loans to the defaulters.

    II. The defaulters may repay the earlier loan to get fresh loan.

    III. The banks may recover the bad loans through such harsh measures.

(a) None is implicit   (b) Only I and II are implicit
(c) All are implicit   (d) Only II and III are implicit
(e) None of these

34. **Statement** : The economic condition continues to be critical even after a good harvest season.

    Assumptions : I. The economic condition was not critical before the harvest season.

    II. The economic condition could not have improved without a good harvest season.

    III. The economic condition was expected to improve after a good harvest season.

(a) Only I and II are implicit   (b) Only II is implicit
(c) Only II and III are implicit   (d) Only III is implicit
(e) Only I and III are implicit

35. **Statement** : The school authority decided to open a summer school this year in the school compound for the students in the age range of 7-14 years.   **(Bank P.O. 1994)**

Assumptions : I. All the students will attend the summer school.

II. All the parents will prefer to remain in the city than going out of town for enabling their children to attend the summer school.

III. Those who cannot afford to go out of station will send their children to summer school.

(*a*) None is implicit   (*b*) Only II is implicit

(*c*) Only II and III are implicit   (*d*) Only III is implicit

(*e*) All are implicit

36. Statement : "Do not lean out of the moving train" — a warning in the railway compartment.

Assumptions : I. Such warnings will have some effect.

II. Leaning out of a moving train is dangerous.

III. It is the duty of railway authorities to take care of passengers' safety.

(*a*) Only I and II are implicit   (*b*) Only II and III are implicit

(*c*) Only II is implicit   (*d*) Only I and III are implicit

(*e*) All are implicit

37. Statement : The Central Government has directed the State Governments to reduce government expenditure in view of the serious resource crunch and it may not be able to sanction any additional grant to the states for the next six months.

Assumptions : I. The State Governments are totally dependent on Central Government for its expenditures.

II. The Central Government has reviewed the expenditure account of the State Government.

III. The State Governments will abide by the directive.

(*a*) None is implicit   (*b*) Only II and III are implicit

(*c*) Only III is implicit   (*d*) All are implicit

(*e*) None of these   **(Bank P.O. 1994)**

38. Statement : State Council For Teacher Education (SCTE) has laid down guidelines in respect of minimum qualifications for a person to be employed as a teacher in universities or in recognised institutions. **(Bank P.O. 1996)**

Assumptions : I. The authorities will now appoint only qualified teachers.

II. Only qualified people will apply for the teaching post.

III. SCTE decides all the norms of educational qualification for teaching faculty.

(*a*) None is implicit   (*b*) Only I is implicit

(*c*) Only I and II are implicit   (*d*) Only I and III are implicit

(*e*) All are implicit

39. Statement : "All are cordially invited to attend the entertainment programme. It is free" — an announcement in a newspaper.

Assumptions : I. People generally do not go to entertainment programmes which are free.

II. Some people, though interested in entertainment programmes, cannot afford purchasing the tickets.

III. Generally, a free entertainment programme is of a good quality.

(a) Only I is implicit
(b) Only I and II are implicit
(c) Only II is implicit
(d) Only II and III are implicit
(e) Only I and III are implicit

40. **Statement** : Keeping in view the financial constraint, the management institution has decided to charge at the time of providing employment in various organisations, a placement fee of Rs 25000 from the organisations in which the student will be provided the employment.   **(Bank P.O 1995)**

Assumptions : I. It will help in increasing the demand of the students belonging to the management institution.

II. The amount collected in this way will be purposeful.

III. It may be possible that the organisation providing employment may select less number of students in future.

(a) None is implicit
(b) Only I is implicit
(c) Only I and II are implicit
(d) Only II and III are implicit
(e) None of these

41. **Statement** : To improve the employment situation in India, there is a need to recast the present educational system towards implementation of scientific discoveries in daily life.

Assumptions : I. The students after completing such education may be able to earn their livelihood.

II. This may bring meaning of education in the minds of the youth.

III. The state may earn more revenue as more and more people will engage themselves in self-employment.

(a) None is implicit
(b) Only I and II are implicit
(c) Only III is implicit
(d) Only I and III are implicit
(e) None of these

42. **Statement** : Inspite of the heavy rains the traffic has not been disrupted this year.

Assumptions : I. The traffic is disrupted in rainy seasons only.

II. Rains do not affect traffic movement.

III. Adequate precautions were taken for traffic management during rainy season.

(a) Only I and II are implicit
(b) Only I is implicit
(c) Only II and III are implicit
(d) Only III is implicit
(e) None is implicit

43. **Statement** : "X-chocolate is ideal as a gift for someone you love" — an advertisement.   **(Bank P.O. 1994)**

Assumptions : I. People generally give gifts to loved ones.

II. Such advertisements generally influence people.

III. Chocolate can be considered as a gift item.

(a) Only I and II are implicit   (b) Only II and III are implicit
(c) Only I and III are implicit   (d) All are implicit
(e) None of these

44. Statement   : "If you are beautiful, we will catch your beauty. If you are not, we will make you beautiful" — an advertisement of a photo studio.

   Assumptions : I. How to look beautiful, is a problem of youngsters.
                      II. A photograph can be beautiful even if a person is not.
                      III. People like to be considered beautiful.

(a) Only I and II are implicit   (b) Only II and III are implicit
(c) Only III is implicit   (d) Only I and III are implicit
(e) All are implicit

45. Statement   : These apples are too cheap to be good.

   Assumptions : I. When the apple crop is abundant, the prices go down.
                      II. The lower the selling price, the inferior is the quality of the commodity.
                      III. Very cheap apples are also good.

(a) Only II is implicit   (b) Only II and III are implicit
(c) None is implicit   (d) Only I and III are implicit
(e) All are implicit

46. Statement   : This book is so prepared that even a layman can study science in the absence of a teacher.

   Assumptions : I. A layman wishes to study science without a teacher.
                      II. A teacher may not always be available to teach science.
                      III. A layman generally finds it difficult to learn science on its own.

(a) Only I and II are implicit   (b) Only II and III are implicit
(c) Only I and III are implicit   (d) All are implicit
(e) None of these

47. Statement   : The company has decided to increase the price of all its products to tackle the precarious financial position.

   Assumptions : I. The company may be able to wipe out the entire losses incurred earlier by this decision.
                      II. The buyers may continue to buy its products even after the increase.
                      III. The company has adequate resources to continue production for few more months.

(a) Only I and III are implicit   (b) Only II is implicit
(c) Only II and III are implicit   (d) None is implicit
(e) None of these

                                                            (Bank P.O. 1997)

48. Statement   : Ten candidates, who were on the waiting list, could finally be admitted to the course.

   Assumptions : I. Wait-listed candidates do not ordinarily get admission.
                      II. A large number of candidates were on the waiting list.
                      III. The number of candidates to be admitted is small.

(a) None is implicit   (b) Only I and II are implicit

(c) Only II and III are implicit   (d) Only I and III are implicit

(e) All are implicit

49. Statement : Considering the tickets sold during the last seven days, the circus authorities decided to continue the show for another fortnight which includes two weekends.

Assumptions : I. People may not turn up on week days.

II. The average number of people who will be visiting circus will be more or less same as that of the last seven days.

III. There may not be enough response at other places.

(a) All are implicit   (b) None is implicit

(c) Only II is implicit   (d) Only I and II are implicit

(e) None of these   **(Bank P.O. 1994)**

50. Statement : "Television X — the neighbour's envy, the owner's pride" — A T.V. advertisement.

Assumptions : I. Catchy slogans appeal to people.

II. People are envious of their neighbours' superior possessions.

III. People want to be envied by their neighbours.

(a) Only I and II are implicit   (b) Only II and III are implicit

(c) Only I and III are implicit   (d) All are implicit

(e) None of these

ANSWERS

1. (c) : Since A has decided to gift a book to Ajay on his birthday, it is quite evident that he will be invited by Ajay and that a book is an acceptable gift. So, both I and III are implicit. Nothing about the state of health of the person can be deduced from the statement. So, II is not implicit.

2. (b) : The advertisement depicts only the requirement, not the availability of flats in court area. So, I is not implicit. Such advertisements are given with the expectation of a response which can make such a flat available. So, II is implicit. Assumption III does not follow from the statement and so is not implicit.

3. (b) : The statement mentions that situation in the area is tense. So, I is implicit. Since people have been requested not to go out and remain in homes for safety, so II is implicit. It cannot be inferred when the normalcy will be restored. So, III is not implicit.

4. (a) : Artificial honey can be made. That is why the word 'natural' needs to be mentioned in the advertisement. So, I is implicit. No comparison is made of the prices of natural and artificial honey. So, II is not implicit. Nothing about the quality of honey of other companies can be deduced. So, III is also not implicit.

5. (e) : Clearly, the advertisement is meant to lure the passengers into travelling by the airline. So, I is implicit. Also, the advertisement promises an enjoyable flight. So, II is also implicit. The facilities offered by other airlines cannot be deduced from the statement. So, III is not implicit.

6. (b) : Nothing about the environment in the new company is mentioned in the statement. So, I is not implicit. Since Arun is not satisfied with the present salary, it is evident that the present company offers moderate pay packets. So, II is implicit. The statement talks only of Arun and not all the employees of the new company. So, III is not implicit.

7. (*c*) : The notice directs all the employees to come on time. This does not mean that all of them come late. So, I is not implicit. Since the officer orders the assistant to put the notice on the board, it is evident that employees read such notice on the board. So, II is implicit. Also, the employees have to comply with the orders of the officer. So, III is implicit.

8. (*a*) : The advertisement seeks to attract the students by ensuring their success. So, both I and II are implicit. Assumption III does not follow from the statement and so is not implicit.

9. (*d*) : The effect of the advertisement cannot be deduced. So, I is not implicit. However, the advertisement is given so as to influence people and encourage them to buy Z-T.V. So, II is implicit. Also, it is quite possible that the sale of Z-T.V. is declining, which has provoked the company owners to advertise for their products. So, III is implicit.

10. (*c*) : It can be inferred from the statement that people also like to see a product before buying. So, I is not implicit. Also, the statement is just an attempt to arouse the people to come and see the shop. So, both II and III are implicit.

11. (*a*) : Clearly, since Pramod decides to get the reservation in May for the journey in July, so I is implicit. The number of trains to Madras or the position of vacancies in different classes cannot be deduced from the given statement. So, both II and III are not implicit.

12. (*b*) : Whether B listens to A's advice or not, is not given in the statement. So, I is not implicit. The advice is given on the behaviour that should be followed to pass the examination. This shows the necessity to pass the examination. So, II is implicit. Passing the examination is a form of success to be attained by hard practice. So, III is also implicit.

13. (*d*) : The Corporation's response to the letter cannot be deduced from the statement. So, I is not implicit. The municipality's position in regard to water supply is also not mentioned. So, II is also not implicit. Since the residents talk of 'restoring' normalcy, it means that water supply was adequate in the past. So, III is implicit.

14. (*d*) : Assumption I follows from the statement and so it is implicit. The second assumption is vague and so it is not implicit. Also, advertisements are given with the hope that people would know the qualities of the product and buy it. So, III is implicit.

15. (*e*) : Since the Director talks of being prepared to face any eventuality, so I is implicit. It is mentioned that a schedule for completing the assignments has been drawn up. So, II is implicit. The fact that the statement is directed to all the faculty members makes III implicit.

16. (*b*) : Assumptions I and III directly follow from the statement and so both are implicit. Also, the basic quality of a successful man is that he can judge himself. This means that he need not judge others. So, II is also implicit.

17. (*d*) : Assumptions I and II cannot be deduced from the statement and so they are not implicit. Assumption III directly follows from the statement and so it is implicit.

18. (*e*) : Clearly, the notification has been issued to caution people against delayed payment of bills. So, both I and III are implicit. The purpose served by the money collected as penalty is not mentioned. So, II is not implicit.

19. (*d*) : The statement mentions that the present staff is insufficient, not incompetent. So, I is not implicit. Also, the purpose for appointing more staff is to control the expanding business, not to expand it further. So, II is not implicit. Since the company owner talks of appointing more staff, so III is implicit.

20. (*a*) : The statement mentions that if the degrees have no connection with jobs, boys will consider and reconsider whether they should join college. So, I is implicit. In the present system, degrees are not delinked with jobs. This means that job is not available without degrees. So, II is not implicit. Nothing about the girls is mentioned in the statement. So, III is also not implicit.

21. (*c*) : I does not follow from the statement and so it is not implicit. Also, knowing that he has to catch the flight at 6 p.m., Ravi would leave accordingly, keeping enough time to search for a vehicle and to reach the airport well before time.

22. (*a*) : Assumptions I and II provide reasons for the step taken by the government. So, both I and II are implicit. Since the foodgrains have been released during pre-harvest kharif season, it is evident that the next kharif crop would replenish the stock. So, III is also implicit.

23. (*c*) : A special warning has been printed to caution people against adverse effects of smoking. So, II is implicit while I is not. Also, the fact that smoking is injurious to health does not imply that non-smoking promotes health. So, III is not implicit.

24. (*a*) : The government's decision is clearly a measure to increase supply and control rates. So, both I and II are implicit, while III is not.

25. (*b*) : Nothing about the present method of admission or the qualification of the Chairman is mentioned in the statement. So, neither I nor III is implicit. Assumption II directly follows from the statement. So, II is implicit.

26. (*c*) : Since the consultant talks of borrowing money from financial institutions, so I is implicit. That the owners wish to make the company 'commercially viable' makes II implicit. Also, it is mentioned that staff strength is to be reduced to make the company 'commercially viable'. So, III is not implicit.

27. (*a*) : Since the response was 'surprising', so I is implicit. Nothing about the real management of service sector can be deduced from the statement. So, II is not implicit. Also, the statement talks of the media's response to only a particular session on service sector and not all in general. So, III is also not implicit.

28. (*b*) : Clearly the statement shows that the present taxes are not sufficient to meet the deficit but they may still be high. So, I is not implicit. Since the statement talks of covering the deficit, so II is implicit, Also, the taxes are increased to meet the deficit. So, III is also implicit.

29. (*e*) : Clearly, none of the given assumptions can be deduced from the given statement. So, none is implicit.

30. (*e*) : The firm has decided to start the air service. This implies that there are enough passengers and people in towns A and B can afford to travel by air. So, I and III are implicit. Assumption II is vague and so it is not implicit.

31. (*b*) : Clearly, I does not follow from the statement. So, it is not implicit. The statement mentions that quality of life does not depend only. This means that there are some other factors as well, which govern the quality of life. But this does not imply that wealth does not contribute at all. So, II is implicit while III is not.

32. (*d*) : Since the State Government has increased the octroi, so I is implicit. Since the decision has been taken without the approval of the Central Government, it implies that Central Government would not confront the new policy. So, II is implicit. Since octroi is collected by the state on all commodities entering the state, so III is also implicit.

33. (*c*) : Clearly, loans to only major defaulters is being refused. So, the banks may still give loans to some defaulters. Thus, I is implicit. Also, the RBI's decision is a measure to recover the previous loans, since one would have to clear the old debts so as to get a fresh loan. So, both II and III are also implicit.

34. (*d*) : It is mentioned that 'the economic condition continues to be critical.' This means that it was critical before the harvest season also. So, I is not implicit. Also, the statement does not imply that only a good harvest season could improve the economic condition. So, II is not implicit. However, since a surprise has been expressed over the condition being critical even after good harvest season, it means that it was expected to improve after a good harvest season. So, III is implicit.

35. (*a*) : The statement talks of the policy of opening a summer school. But the response of the children and their parents cannot be deduced from it. So, none is implicit.

36. (*e*) : The warning against leaning out of moving train is made to heed against the dangers involved. So, both I and II are implicit. Since the warning has been put up in the railway compartment, so III is also implicit.

37. (*b*) : Nothing about the sources of income of the State Governments is mentioned in the statement. So, I is not implicit. Since the Central Government has directed the State Governments to reduce expenditure, so II is implicit. Also, III follows from the statement and so it is implicit.

38. (*e*) : Since the SCTE has laid down the necessary qualifications for a person to be employed as a teacher in all universities and institutions, so all are implicit.

39. (*c*) : Since the announcement invites the people to the programme saying that it is free, so I is not implicit while II follows. The quality of the programme is not being talked about in the statement. So, III is not implicit.

40. (*d*) : Since the management has imposed a fee of Rs 25000 for the employment of each student by the organisation, so III is implicit while I is not. Since the statement mentions that the fee is being charged to cover up the financial constraint, so II is implicit.

41. (*b*) : The statement mentions that such education can improve employment situation. So, both I and II are implicit. Nothing about the aspect of revenue collection is mentioned in the statement. So, III is not implicit.

42. (*d*) : The statement expresses surprise at the traffic situation remaining normal even after rains. This means that rains affect traffic. So, II is not implicit. But this does not mean that only rains affect traffic. So, I is also not implicit. Since the traffic was not affected during rains as expected, so III is implicit.

43. (*d*) : Clearly, all the three directly follow from the given statement.

44. (*c*) : Clearly, nothing is mentioned in the advertisement about the problem of youngsters. So, I is not implicit. Nothing is mentioned about the nature of the photograph of a person who is not beautiful. So, II is not implicit. Also, the advertisement is meant for persons who desire to be beautiful. So, III is implicit.

45. (*a*) : It is mentioned that the apples are so cheap that they cannot be good. This means that the prices of good apples are never too low. So, I is not implicit. Assumption II clearly follows from the statement that apples are of inferior quality because they are cheap. So, it is implicit. Also, the statement means that the apples are so cheap that they cannot be good. This means that very cheap apples are never good. So, III is not implicit.

46. (*b*) : Clearly, the statement is made to impress the usefulness of the book. It does not mention the desire of a layman. So, I is not implicit. Also, the book is intended to guide one when a teacher is not available. So, both II and III are implicit.

47. (*a*) : It is mentioned that the company has taken the decision to make up for the financial deficit. So, I is implicit. The response of the buyers to the increased prices cannot be deduced from the statement. So, II is not implicit.

48. (*a*) : Since the wait-listed candidates have been admitted, so I is not implicit. Also, nothing about the number of candidates on the waiting list or the number to be admitted can be deduced from the statement. So, neither I nor II is implicit.

49. (*c*) : Clearly, the fortnight would include week days also. So, I is not implicit. Also, the authorities decided to continue the show with the hope that people would visit the circus in the same numbers as they had done in the last seven days. So, II is implicit. III is vague and so is not implicit.

50. (*a*) : Clearly, both I and II directly follow from the statement. Also, it is clear that people wish to buy a thing which they can be proud of. So, III is not implicit.

4. STATEMENT — COURSES OF ACTION

A course of action is 'a step or administrative decision to be taken for improvement, follow-up or further action in regard to the problem, policy *etc.* on the basis of the information given in the statement'.

The questions in this section, thus, involve finding the appropriate course of action, assuming the problem or policy being talked about in the statement.

TYPE 1

In this type of questions, a statement is given followed by two courses of action numbered I and II. The candidate is required to grasp the statement, analyse the problem or policy it mentions and then decide which of the courses of action logically follow.

ILLUSTRATIVE EXAMPLES

Ex. 1. Statement — Many cases of cholera were reported from a nearby village.

Courses of action —
I. The question should be raised in the Legislative Assembly.
II. A team of doctors should be rushed to the village.

Sol. Clearly, the disease has to be eradicated. For this, proper and immediate medication and preventive measures by doctors is necessary. So, only course II follows.

Ex. 2. Statement — Japan is not likely to grant India's request for a $500 million fast disbursing loan for the current year.

Courses of action —
I. India should approach other countries to get a loan.
II. India should persuade Japan to grant the loan to meet its immediate demand of foreign exchange.

Sol. Clearly, to remedy the problem, India can either stress its urgency and persuade Japan itself or it shall look to another country for the same purpose. Thus, either I or II course of action can follow.

Ex. 3. Statement — People residing in some tribal areas are far from education.

Courses of action —
I. Schools for children and adults should be opened there.
II. Social workers should be entrusted with the job of educating them.

Sol. Clearly, to make permanent arrangements for education in remote tribal areas, schools have to be opened in those very areas. Education by social workers shall be a temporary remedy. So, only the course of action I follows.

Ex. 4. Statement — India today is midstream in its demographic transaction. In the last 60 years there has been an almost continuous decline in mortality; while fertility has declined over the last 20 years. The consequence is that there has been a rapid growth in population over the last 50 years.

Courses of action —
I. India should immediately revitalise its family planning programme.

85

II. The Government should immediately launch a massive education programme through mass media highlighting the implication of population growth at the present rate.

Sol. Clearly, to face the problem of the ever growing population, an effective family planning programme, for the people to have small families, is a must. Education shall further stress the advantages of having less number of children and the disasters of the fast growth in population. Thus, both the courses of action will follow.

EXERCISE 4A

Directions : *In each question below is given a statement followed by two courses of action numbered I and II. You have to assume everything in the statement to be true, then decide which of the two suggested courses of action logically follows for pursuing.*

Give answer (a) if only I follows; (b) if only II follows; (c) if either I or II follows; (d) if neither I nor II follows and (e) if both I and II follow.

1. Statement   There are more than 200 villages in the hill area of Uttar Pradesh which are severely damaged due to cyclone and it causes an extra burden of Rs 200 crore on State Government for relief and rehabilitation work.   **(Bank P.O. 1993)**

Courses of action
I. People of hill area should be shifted to other safer places.
II. State Government should ask more financial support from Central Government.

2. Statement   The Minister said that the teachers are still not familiarised with the need, importance and meaning of population education in the higher education system. They are not even clearly aware about their role and responsibilities in the population education programme.   **(Bank P.O. 1996)**

Courses of action
I. Population education programme should be included in the college curriculum.
II. Orientation programme should be conducted for teachers on population education.

3. Statement   A group of school students was reported to be enjoying at a picnic spot during school hours.

Courses of action
I. The Principal should contact the parents of those students and tell them about the incident with a real warning for future.
II. Some disciplinary action must be taken against those students and all other students should be made aware of it.

4. Statement   Financial stringency prevented the State Government from paying salaries to its employees since April this year.

Courses of action
I. The State Government should immediately curtail the staff strength at least by 30%.
II. The State Government should reduce wasteful expenditure and arrange to pay the salaries of its employees.

5. Statement   The State Government has decided to declare 'Kala Azar' as a notifiable disease under the Epidemics Act. Family members or neighbours of the patient are liable to be punished in case they did not inform the State authorities.

Courses of action	I. Efforts should be made to effectively implement the Act. II. The cases of punishment should be propagated through mass media so that more people become aware of the stern actions.
6. Statement	One of the problems facing the food processing industry is the irregular supply of raw material. The producers of raw material are not getting a reasonable price.
Courses of action	I. The government should regulate the supply of raw material to other industries also. II. The government should announce an attractive package to ensure regular supply of raw material for food processing industry. **(Bank P.O. 1993)**
7. Statement	The Officer Incharge of a Company had a hunch that some money was missing from the safe.
Courses of action	I. He should get it recounted with the help of the staff and check it with the balance sheet. II. He should inform the police.
8. Statement	The Government has decided not to provide financial support to voluntary organisations from next five year plan and has communicated that all such organisations should raise funds to meet their financial needs.
Courses of action	I. Voluntary organisations should collaborate with foreign agencies. II. They should explore other sources of financial support. **(Bank P.O. 1993)**
9. Statement	Some serious blunders were detected in the Accounts section of a factory.
Courses of action	I. An efficient team of auditors should be appointed to check the Accounts. II. A show cause notice should be issued to all the employees involved in the irregularity.
10. Statement	If the retired Professors of the same Institutes are also invited to deliberate on restructuring of the organisation, their contribution may be beneficial to the Institute.
Courses of action	I. Management may seek opinion of the employees before calling retired professors. II. Management should involve experienced people for the systematic restructuring of the organisation. **(Bank P.O. 1996)**
11. Statement	Doordarshan is concerned about the quality of its programmes particularly in view of stiff competition it is facing from STAR and other satellite TV channels and is contemplating various measures to attract talent for its programmes.
Courses of action	I. In an effort to attract talent, the Doordarshan has decided to revise its fee structure for the artists. II. The fee structure should not be revised until other electronic media also revise it. **(Bank P.O. 1993)**
12. Statement	Youngsters are often found staring at obscene posters.
Courses of action	I. Children should be punished and penalized if they are found doing so.

II. Any display of such material should be banned.

13. Statement
Since its launching in 1981, Vayudoot has so far accumulated losses amounting to Rs 153 crore during the last ten years.

Courses of action
I. Vayudoot should be directed to reduce wasteful expenditure and to increase passenger fare.

II. An amount of about Rs 300 crore should be provided to Vayudoot to make the airliner economically viable.   **(Bank P.O. 1992)**

14. Statement
The Indian electronic component industry venturing into the West European markets faces tough competition from the Japanese.

Courses of action
I. India should search for other international markets for its products.

II. India should improve the quality of the electronic components to compete with the Japanese in capturing these markets.

15. Statement
A recent study shows that children below five die in the cities of the developing countries mainly from diarrhoea and parasitic intestinal worms.   **(Bank P.O. 1992)**

Courses of action
I. Governments of the developing countries should take adequate measures to improve the hygienic conditions in the cities.

II. Children below five years in the cities of the developing countries need to be kept under constant medication.

16. Statement
The sale of a particular product has gone down considerably causing great concern to the company.

Courses of action
I. The company should make a proper study of rival products in the market.

II. The price of the product should be reduced and quality improved.

17. Statement
Every year, at the beginning or at the end of the monsoons, we have some cases of conjunctivitis, but this year, it seems to be a major epidemic, witnessed after nearly four years.

Courses of action
I. Precautionary measures should be taken after every four years to check this epidemic.

II. People should be advised to drink boiled water during rainy season.

18. Statement
Footpaths of a busy road are crowded with vendors selling cheap items.

Courses of action
I. The help of police should be sought to drive them away.

II. Some space should be provided to them where they can earn their bread without blocking footpaths.

19. Statement
Researchers are feeling agitated as libraries are not equipped to provide the right information to the right users at the right time in the required format. Even the users are not aware about the various services available for them.

Courses of action
I. All the information available to the libraries should be computerised to provide faster services to the users.

II. Library staff should be trained in computer operations.

20. Statement	Exporters in the capital are alleging that commercial banks are violating a Reserve Bank of India directive to operate a post shipment export credit denominated in foreign currency at international interest rates from January this year.
Courses of action	I. The officers concerned in the commercial banks are to be suspended.
	II. The RBI should be asked to stop giving such directives to commercial banks. **(Bank P.O. 1992)**
21. Statement	The police department has come under a cloud with recent revelations that at least two senior police officials are suspected to have been involved in the illegal sale of a large quantity of weapons from the state police armoury.
Courses of action	I. A thorough investigation should be ordered by the State Government to bring out all those who are involved into the illegal sale of arms.
	II. State police armoury should be kept under Central Government's control.
22. Statement	India's performance in the recent Olympic Games was very poor. Not even a single medal could be bagged by the players. Government has spent Rs 5 crores in training and deputing a team of players to participate in the Olympic Games.
Courses of action	I. India should stop sending players to the future Olympic Games.
	II. Government should immediately set up an enquiry commission to find out the reason for India's dismal performance.
	(Bank P.O. 1992)
23. Statement	Courts take too long in deciding important disputes of various departments.
Courses of action	I. Courts should be ordered to speed up matters.
	II. Special powers should be granted to officers to settle disputes concerning their department.
24. Statement	The Committee has criticized the Institute for its failure to implement a dozen of regular programmes despite an increase in the staff strength and not drawing up a firm action plan for studies and research.
Courses of action	I. The broad objectives of the Institute should be redefined to implement a practical action plan.
	II. The Institute should give a report on reasons for not having implemented the planned programmes.
25. Statement	Mr. X, an active member of the Union, often insults his superiors in the office with his rude behaviour.
Courses of action	I. He should be transferred to some other department.
	II. The matter should be referred to the Union.
26. Statement	A leading U.S. multinational engineering and construction firm is keen to invest in India in a variety of sectors ranging from power to land management. **(Bank P.O. 1992)**
Courses of action	I. Such multinational companies should not be allowed to operate in India.

II. India should encourage multinational companies from other developed countries to invest in power sectors to bring in competitive climate.

27. Statement
The Government could consider the possibility of increasing the software budget from the current Rs 20 crore to Rs 100 crore in the Eighth Plan, provided there are concrete suggestions for the utilisation of the funds.

Courses of action
I. The Government should consult the trade unions in this regard.
II. Software companies should submit detailed proposals to the Government. **(Bank P.O. 1993)**

28. Statement
The Chairman stressed the need for making education system more flexible and regretted that the curriculum has not been revised in keeping with the pace of the changes taking place. **(Bank P.O. 1996)**

Courses of action
I. Curriculum should be reviewed and revised periodically.
II. System of education should be made more flexible.

29. Statement
A shopkeeper was reported to be selling adulterated grains.

Courses of action
I. He should be fined and his shop sealed.
II. He should be asked to leave the town and open a shop elsewhere.

30. Statement
Inspite of the Principal's repeated warnings, a child was caught exploding crackers secretly in the school.

Courses of action
I. All the crackers should be taken away from the child and he should be threatened not to do it again.
II. The child should be severely punished for his wrong act.

31. Statement
A train derailed near a station while moving over a bridge and fell into a river.

Courses of action
I. The Railway Authorities should clarify the reason of the accident to the Government.
II. The Government should allocate funds to compensate the destruction caused.

32. Statement
Most of the children in India are not able to get education, because they get employed to earn livelihood in their childhood only.

Courses of action
I. Education should be made compulsory for all children upto the age of 14.
II. Employment of children below the age of 14 years, should be banned.

33. Statement
Ministry of Tourism in its one of the reports revealed that due to recent social disturbances in the country the number of foreign tourists has been decreased considerably, which resulted in a financial loss of Rs 100 crore.

Courses of action
I. Government should provide financial support to the tourism sector.
II. Foreign tourists should be informed to visit the country at their risk.

34. Statement   The Central Bureau of Investigation receives the complaint of an officer taking bribe to do the duty he is supposed to.

Courses of action   I. CBI should try to catch the officer red-handed and then take a strict action against him.

II. CBI should wait for some more complaints about the officer to be sure about the matter.

35. Statement   The Finance Minister submits his resignation a month before the new budget is to be presented in the Parliament.

Courses of action   I. The resignation should be accepted and another person should be appointed as the Finance Minister.

II. The resignation should not be accepted.

36. Statement   The Librarian finds some cases in which the pages from certain books issued from the library, are torn.

Courses of action   I. The Librarian should keep a record of books issued by each student, and if the pages are found torn, strict measures should be taken against the child who had been issued that book.

II. Some funds should be collected from the children collectively to renovate the library.

37. Statement   The Asian Development Bank has approved a $ 285 million loan to finance a project to construct coal ports by Paradip and Madras Port Trusts.   **(Bank P.O. 1992)**

Courses of action   I. India should use financial assistance from other international financial organisations to develop such ports in other places.

II. India should not seek such financial assistance from the international financial agencies.

38. Statement   The Secretary lamented that the electronic media was losing its credibility and that it should try to regain it by establishing better communications with the listeners and the viewers. He also emphasised the need for training to improve the functioning.   **(Bank P.O. 1993)**

Courses of action   I. Efforts should be made to get organised feedback on the programme.

II. The critical areas in which the staff requires training should be identified.

39. Statement   The killer entric fever has so far claimed 100 lives in some tribal villages in M.P. during the past three weeks.

Courses of action   I. The residents of these villages should immediately be shifted to a non-infected area.

II. The Government should immediately send a medical squad to this area to restrict spread of the killer disease.

40. Statement   Orissa and Andhra Pradesh have agreed in principle to set up a joint control board for better control, management and productivity of several inter-state multipurpose projects.

I. Other neighbouring states should set up such control boards.

II. The proposed control board should not be allowed to function as such joint boards are always ineffective. **(Bank P.O. 1992)**

41. Statement | Certain mining industries in Gujarat may come to a standstill because of the notification issued by the Department of Environment and Forest banning mining operations and industries alike within 25 kms of National Park, the game sanctuary and reserve forest areas.

Courses of action
I. The Department should be asked to immediately withdraw the notification.
II. The Government should make effort to shift the parks, sanctuaries and reserve forests to other non-mining areas.

42. Statement | Most of the development plans develop in papers only.

Courses of action
I. The incharges should be instructed to supervise the field-work regularly.
II. The supply of paper to such departments should be cut short.

43. Statement | Some serious blunders were detected in the Accounts Section of a factory.

Courses of action
I. An efficient team of auditors should be appointed to check the Accounts.
II. A show cause notice should be issued to all the employees involved in the irregularity.

44. Statement | The Government will slap legally enforceable penalties on coal companies defaulting on quality and quantity of coal supplies to bulk consumers, especially to the thermal power stations.

Courses of action
I. The requirement of coal for thermal power stations should be assessed realistically.
II. The coal companies should introduce welfare measures for their employees. **(Bank P.O. 1993)**

ANSWERS

1. (e) : Since severe damage has been caused by cyclone, people in affected villages ought to be shifted to safer places. Also, since relief work entails huge amounts, financial help from Central Government is a must. So, both the courses follow.

2. (b) : Clearly, the statement stresses on teachers' lack of awareness and knowledge in population education and as such the best remedy would be to guide them in this field through orientation programmes. So, only course II follows.

3. (e) : Clearly, both warning and future prevention are necessary. So, both the courses follow.

4. (b) : Clearly, curtailing of the staff strength will only increase the panic and discontent, and the satisfaction of the employees is a must. So, the Government should arrange for payment of wages. Thus, only course II follows.

5. (e) : The Act is aimed at eradication of the disease and so it needs to be proclaimed and promoted. So, both the courses follow.

6. (b) : Clearly, to remedy the problem of food processing industry, a regular supply of raw material should be ensured. So, course II shall follow.

7. (a) : Clearly, a suspicion first needs to be confirmed and only when it is confirmed, should an action be taken. So, only course I follows.

8. (b) : The problem arising is shortage of funds. So, alternative sources of financial support need to be worked out first. Thus, only course II follows.

9. (e) : Clearly, the situation demands that the faults in Accounts be properly worked out and the persons involved be interrogated about the matter. So, both the courses follow.

10. (b) : Clearly, the statement stresses that the contribution of retired Professors shall be beneficial. This means that these people's experience regarding working of the organisation is helpful. So, only course II follows.

11. (a) : Clearly, the decision to revise its fee structure for artists is taken by Doordarshan as a remedy to the challenging problem that had arisen before it. It cannot wait till other media take action. So, only course I follows.

12. (b) : Bad things attract more and punishment after the act has been committed is no remedy. The act should be prevented So, only course II follows.

13. (a) : Clearly, for better economic gain, losses should be reduced and income should be increased. So, only course I follows.

14. (b) : An escapist's attitude does not help much. The need is to complete and emerge successful. So, only course II follows.

15. (e) : Clearly the two diseases mentioned are caused by unhygienic conditions. So, improving the hygienic conditions is a step towards their eradication. Also, constant medication will help timely detection of the disease and hence a proper treatment. So, both I and II follow.

16. (a) : Clearly, a study of rival products in the market will help assess the cause for the lowering down of the prices and then a suitable action will be taken.

17. (b) : The disease occurs at the end of monsoons every year. So, precautionary measures every four years shall not help. The second course of action shall be a preventive measure. So, only course II follows.

18. (e) : The footpaths are meant for an entirely different purpose. So, they need to be kept empty. For this, police has to be sought. Also, the vendors cannot be deprived of a living. So, both the courses follow.

19. (e) : Clearly, the library needs to be provided with the essential facilities and trained personnel for better services. So, both the courses follow.

20. (d) : The statement mentions that the commercial banks violate a directive issued by the RBI. The remedy is only to make the banks implement the Act. So, none of the courses follows.

21. (a) : Clearly, the situation demands finding out the real culprits first. So, only I follows.

22. (b) : Clearly, to compete against a challenge, the first step must be to find out where the lackening is. So, only course II follows.

23. (e) : For quick disposal of cases, either the matters in the court should be speeded up or the matters should be cleared up in their respective departments to prevent the delay. So, both the courses follow.

24. (e) : The problem is that despite an increase in staff strength, the Institute has failed in its objective of implementing its plan. So, either there should be reasons for the lackening or the plans are a failure and must be revised for practical implementation. Thus, both the courses follow.

25. (d) : Clearly, the only remedy is to somehow attempt to change the habit. If transferred, the habit will create problem elsewhere. Also, it is no legal complaint to be referred to the Union. So, none of the courses follows.

26. (b) : Clearly, financing is the major problem in starting any project. The investment by multinational companies shall, therefore, be a way to development. So, course II should follow.

27. (b) : Clearly, the suggestions shall be offered to the Government only through detailed proposals by software companies. So, course II shall follow.

28. (e) : Clearly, the situation demands making the education system more flexible and changing it periodically according to the needs of the time. So, both the courses follow.

29. (a) : Clearly, if allowed to continue without being punished, the shopkeeper would create a problem elsewhere. So, course I shall follow.

30. (b) : Since the act has been repeated despite various warnings, so course I would only be another warning and would not help. Severe punishment to set example for him and others is inevitable. Thus, course II shall follow.

31. (d) : What is necessary is the preventive measures to protect the passengers and pay them adequate compensation. So, none of the courses follows.

32. (e) : To educate all children, enforcement of education is necessary. Also, the reason is that they are employed. So, ban on such employment is also needed. Thus, both the courses follow.

33. (d) : Clearly, the situation demands maintaining peace in the country so as to restore the original number of tourists and not suffer a fall in the revenue earned. Thus, none of the courses follows.

34. (a) : Clearly, one complaint is enough for a wrong doing. This should be confirmed by catching the guilty red handed and then strict action taken against him. So, only course I follows.

35. (b) : Clearly, an already working Finance Minister shall know better all the plans and resources of the Government and he alone can present a suitable budget. So, course II should be followed.

36. (a) : Clearly, precaution should be taken to catch the guilty person and punish him for the act. This alone will help curb the wrong practice. So, only course I will follow.

37. (a) : Clearly, such projects shall be an asset and a source of income to the country later on. So, course I shall follow.

38. (e) : Clearly, both the courses directly follow from the pre-requisites mentioned in the statement.

39. (b) : Clearly, the first course of action is vague because if people are shifted to a non-infected area, the infection will spread there as well. The remedy is only to fight the disease and restrict its spread. So, course II will follow.

40. (a) : The effectiveness of such Control Boards is established by the fact that Orissa and A.P. have agreed to it for better control of its multipurpose projects. So, only course I follows.

41. (d) : Clearly, none of the courses of action follows because firstly, the notification is issued to promote the natural environment is issued to promote the natural environment and so cannot be withdrawn and secondly, the sanctuaries etc., cannot be shifted.

42. (a) : Clearly, proper supervision alone can see the development in practice. So, only course I follows.

43. (a) : Clearly, the urgent need is to detect the blunder and improve it. Reasons do not matter much. So, only course I follows.

44. (d) : Clearly, none of the courses of action is a suitable follow up of the Government's act against defaultation. So, neither I nor II follows.

EXERCISE 4B

Directions : *In each question below is given a statement followed by three courses of action numbered I, II and III. You have to assume everything in the statement to be true, then decide which of the three given suggested courses of action logically follows for pursuing.*

Questions 1 to 5 (Bank P.O. 1995)

1. Statement   In one of the worst accidents in railway level crossing fifty people died when a bus carrying them collided on to a running train.

Courses of action	I. The train driver should immediately be suspended.
	II. The driver of the bus should be tried in court for negligence on his part.
	III. The railway authority should be asked to man all its level crossings.

(a) None follows   (b) Only I and II follow   (c) Only III follows
(d) Only II and III follow   (e) None of these

2. Statement   There was a spurt in criminal activities in the city during the recent festival season.

Courses of action
I. The police should immediately investigate into the causes of this increase.
II. In future the police should take adequate precaution to avoid recurrence of such situation during festival.
III. The known criminals should be arrested before any such season.

(a) None follows   (b) Only I and II follow   (c) Only II and III follow
(d) All follow   (e) None of these

3. Statement   A mass mortality of shrimps in ponds on entire Andhra coast has recently been reported due to the presence of a virus.

Courses of action
I. The water of the ponds affected should immediately be treated for identifying the nature of the virus.
II. The catching of shrimps from the ponds should temporarily be stopped.
III. The fishermen should be asked to watch for the onset of such phenomenon in nature.

(a) Only I follows   (b) Only I and II follow   (c) All follow
(d) Only II and III follow   (e) None of these

4. Statement   The weather bureau has through a recent bulletin forecast heavy rainfall during the next week which may cause water logging in several parts of the city.

Courses of action
I. The bulletin should be given wide publicity through the mass media.
II. The civic authority should keep in readiness the pumping system for removal of water from these parts.
III. The people should be advised to stay indoors during the period.

(a) None follows   (b) Only I and II follow   (c) Only II follows
(d) Only II and III follow   (e) None of these

5. Statement   The world will have to feed more than 10 billion people in the next century of whom half will be in Asia and will eat rice as their staple.

Courses of action
I. More funds should immediately be allocated for rice research to help ensure adequate supplies.
II. The people in Asia should be encouraged to change their food habit.
III. The rice should be grown in countries outside Asia to meet the demand.

(a) Only I and II follow   (b) Only II and III follow   (c) All follow
(d) Only I and III follow   (e) None of these

Questions 6 to 10   (Bank P.O. 1993)

6. Statement | If the faculty members also join the strike, there is going to be a serious problem.

Courses of action
I. The faculty members should be persuaded not to go on strike.
II. Those faculty members who join the strike should be suspended.
III. The management should not worry about such small things.

(*a*) None follows   (*b*) Only I follows   (*c*) Only I and II follow
(*d*) Only II and III follow   (*e*) All follow

7. Statement | Higher disposal costs encourage those who produce waste to look for cheaper ways to get rid of it.

Courses of action
I. The disposal costs should be made higher.
II. The disposal costs should be brought down.
III. A committee should be set up to study the details in this respect.

(*a*) All follow   (*b*) Only I follows   (*c*) Only II follows
(*d*) Either I or II follows   (*e*) Only II and III follow

8. Statement | The army has been alerted in the district following floods triggered by incessant rains.

Courses of action
I. Relief to flood affected people should be arranged.
II. Supply of food articles should be arranged.
III. Adequate medical facilities should be arranged.

(*a*) None follows   (*b*) Only I follows   (*c*) Only II follows
(*d*) Only I and III follow   (*e*) All follow

9. Statement | Faced with a serious resource crunch and a depressing overall economic scenario, Orissa is unlikely to achieve the targetted percent compound annual growth rate during the 8th plan.

Courses of action
I. The target growth should be reduced for the next year.
II. The reasons for the failure should be studied.
III. Orissa's performance should be compared with that of other states.

(*a*) None follows   (*b*) Only I follows   (*c*) Only II and III follow
(*d*) Only I and III follow   (*e*) All follow

10. Statement | Over 27,000 bonded labourers identified and freed are still awaiting rehabilitation.

Courses of action
I. More cases of bonded labourers should be identified.
II. Till the proper rehabilitation facilities are available, the bonded labourers should not be freed.
III. The impediments in the way of speedy and proper rehabilitation of bonded labourers should be removed.

(*a*) None follows   (*b*) Only I follows   (*c*) Only II follows
(*d*) Only III follows   (*e*) Only II and III follow

Questions 11 to 15   (S.B.I.P.O. 1994)

11. Statement | In the Teacher's Day function, Shri Roy, a state awardee and a retired Principal, had questioned the celebration of Teacher's Day in "today's materialistic world".

Courses of action

I. The expenditure on Teacher's Day celebration should be reduced.

II. More funds should be allocated for the celebration of Teacher's Day.

III. The role and responsibilities of teachers should be seen in today's perspective.

(*a*) None follows   (*b*) Only II and II follow   (*c*) All follow
(*d*) Either I or II follows   (*e*) Only III follows

12. **Statement**   Lack of coordination between the University, its colleges and various authorities has resulted in students ousted from one college seeking migration to another.

Courses of action

I. If a student is ousted from a college, the information should be sent to all the other colleges of the University.

II. The admissions to all the colleges of the University should be handled by the University directly.

III. A separate section should be made for taking strict action against students indulging in anti-social activities.

(*a*) Only I follows   (*b*) Only II follows   (*c*) Only III follows
(*d*) Only I and III follow   (*e*) Only II and III follow

13. **Statement**   According to the officials, paucity of funds with the organisation has led to the pathetic condition of this brilliant architectural structure.

Courses of action

I. A new architectural structure for the building should be designed.

II. The reasons for the poor condition of the structure should be found out.

III. Grant should be given to improve the condition of the structure.

(*a*) Only I follows   (*b*) Only II follows   (*c*) Only II and III follow
(*d*) Only III follows   (*e*) Only I and III follow

14. **Statement**   The Institute has fixed for the investors a validity period of one year for transfer forms for some of its listed schemes.

Courses of action

I. The Institute should consult investors before fixing the duration of validity period.

II. The investors should be duly informed about the validity period.

III. List of schemes covered under this validity period should be communicated.

(*a*) Only I and II follow   (*b*) Only III follows   (*c*) Only I and III follow
(*d*) Only II and III follow   (*e*) All follow

15. **Statement**   In the city, over 75 percent of the people are living in slums and sub-standard houses which is a reflection on the housing and urban development policies of the Government.

Courses of action

I. There should be a separate department looking after housing and urban development.

II. The policies in regard to urban housing should be reviewed.

III. The policies regarding rural housing should also be reviewed so that such problems could be avoided in rural areas.

(*a*) Only I follows   (*b*) Only I and II follow   (*c*) Only II follows
(*d*) Either II or III follows   (*e*) Only II and III follow

Questions 16 to 20   (Bank P.O. 1994)

16. **Statement** | Any further increase in the pollution level in the city by way of industrial effluents and automobile exhaustions would pose a severe threat to the inhabitants.

Courses of action
I. All the factories in the city should immediately be closed down.
II. The automobiles should not be allowed to ply on the road for more than four hours a day.
III. The Government should restrict the issue of fresh licences to factories and automobiles.

(a) None follows   (b) Only II follows   (c) Only III follows
(d) All follow   (e) None of these

17. **Statement** | Every year thousands of eligible students do not get admission in colleges both in urban and rural areas after passing their school leaving certificate examination.

Courses of action
I. More colleges should be set up in both urban and rural areas.
II. The number of schools in both urban and rural areas should be reduced.
III. More schools should offer vocational courses to equip students for taking up their vocation after completing their school education.

(a) Only I follows   (b) Only I and III follow   (c) Only II and III follow
(d) All follow   (e) None of these

18. **Statement** | Without the active cooperation between the proprietor and the employees of the mill, it cannot remain a profitable concern for long.

Courses of action
I. The mill should be closed down.
II. The workers should be asked to cooperate with the owners.
III. The owner should be asked to cooperate with the employees.

(a) None follows   (b) Only I and II follow   (c) All follow
(d) Only II and III follow   (e) None of these

19. **Statement** | Incessant rain for the past several days has posed the problem of overflowing and flood as the river bed is full of silt and mud.

Courses of action
I. The people residing near the river should be shifted to a safe place.
II. The people should be made aware about the imminent danger over radio/television.
III. The slit and mud from the river bed should be cleared immediately after the receding of the water level.

(a) Only I and II follow   (b) None follows   (c) Only II and III follow
(d) All follow   (e) Only I and III follow

20. **Statement** | Some strains of mosquito have become resistant to chloroquine — the widely used medicine for malaria patients.

Courses of action
I. Selling of chloroquine should be stopped.
II. Researchers should develop a new medicine for patients affected by such mosquitoes.
III. All the patients suffering from malaria should be checked for identification of causal mosquito.

(a) None follows   (b) Only I and III follow   (c) All follow
(d) Only II and III follow   (e) None of these

Questions 21 to 25   **(Bank P.O. 1995)**

21. Statement   Drinking water supply to New Bombay has been suspended till further orders from Maharashtra Pollution Control Board following pollution of Patalganga river, caused by discharge of effluents from some chemical industries.

Courses of action   I. The industries responsible for discharging effluents into the river should be asked to close down immediately.

      II. The river water should immediately be treated chemically before resuming supply.

    III. The Pollution Control Board should check the nature of effluents being discharged into the river by industries at regular intervals.

(a) All follow   (b) Only I follows   (c) Only II and III follow
(d) Only III follows   (e) None of these

22. Statement   The Department of Education has recommended that the primary level admission to Government and Government aided schools should be done purely by random selection and not by admission tests. This is necessitated as the number of admission seekers are much more than the available seats.

Courses of action   I. The Government should instruct the private schools also to follow the same practice.

      II. The Government should set up an independent body to regulate the primary level admissions.

    III. The schools should be asked to select students only from those who stay in the neighbouring area of the school.

(a) None follows   (b) Only I and II follow   (c) Only II and III follow
(d) Only II follows   (e) None of these

23. Statement   The vehicular traffic has increased so much in the recent past that it takes at least two hours to travel between the city and the airport during peak hours.

Courses of action   I. Non-airport bound vehicles should not be allowed to ply on the road connecting the city and the airport.

      II. The load of vehicular traffic should be diverted through various link roads during peak hours.

    III. The departure and arrival of flights should be regulated so as to avoid congestion during peak hours.

(a) Only I follows   (b) Only II follows   (c) Only I and II follow
(d) All follow   (e) None of these

24. Statement   Due to cancellation of a huge export order for not adhering to the time frame, the company is likely to get into incurring losses in the current financial year.

Courses of action   I. The officer in charge of the production should be immediately suspended.

II. The goods manufactured for the export order should be sold to other party.

III. The company should change its machinery to maintain the time frame.

(a) None follows   (b) Only II follows   (c) Only I and II follow

(d) All follow   (e) None of these

25. Statement   A devastating earthquake has ravaged the city killing hundreds of people and rendering many more homeless.

Courses of action   I. The entry of outsiders into the city should be stopped immediately.

II. The civic administration should immediately make alternate temporary housing arrangement for the victims.

III. The affected people should immediately be shifted to a safer place.

(a) Only I follows   (b) Only II and III follow

(c) Only III follows   (d) Only either II or III follows

(e) None of these

ANSWERS

1. (c)	2. (b)	3. (a)	4. (d)	5. (a)	6. (b)	7. (e)	8. (e)	9. (c)	10. (d)
11. (e)	12. (a)	13. (d)	14. (d)	15. (b)	16. (c)	17. (b)	18. (d)	19. (d)	20. (d)
21. (c)	22. (a)	23. (b)	24. (b)	25. (b)					

---

5. STATEMENT — CONCLUSIONS

'Conclusion' means 'a fact that can be truly inferred from the contents of a given sentence or passage'. The questions in this section thus consist of a statement/group of statements, followed by certain inferences based on the facts contained in the given statements. The candidate is required to analyse the given statements, understand their indirect implications and then decide which of the given conclusions follows logically and for sure, from the given statements.

TYPE 1

In this type of questions, a statement is given followed by two conclusions. The candidate is required to find out which of these conclusions definitely follows from the given statement and choose the answer accordingly.

ILLUSTRATIVE EXAMPLES

Directions : *In each of the following questions, a statement is given followed by two conclusions I and II. Give answer (a) if only conclusion I follows; (b) if only conclusion II follows; (c) if either I or II follows; (d) if neither I nor II follows and (e) if both I and II follow.*

Ex. 1. Statement : Sealed tenders are invited from competent contractors experienced in executing construction jobs.

Conclusions : I. Tenders are invited only from experienced contractors.

II. It is difficult to find competent tenderers in construction jobs.

Sol. According to the statement, tenders are invited from contractors experienced in executing construction jobs. So, conclusion I follows. The availability of competent tenderers in construction is not mentioned. So, conclusion II does not follow.

Hence, the answer is (a).

Ex. 2. Statement : The distance of 900 km by road between Bombay and Jafra will be reduced to 280 km by sea. This will lead to a saving of Rs 7.92 crores per annum on fuel.

Conclusions : I. Transportation by sea is cheaper than that by road.

II. Fuel must be saved to the greatest extent.

Sol. According to the statement, sea transport is cheaper than road transport in the case of route from Bombay to Jafra, not in all the cases. So, conclusion I does not follow. The statement stresses on the saving of fuel. So, conclusion II follows.

Hence, the answer is (*b*).

Ex. 3. Statement : The manager humiliated Sachin in the presence of his colleagues.

Conclusions : I. The manager did not like Sachin.

II. Sachin was not popular with his colleagues.

Sol. Clearly, none of the given conclusions is either mentioned in or can be drawn from the facts given in the statement.

Hence, the answer is (*d*).

Ex. 4. Statement : Any young man who makes dowry as a condition for marriage discredits himself and dishonours womanhood.

Conclusions : I. Those who take dowry in marriage should be condemned by society.

II. Those who do not take dowry in marriage respect womanhood.

Sol. Clearly, the statement declares dowry as an evil practice and reflects its demerits. Thus, conclusion I follows. Also, it is given that those who take dowry dishonour womanhood. This implies that those who do not take dowry respect womanhood. So, conclusion II follows.
Hence, the answer is (e).

EXERCISE 5A

Directions : *In each of the following questions, a statement is given, followed by two conclusions. Give answer (a) if only conclusion I follows; (b) if only conclusion II follows; (c) if either I or II follows; (d) if neither I nor II follows and (e) if both I and II follow.*

1. **Statement** : Morning walks are good for health.
   Conclusions : I. All healthy people go for morning walks.
   II. Evening walks are harmful.

2. **Statement** : Company X has marketed the product. Go ahead, purchase it if price and quality are your considerations. **(Bank P.O. 1996)**
   Conclusions : I. The product must be good in quality.
   II. The price of the product must be reasonable.

3. **Statement** : The best way to escape from a problem is to solve it.
   Conclusions : I. Your life will be dull if you don't face a problem.
   II. To escape from problems, you should always have some solutions with you.

4. **Statement** : A neurotic is a non-stupid person who behaves stupidly.
   Conclusions : I. Neuroticism and stupidity go hand in hand.
   II. Normal persons behave intelligently.

5. **Statement** : Vegetable prices are soaring in the market.
   Conclusions : I. Vegetables are becoming a rare commodity.
   II. People cannot eat vegatables.   **(Assistant Grade, 1995)**

6. **Statement** : India's economy is depending mainly on forests.
   Conclusions : I. Trees should be preserved to improve Indian economy.
   II. India wants only maintenance of forests to improve economic conditions.

7. **Statement** : This world is neither good nor evil; each man manufactures a world for himself.   **(Bank P.O. 1997)**
   Conclusions : I. Some people find this world quite good.
   II. Some people find this world quite bad.

8. **Statement** : Video-libraries are flourishing very much these days.
   Conclusions : I. People in general have got a video craze.
   II. It is much cheaper to see as many movies as one likes on videos rather than going to the cinema hall.

9. Statement : Company X has a record of manufacturing cameras of quality and the latest design so that you do not spoil even a single shot irrespective of the weather conditions. **(Bank P.O. 1996)**

Conclusions : I. No other company except X is reputed in the camera industry.

II. Anyone can take an acceptable shot with camera X.

10. Statement : Recent trends also indicate that the number of child migrants in large cities is increasing. These children leave their families to join the ranks of urban poor doing odd jobs in markets, workshops, hotels or in service sectors.

Conclusions : I. Migration to big cities should be checked.

II. The plight of poor children should be thoroughly studied.

11. Statement : Jade plant has thick leaves and it requires little water.

Conclusions : I. All plants with thick leaves require little water.

II. Jade plants may be grown in places where water is not in abundance. **(C.B.I. 1995)**

12. Statement : After this amendment to the Constitution, no child below the age of 14 years will be employed to work in any factory or mine or engaged in any other hazardous employment.

Conclusions : I. Before this amendment, children below 14 years were employed to work in factory or mine.

II. The employers must now abide by this amendment to the Constitution.

3. Statement : Good voice is a natural gift but one has to keep practising to improve and excel well in the field of music. **(S.B.I.P.O. 1997)**

Conclusions : I. Natural gifts need nurturing and care.

II. Even though your voice is not good, one can keep practising.

4. Statement : Domestic demand has been increasing faster than the production of indigenous crude oil.

Conclusions : I. Crude oil must be imported.

II. Domestic demand should be reduced.

5. Statement : All the organised persons find time for rest. Sunita, inspite of her very busy schedule, finds time for rest.

Conclusions : I. Sunita is an organised person.

II. Sunita is an industrious person. **(Central Excise, 1995)**

6. Statement : Until our country achieves economic equality, political freedom and democracy would be meaningless. **(U.T.I. 1993)**

Conclusions : I. Political freedom and democracy go hand in hand.

II. Economic equality leads to real political freedom and democracy.

7. Statement : National Aluminium Company has moved India from a position of shortage to self-sufficiency in the metal.

Conclusions : I. Previously, India had to import aluminium.

II. With this speed, it can soon become a foreign exchange earner.

18. Statement : In case of outstanding candidates, the condition of previous experience of social work may be waived by the admission committee for M.A. (Social Work).   **(Bank P.O. 1996)**

Conclusions : I. Some of the students for M.A. (social work) will have previous experience of social work.

II. Some of the students for M.A. (social work) will not have previous experience of social work.

19. Statement : Death keeps no calendar.

Conclusions : I. Man must die one day.

II. Death can come at any time.

20. Statement : Water supply in wards A and B of the city will be affected by about 50% on Friday because repairing work of the main lines is to be carried out.   **(Assistant Grade, 1998)**

Conclusions : I. The residents in these wards should economise on water on Friday.

II. The residents in these wards should store some water on the previous day.

21. Statement : Parents are prepared to pay any price for an elite education to their children.

Conclusions : I. All parents these days are very well off.

II. Parents have an obsessive passion for a perfect development of their children through good schooling.

22. Statement : The government of country X has recently announced several concessions and offered attractive package tours for foreign visitors.

Conclusions : I. Now, more number of foreign tourists will visit the country.

II. The government of country X seems to be serious in attracting tourists.   **(Bank P.O. 1997)**

23. Statement : Prime age school-going children in urban India have now become avid as well as more regular viewers of television, even in households without a T.V. As a result there has been an alarming decline in the extent of readership of newspapers.

Conclusions : I. Method of increasing the readership of newspapers should be devised.

II. A team of experts should be sent to other countries to study the impact of T.V. on the readership of newspapers.

24. Statement : From the next academic year, students will have the option of dropping Mathematics and Science for their school leaving certificate examination.   **(S.B.I.P.O. 1997**

Conclusions : I. Students who are weak in Science and Mathematics will be admitted.

II. Earlier students did not have the choice of continuing their education without taking these subjects.

25. Statement : Reading maketh a full man, conference a ready man and writing an exact man.

Conclusions : I. Pointed and precise expression comes only through extensive writing.

II. Extensive reading makes a complete man.

26. Statement : Industrial Revolution which first of all started in Europe has brought about modern age. **(Assistant Grade, 1995)**

Conclusions : I. Disparity between rich and poor results in revolution.

II. Revolution overhauls society.

27. Statement : Government has spoiled many top ranking financial institutions by appointing bureaucrats an Directors of these institutions.

Conclusions : I. Government should appoint Directors of the financial institutes taking into consideration the expertise of the person in the area of finance.

II. The Director of the financial institute should have expertise commensurate with the financial work carried out by the institute.

28. Statement : The General Manager asked four managers to either submit their resignations by the next day or face termination orders from service. Three of them had submitted their resignations by that evening. **(Bank P.O. 1990)**

Conclusions : I. The next day, the remaining manager would also resign

II. The General Manager would terminate his services the next day.

29. Statement : No country is absolutely self-dependent these days.

Conclusions : I. It is impossible to grow and produce all that a country needs.

II. Countrymen in general have become lazy.

30. Statement : Today out of the world population of several thousand million, the majority of men have to live under governments which refuse them personal liberty and the right to dissent.

Conclusions : I. People are indifferent to personal liberty and the right to dissent.

II. People desire personal liberty and the right to dissent. **(Bank P.O. 1996)**

31. Statement : To cultivate interest in reading, the school has made it compulsory from June 96 for each student to read two books per week and submit a weekly report on the books.

Conclusions : I. Interest in reading can be created by force.

II. Some students eventually will develop interest in reading. **(S.B.I.P.O. 1996)**

32. Statement : The use of non-conventional sources of energy will eliminate the energy crisis in the world.

Conclusions : I. Modern technology is gradually replacing the conventional sources of energy.

II. The excessive exploitation of environment has led to depletion of conventional sources of energy.

33. **Statement** : Adversity makes a man wise.   **(Hotel Management, 1991)**
    Conclusions : I. The poor are wise.
                     II. Man learns from bitter experience.

34. **Statement** : The T.V. programmes, telecast specially for women are packed with a variety of recipes and household hints. A major portion of magazines for women also contains the items mentioned above.
    Conclusions : I. Women are not interested in other things.
                     II. An average woman's primary interest lies in home and specially in the kitchen.

35. **Statement** : The standard of education in private schools is much better than municipal and Zila parishand-run schools.
    Conclusions : I. The municipal and Zila parishad should make serious efforts to improve standard of their schools.
                     II. All municipal and Zila parishad schools should be closed immediately.   **(Bank P.O. 1997)**

36. **Statement** : About 50 per cent of the animal by-products — hair, skin, horns *etc.*, is edible protein. American chemists have developed a method of isolating 45 per cent of this protein. They used an enzyme developed in Japan to break down soya protein.
    Conclusions : I. Americans have not been able to develop enzymes.
                     II. Animal by-products protein has the same composition as soya protein.

37. **Statement** : Although the education system has progressed from the point of view of the number of schools, most of them are ill-equipped and have not achieved excellence in imparting education.
    Conclusions : I. In future, we should provide good teachers and equipment to these schools.
                     II. We need not open any more schools in the future.
                                                                         (Bank P.O. 1996)

38. **Statement** : All those political prisoners were released on bail who had gone to jail for reasons other than political dharnas. Bail was not granted to persons involved in murders.
    Conclusions : I. No political prisoner had committed murder.
                     II. Some politicians were not arrested.

39. **Statement** : The best evidence of India's glorious past is the growing popularity of Ayurvedic medicines in the west.   **(S.B.I.P.O. 1997)**
    Conclusions : I. Ayurvedic medicines are not popular in India.
                     II. Allopathic medicines are more popular in India.

40. **Statement** : Players who break various records in a fair way get special prizes. Player X broke the world record but was found to be under the influence of a prohibited drug.
    Conclusions : I. X will get the special prize.
                     II. X will not get the special prize.

41. **Statement** : People who speak too much against the dowry are those who had taken it themselves.   **(Assistant Grade, 1998)**

Conclusions : I. It is easier said than done.

II. People have double standards.

42. Statement : In Japan, the incidence of stomach cancer is very high, while that of bowel cancer is very low. But Japanese emigrate to Hawaii, this is reversed — the rate of bowel cancer increases but the rate of stomach cancer is reduced in the next generation. All this is related to nutrition — the diets of Japanese in Hawaii are different than those in Japan.

Conclusions : I. The same diet as in Hawaii should be propagated in Japan also.

II. Bowel cancer is less severe than stomach cancer.

43. Statement : In India, more emphasis should be placed on areas such as agriculture, engineering and technology instead of basic and pure sciences. **(Bank P.O. 1996)**

Conclusions : I. India has achieved sufficient progress in basic and pure sciences.

II. In the past, the productivity factor in our economy was neglected.

44. Statement : The old order changeth yielding place to new.

Conclusions : I. Change is the law of nature.

II. Discard old ideas because they are old.

45. Statement : Our securities investment carry market risk. Consult your investment advisor or agent before investing.

Conclusions : I. One should not invest in securities.

II. The investment advisor calculates the market risk with certainty. **(Bank P.O. 1996)**

46. Statement : In a highly centralised power structure, in which even senior cabinet ministers are prepared to reduce themselves to pathetic countries or yesmen airing views that are primarily intended to anticipate or reflect the Prime Minister's own performances, there can be no place for any consensus that is quite different from real or contrived unanimity of opinion, expressed through a well orchestrated endorsement of the leader's actions.

Conclusions : I. The ministers play safe by not giving anti government views.

II. The Prime Minister does not encourage his colleagues to render their own views.

47. Statement : Any student who does not behave properly while in the school brings bad name to himself and also for the school.

Conclusions : I. Such student should be removed from the school.

II. Stricter discipline does not improve behaviour of the students. **(Bank P.O. 1996)**

48. Statement : Smoking is one of those human weaknesses which tend to test the will power of the smoker to the edge.

Conclusions : I. It is very difficult for the smokers to give up smoking even if they want to do so.

II. Human beings have other weaknesses as well.

49. Statement : The secret of success is constancy of purpose.

 Conclusions : I. Constant dripping wears the stone.

 II. Single-minded devotion is necessary for achieving success.

50. Statement : The percentage of the national income shared by the top 10 per cent of households in India is 35.

 Conclusions : I. When an economy grows fast, concentration of wealth in certain pockets of population takes place.

 II. The national income is unevenly distributed in India.

51. Statement : The Prime Minister emphatically stated that his government will make every possible effort for the upliftment of poor farmers and farmhands.

 Conclusions : I. Except poor formers and farmhands, all others have got benefits of fruits of development.

 II. No serious efforts have been made in the past for upliftment of any section of the society.   **(Bank P.O. 1997)**

52. Statement : He stressed the need to stop the present examination system and its replacement by other methods which would measure the real merit of the students.

 Conclusions : I. Examinations should be abolished.

 II. The present examination system does not measure the real merit of the students.

53. Statement : A large majority of the work force in India is unorganised. Most of them earn either the minimum or uncertain wages while others are engaged in sundry jobs.

 Conclusions : I. The workers in the organised sector get better facilities and stay longer in their jobs.

 II. Some workers in the unorganised sector of the work force have a regular and fixed income.   **(Bank P.O. 1996)**

54. Statement : The T.V. staff deserves an applaud for showing booth capture.

 Conclusions : I. T.V. aims at showing things in their true perspective.

 II. People involved in booth capturing have been recognised and are being tried by law.

55. Statement : The national norm is 100 beds per thousand population but in this state, 150 beds per thousand are available in the hospitals.

 Conclusions : I. Our national norm is appropriate.

 II. The state's health system is taking adequate care in this regard.
                                                                    (S.B.I.P.O. 1997)

56. Statement : In a one day cricket match, the total runs made by a team were 200. Out of these 160 runs were made by spinners.

 Conclusions : I. 80% of the team consists of spinners.

 II. The opening batsmen were spinners.

57. Statement : America's defence secretary reiterated that they would continue to supply arms to Pakistan.   **(Assistant Grade, 1995)**

 Conclusions : I. Pakistan is incapable of manufacturing arms.

 II. It would ensure peace in the region.

58. Statement : Nation X faced growing international opposition for its decision to explode eight nuclear weapons at its test site.

Conclusions : I. The citizens of the nation favoured the decision.

II. Some powerful countries do not want other nations to become as powerful as they are.

59. Statement : Money plays a vital role in politics.

Conclusions : I. The poor can never become politicians.

II. All the rich men take part in politics.

60. Statement : Fortune favours the brave. **(Hotel Management, 1991)**

Conclusions : I. Risks are necessary for success.

II. Cowards die many times before their death.

61. Statement : I know nothing except the fact of my ignorance.

Conclusions : I. Writer's knowledge is very poor.

II. The world of knowledge is too vast to be explored by a single person.

62. Statement : A man must be wise to be a good wrangler. Good wranglers are talkative and boring. **(I. Tax & Central Excise, 1995)**

Conclusions : I. All the wise persons are boring.

II. All the wise persons are good wranglers.

63. Statement : Monitoring has become an integral part in the planning of social development programmes. It is recommended that Management Information System be developed for all programmes. This is likely to give a feedback on the performance of the functionaries and the efficacy with which services are being delivered.

Conclusions : I. All the social development programmes should be evaluated.

II. There is a need to monitor the performance of workers.

64. Statement : It is almost impossible to survive and prosper in this world without sacrificing ethics and morality. **(S.B.I.P.O. 1996)**

Conclusions : I. World appreciates some concepts but may not uphold it.

II. Concept of ethics and morality are not practicable in life.

65. Statement : Quality has a price tag. India is allocating lots of funds to education. **(Assistant Grade, 1994)**

Conclusions : I. Quality of education in India would improve soon.

II. Funding alone can enhance quality of education

66. Statement : The average number of persons per household is 5 in urban areas whereas it is 7 in rural areas. The national average is 6.

Conclusions : I. The population per unit area in the rural areas is higher than in the urban areas.

II. More persons live in the same household in the rural areas as compared to those in the urban areas.

67. Statement : The interview panel may select a candidate who neither possesses the desired qualifications nor the values and attributes.

(Bank P.O. 1996)

Conclusions : I. The inclusion of specialists on the interview panel does not guarantee that the selection will be proper.

II. The interview test has certain limitations in the matter of selection of candidates.

68. Statement : Inspite of the claim of the government of terrorism being under check, killing continues.

Conclusions : I. The terrorists have not come to an understanding with the government.

II. The government has been constantly telling a lie.

69. Statement : Modern man influences his destiny by the choice he makes unlike in the past. **(S.B.I.P.O. 1996)**

Conclusions : I. Earlier there were less options available to man.

II. There was no desire in the past to influence the destiny.

70. Statement : Leaders, who raise much hue and cry about the use of Hindi, generally send their children to English medium schools.

Conclusions : I. India lacks good Hindi medium schools.

II. There is a world of difference between preaching and practising

ANSWERS

1. (*d*) : The statement mentions that morning walks improve health. But this does not mean that all healthy people go for morning walks. So, I does not follow. Also, nothing is mentioned about evening walks in the statement. So, II does not follow.

2. (*e*) : It is mentioned in the statement that one who considers price and quality before buying a product should buy the product of company X. So, both I and II follow.

3. (*d*) : Clearly, both I and II do not follow from the given statement.

4. (*a*) : It is mentioned in the statement that a neurotic is a person who behaves stupidly. So, I follows. The behaviour of normal persons cannot be deduced from the given statement. So, II does not follow.

5. (*d*) : The availability of vegetables is not mentioned in the given statement. So, I does not follow. Also, II is not directly related to the statement and so it also does not follow.

6. (*a*) : It is mentioned in the statement that India's economy depends mainly on forests. This means that forests should be preserved. So, I follows. But, that only preservation of forests can improve the economy, cannot be said. So, II does not follow.

7. (*e*) : The statement mentions that the world for a man is as he makes it himself. So some people might find it good and some quite bad. Thus, both I and II follow.

8. (*e*) : Since both I and II provide suitable explanations to the given statement, so both follow.

9. (*b*) : Clearly, the statement talks of company X only and no other company. So, I does not follow. Also, it is mentioned that one can take a good shot even in bad weather conditions with a camera of company X. So, II follows.

10. (*d*) : The statement mentions the problem of increased migration of children to cities. But the ways to deal with the problem cannot be deduced from it. So, neither I nor II follows.

11. (*b*) : The statement talks of jade plants only and not 'all plants with thick leaves'. So, I does not follow. Also, since jade plants require little water, so they can be grown in place where water is not in abundance. So, II follows.

12. (*e*) : The statement mentions that after the amendment, no child below 14 years will be engaged in hazardous employment. This means that before the amendment, the practice of employing children below 14 years was in vogue. This in turn means that employers will have to abide by the amendment. So, both I and II follow.

13. (*a*) : Clearly, I follows directly from the given statement. However, II is not related to the given statement and so does not follow.

14. (*c*) : The statement mentions that demand for oil is increasing faster than the production. So, either the demand must be reduced or oil must be imported to cope with the increasing demand. Thus, either I or II follows.

15. (*e*) : Sunita has a very busy schedule. This means that she is industrious. But still she finds time for rest. This means that she is an organised person. So, both I and II follow.

16. (*b*) : Nothing about the relation between political freedom and democracy is mentioned in the statement. So, I does not follow. But II directly follows from the given statement.

17. (*e*) : According to the statement, National Aluminium Company has moved India from a position of shortage in the past to self-sufficiency in the present. This means that previously, India had to import aluminium. So, I follows. Also it can be deduced that if production increases at the same rate, India can export it in future. So, II also follows.

18. (*e*) : According to the statement, previous experience is an essential condition for candidates but in case of outstanding candidates, this condition shall be waived. This means that some candidates will have previous experience while some will not. So, both I and II follow.

19. (*e*) : Both I and II directly follow from the statement.

20. (*e*) : Clearly, the information has been given beforehand so that the residents can collect water on the previous day and use less water on Friday. So, both I and II follow.

21. (*b*) : The statement implies that people are inclined towards giving their children good education. So, only II follows while I does not.

22. (*e*) : Clearly, the government has taken the step to attract more tourists. So, both I and II follow.

23. (*d*) : The statement concentrates on the increasing viewership of T.V. and does not stress either on increasing the readership of newspapers or making studies regarding the same. So, both I and II do not follow.

24. (*e*) : Since the new system gives the students the option of dropping Science and Mathematics, so students weak in these subjects can also be admitted. So, I follows. Also, it is mentioned that the new system will come into effect from the next academic year. This means that it did not exist previously. So, II also follows.

25. (*e*) : Clearly, I follows from the fact that writing makes an exact man. Conclusion II also directly follows from the statement.

26. (*b*) : The cause of revolution cannot be deduced from the given statement. So, I does not follow. However, the statement mentions that Industrial Revolution brought about modern age. This means that revolution overhauls society. So, II follows.

27. (*e*) : According to the statements, Government has spoiled financial institutions by appointing bureaucrats as Directors. This means that only those persons should be appointed as Directors who are experts in finance and are acquainted with the financial work of the Institute. So, both I and II follow.

28. (*c*) : It is mentioned in the statement that either the managers should resign by the next day or their services would be terminated. So, either I or II follows.

29. (*a*) : Clearly, only I provides a suitable explanation to the given statement. So, only I follows.

30. (*b*) : It is mentioned in the statement that most people are forced to live under Governments which refuse them personal liberty and the right to dissent. This means that they are not indifferent to these rights but have a desire for them. So, only II follows.

31. (*b*) : Clearly, the new scheme intends to develop interest in reading by incorporating the habit in their routine. So, only II follows while I does not.

32. (*e*) : Both I and II directly follow from the given statement.

33. (*b*) : Clearly, only II correctly explains the statement while I cannot be deduced from it.

34. (*b*) : Clearly, nothing about 'other things' is mentioned in the statement. So, I does not follow. Also, since it is mentioned that programmes and magazines for women are stuffed with kitchen recipes and other household hints. This means that women have special interest in these areas. So, II follows.

35. (*a*) : Clearly, the solution to the problem is not to close down the municipal and Zila parishad-run schools but to strive to improve the standard of education of these schools. So, only I follows while II does not.

36. (*d*) : That the American chemists used an enzyme developed in Japan, does not mean that Americans have not been able to develop enzymes. So, I does not follow. Also, nothing about the compositions of animal by-products protein and soya protein is mentioned in the statement. So, II also does not follow.

37. (*a*) : Clearly, the statement stresses the need to provide good teachers and equipment to schools. So, I follows. However, the fact that education system in India is progressing with regard to schools does not imply that no more schools should be opened. So, II does not follow.

38. (*a*) : According to the statement, the political prisoners can be divided into two groups — those who were released and those who were put in jail for political dharnas. However, no person involved in murder was released. This means that no political prisoner had committed murder. So, I follows. Clearly, II is not directly related to the statement and does no follow.

39. (*d*) : The popularity of Ayurvedic or allopathic medicines in India is not being talked about in the statement. So, neither I nor II follows.

40. (*b*) : Clearly, X will not get the special prize because although he broke the world record, he was found to use unfair means. So, II follows while I does not.

41. (*e*) : The statement clearly implies that it is easier to say than to do something and what people say is different from what they do. So, both I and II follow.

42. (*d*) : The statement neither propagates the diet of any of the countries nor compares the two types of cancer. So, neither I nor II follows.

43. (*b*) : That more emphasis should be laid on productivity areas instead of sciences does not mean that the country has achieved sufficient progress in sciences. But it implies that productivity factor was previously being neglected. So, II follows while I does not.

44. (*a*) : Clearly, I directly follows from the given statement. Also, it is mentioned that old ideas are replaced by new ones, as thinking changes with the progressing time. So, II does not follow.

45. (*b*) : Investment in securities involves risk. This does not mean that one should not invest in securities. So, I does not follow. Since the statement advises one to consult investment advisor before investing, so II follows.

46. (*a*) : According to the statement, even senior cabinet ministers are always ready to conform to the Prime Ministers' views. So, I follows. However, II contradicts the given statement and so does not follow.

47. (*d*) : Clearly, I cannot be deduced from the statement. Also, nothing about discipline is mentioned in the statement. So, neither I nor II follows.

48. (*e*) : The statement mentions that a very strong will power is required to give up smoking and so it is very difficult. So, I follows. Also, it is mentioned that smoking is one of the human weaknesses. This means that there are other human weaknesses as well. So, II also follows.

49. (*e*) : Both I and II directly follow from the given statement.

50. (*b*) : Nothing about the growth of economy is mentioned in the statement. So, I does not follow. Also, it is given that 35 per cent of national income is shared by 10 per cent of households. This indicates unequal distribution. So, II follows.

51. (*d*) : No other section of society except farmers has been talked about in the statement. So, neither I nor II follows.

52. (*b*) : The statement stresses the need to adopt a new method of examination. So, I does not follow. However, II directly follows from the given statement.

53. (*b*) : The workers in the organised sector are not being talked about in the statement. So, I does not follow. It is mentioned that some workers in the unorganised sector are engaged in sundry jobs. This means that they have fixed income. So, II follows.

54. (*a*) : Clearly, I directly follows from the statement. However, II is not directly related to the given statement and so does not follow.

55. (*b*) : Whether the national norm is appropriate or not cannot be said. So I does not follow. However, more number of beds per thousand population are available in the state. So, II follows.

56. (*d*) : According to the statement, 80% of the total runs were made by spinnners. So, I does not follow. Nothing about the opening batsmen is mentioned in the statement. So, II also does not follow.

57. (*d*) : Pakistan's ability to manufacture arms is not being talked about in the statement. So, I does not follow. The fact in II cannot be deduced from the given statement. So, II also does not follow.

58. (*d*) : Neither the citizens' response to the decision nor the reason for opposition by other nations can be deduced from the statement. So, neither I or II follows.

59. (*d*) : Neither the poor nor the rich, but only the role of money in politics is being talked about in the statement. So, neither I nor II follows.

60. (*a*) : According to the statement, only those who tackle situations bravely achieve success. So, I follows. However, II is vague with regard to the given statement and so does not follow.

61. (*b*) : The statement is a symbolic one and only II correctly explains it.

62. (*d*) : According to the statement, good wranglers are wise men. But it doesn't mean that all wise men are good wranglers. So, neither I nor II follows.

63. (*e*) : According to the statement, monitoring and evaluation of social development programmes — their function, performance and efficiency — is absolutely essential. So, both I and II follow.

64. (*b*) : Clearly, I is vague and so does not follow. However, II directly follows from the given statement.

65. (*a*) : According to the statement, funding is necessary to improve quality and India is allocating funds to education. This means that quality of education will improve in India. So, I follows. But funding alone is sufficient to enhance quality, is not true. So, II does not follow.

66. (*b*) : The population per household and not the population per unit area is being talked about in the statement. So, only II follows while I does not.

67. (*e*) : Clearly, both I and II correctly explain the given statement. So, both follow.

68. (*a*) : The statement implies that the government is continuously making efforts to curb terrorism, but it still continues to prevail. Thus, I follows while II does not.

69. (*a*) : Clearly, I directly follows from the statement while II cannot be deduced from it.

70. (*c*) : Clearly, either I or II could be the reason for the situation expressed in the statement.

OTHER MISCELLANEOUS TYPES

EXERCISE 5B

Directions (*Questions 1 to 27*) : *In each of the following questions, a statement / group of statements is given followed by some conclusions. Choose the conclusion which logically follows from the given statements.*

1. **Statement :**   **(Bank P.O. 1993)**
   To pass the examination one must work hard.
   Conclusions :
   (a) Examination is related with hard work.
   (b) All those who work hard, pass.
   (c) Examination causes some anxiety and those who work hard overcome it.
   (d) Without hard work, one does not pass.
   (e) Hard-working person is a satisfied person.

2. **Statement :**   **(Hotel Management, 1991)**
   This book can help because all good books help.
   Conclusions :
   (a) This is not a good book.   (b) This is a good book.
   (c) No good book helps.   (d) Some good books help.

3. **Statement :**
   Every library has books.
   Conclusions :
   (a) Books are only in library.   (b) Libraries are meant for books only.
   (c) No library is without books .   (d) Some libraries do not have readers.

4. **Statement :**   **(Assistant Grade, 1992)**
   Soldiers serve their country.
   Conclusions :
   (a) Men generally serve their country.
   (b) Those who serve their country are soldiers.
   (c) Some men who are soldiers serve their country.
   (d) Women do not serve their country because they are not soldiers.

5. **Statement :**   **(S.B.I.P.O. 1995)**
   The government is soon going to introduce a bill which would permit the instituting
   of private universities under very strict directions.
   Conclusions :
   (a) The government gives directions to establish anything in private sector.
   (b) Such directions can also be issued without informing the Parliament.
   (c) The demand for more universities is being stepped up.
   (d) Unless and until the directions are given, the private universities can
       charge exorbitant fees.
   (e) We have some private universities in our country even now.

6. **Statement :**   **(S.C.R.A. 1994)**
   A factory worker has five children. No one else in the factory has five children.
   Conclusions :
   (a) All workers in the factory have five children each.
   (b) Everybody in the factory has children.
   (c) Some of the factory workers have more than five children.
   (d) Only one worker in the factory has exactly five children.

7. **Statements :**
   1. None but the rich can afford air-travel.
   2. Some of those who travel by air become sick.
   3. Some of those who become sick require treatment.

Conclusions :
- (a) All the rich persons travel by air.
- (b) Those who travel by air become sick.
- (c) All the rich persons become sick.
- (d) All those who travel by air are rich.

8. Statements : (I.A.S. 1998)
1. Processed meat is a perishable food.
2. All perishable foods are packed in sealed tins.
3. Sealed tins sometimes do not contain processed meat.

Conclusions :
- (a) Non-perishable foods are never packed in sealed tins.
- (b) Processed meat is always packed in sealed tins.
- (c) Processed meat is sometimes not packed in sealed tins.
- (d) Sealed tins always contain perishable food.

9. Statements : (S.S.C. 1996)
1. All students in my class are bright.
2. Manish is not bright.

Conclusions :
- (a) Some students are not bright. (b) Manish must work hard.
- (c) Non-bright ones are not students.
- (d) Manish is not a student of my class.

10. Statement :
Three-fourth of the students of standard VII consisting of 48 boys and 12 girls know swimming.

Conclusions :
- (a) Girls are poor swimmers.
- (b) Swimming is compulsory in this school.
- (c) One-fourth of the boys do not know swimming.
- (d) The percentage of boys who know swimming is more than that of girls.
- (e) None of these

11. Statement : (S.B.I.P.O. 1995)
Every man should have his identity card with him. That card should mention his blood group, complete address and telephone number for contact, in case, some serious accident takes place.

Conclusions :
- (a) Blood cannot be transfused until its group is mentioned in the card.
- (b) The police needs this information specially when the accident is fatal.
- (c) In case of emergency, he may forget his address and may need the card to contact his house.
- (d) None is supposed to forget his phone number under any circumstances.
- (e) When the seriously injured person is helpless to tell his blood group, this information would suffice to indicate the required blood group.

12. Statement :
A forest has as many sandal trees as it has Ashoka trees. Three-fourth of the trees are old ones and half of the trees are at the flowering stage.

Conclusions :
(a) All Ashoka trees are at the flowering stage.
(b) All sandal trees are at the flowering stage.
(c) At least one-half of the Ashoka trees are old.
(d) One-half of the sandal trees are at the flowering stage.
(e) None of these

13. Statement :   **(Bank P.O. 1994)**

In a class, three-fourth of the boys play football, one-half play cricket, one-fourth of those who play cricket do not play football.

Conclusions :
(a) Two-third of the boys play only football.
(b) One-fourth of the boys play neither cricket nor football.
(c) One-third of the boys play neither cricket nor football.
(d) One-eighth of the boys play neither cricket nor football.
(e) Two-fifth of the boys play only football.

14. Statement :   **(Section Officers' 1993)**

Ability is poor man's wealth.

Conclusions :
(a) A poor man is always able.
(b) A poor man has the ability to earn wealth.
(c) A wealthy man is always able.
(d) A poor man can earn wealth if he has ability.

15. Statement :

Hitesh told Mohit a ghost lived by the peepal tree on the outskirts of the village.

Conclusions :
(a) Peepal trees grow on the outskirts of the village.
(b) Ghosts live on peepal trees.
(c) Mohit must be afraid of ghosts.
(d) Hitesh perhaps believed in the stories of ghosts.

16. Statements :   **(I.A.S. 1995)**

1. I watch T.V. only if I am bored.
2. I am never bored when I have my brother's company.
3. Whenever I go to the theatre I take my brother along.

Conclusions :
(a) If I am bored, I seek my brother's company.
(b) If I am not bored, I do not watch T.V.
(c) If I am bored, I watch T.V.
(d) If I am not with my brother then I watch T.V.

17. Statement :   **(S.S.C. 1996)**

Most of the politicians are liars. Harish tells lies.

Conclusions :
(a) Harish is a politician.
(b) Those who do not tell lies are not politicians.
(c) Some politicians do not tell lies.
(d) You can only benefit by telling lies.

18. Statements :
1. Shyam is not the father of Hari.
2. Hari is the son of Suresh.
3. Suresh has three sons.

Conclusions :
(*a*) Shyam is the son of Suresh.   (*b*) Hari is the brother of Shyam.
(*c*) Suresh is the father of Hari.   (*d*) Shyam has no children.

                                                                    (I.A.S. 1998)

19. Statements :
1. All members of Mohan's family are honest.
2. Some members of Mohan's family are not employed.
3. Some employed persons are not honest.
4. Some honest persons are not employed.

Conclusions :
(*a*) All members of Mohan's family are employed.
(*b*) The employed members of Mohan's family are honest.
(*c*) The honest members of Mohan's family are not employed.
(*d*) The employed members of Mohan's family are not honest.

                                                                (S.B.I.P.O. 1995)

20. Statement :
The data given by the U.S. Labour Ministry indicate that till the year 2000, there will be a shortage of 100,000 programmers. A spokesman from the industry said, "We should understand this thoroughly America needs Indian programmers. This is not only the question of investment but also of the talent with which the Indian programmers are equipped."

Conclusions :
(*a*) In other sectors also, there will be shortage of the talented labour till the year 2000.
(*b*) Indian programmers are the most talented in the world.
(*c*) Indian programmers are available on comparatively less salary in comparison to the programmers from other countries.
(*d*) Inspite of entering with huge capital in the Software Training Sector, U.S. could not be able to meet its own needs fully.
(*e*) The Indian Software Market is well equipped to send programmers to other countries.

                                                                    (S.C.R.A. 1993)

21. Statements :
1. Only students can participate in the race.
2. Some participants in the race are females.
3. All female participants in the race are invited for coaching.

Conclusions :
(*a*) All participants in the race are invited for coaching.
(*b*) All participants in the race are males.
(*c*) All students are invited for coaching.
(*d*) All participants in the race are students.

                                                    (I. Tax & Central Excise, 1993)

22. Statement :
All scientists working in America are talented. Some Indian scientists are working in America.

Conclusions :

1. None of Indian scientists is talented.
2. Some talented Indian scientists have migrated to America.
3. All talented scientists are Indians.
4. Some Indian scientists are talented.

The conclusion(s) correctly drawn is/are

(a) 2 and 3   (b) 1 only   (c) 2 and 4   (d) 2 only

23. **Statement :**

(S.C.R.A. 1994)

Few shops on this road have neon lights, but they all have signboards.

Conclusions :

1. Some shops have either signboards or neon lights.
2. Some shops have both signboards and neon lights.
3. Some shops have no neon lights.
4. Some shops have no signboards.

The conclusion(s) correctly drawn is/are

(a) 1 alone   (b) 1 and 4   (c) 2 alone   (d) 2 and 3

24. **Statement :**

Amit and Subhash are friends. Subhash is friendly with all. Amit has many enemies. Rahul and Amit do not like each other.

Conclusions :

1. Amit, Rahul and Subhash form a clique.
2. Rahul and Subhash are friends.
3. Subhash is friendly with Amit's friends.
4. Amit and Rahul are both friends of Subhash.

The conclusion(s) correctly drawn is/are

(a) 3 and 4   (b) 2 and 3   (c) 1 and 2   (d) 2, 3 and 4

25. **Statement :**

(Central Excise, 1993)

All watches sold in that shop are of high standard; some of the HMT watches are sold in that shop.

Conclusions :

1. All watches of high standard were manufactured by HMT.
2. Some of the HMT watches are of high standard.
3. None of the HMT watches is of high standard.
4. Some of the HMT watches of high standard are sold in that shop.

The conclusion(s) correctly drawn is/are

(a) 1 and 2   (b) 1 and 3   (c) 1 and 4   (d) 2 and 4

26. **Statement :**

A wise man saves for a rainy day.
A rainy day signifies adversity.

Conclusions :

1. A fool squanders everything.
2. A wise man is likely to get into adversity.
3. A clear day signifies prosperity.

The conclusion(s) correctly drawn is/are

(a) 1 only   (b) 1 and 2   (c) 2 only   (d) 1 and 3

27. Statement :   (I. Tax & Central Excise, 1993)

Foreigners in Jordan without a valid work permit will be permitted. A few Indian employees in the building industry in Jordan do not possess valid work permits.

Conclusions :

1. All Indians engaged in building industry in Jordan will be deported to India.
2. A few Indians in building industry in Jordan will be deported.
3. A bulk of Indians in Jordan will be deported to India.
4. Indian employees in building industry without work permit will be deported from Jordan.

The conclusion(s) correctly drawn is/are

(a) 1 and 2   (b) 1 and 3   (c) 2 and 4   (d) 3 and 4

Directions (Questions 28 to 32) : *In the following questions there are given some statements followed by conclusions that can be drawn from them. Choose the conclusion which appeals to you to be the most correct.* (M.B.A. 1997)

28. The Taj is in Agra. Agra is in India. Therefore, the Taj is in India.

(a) True   (b) Probably false   (c) False   (d) Can't say

29. The presence of calcium in milk makes it white. Rice, too, is white. Therefore, rice also contains calcium.

(a) False   (b) Probably true   (c) True   (d) Can't say

30. Hydrogen is lighter than oxygen. Hydrogen is lighter than helium. Therefore, oxygen is the heaviest of the three gases.

(a) False   (b) Probably false   (c) True   (d) Can't say

31. People who are bald are generally of the intellectual type. Arun is bald. Therefore Arun is an intellectual.

(a) True   (b) Probably true   (c) False   (d) Can't say

32. Jatin, Kamal and Navin are three mountaineers. Jatin is Kamal's brother. Kamal is Navin's brother. Navin is not Jatin's brother. Therefore, Navin is Jatin's sister.

(a) True   (b) Probably false   (c) False   (d) Can't say

Directions (Questions 33 to 45) : *In each of the following questions, certain statements are given followed by a conclusion based upon them. Choose the alternative which best applies to the given statements and conclusion.*

33. Statements :   (I. Tax & Central Excise, 1994)

1. A triangle has three angles.
2. A square has four angles.

Conclusion : A polygon has many angles.

The conclusion drawn is

(a) definitely true   (b) definitely false
(c) either probably true or probably false   (d) irrelevant

34. Statements :

1. Some persons are weak in Mathematics.
2. All those, who are weak in Mathematics, are musicians.

Conclusion : Some musicians are weak in Mathematics.

The conclusion drawn is

(a) definitely true   (b) irrelevant   (c) probably true   (d) definitely false

35. Statements :
1. Some very effective medicines are made from spider venom.
2. Poison of snake is also used for curing certain diseases.

Conclusion : All poisons cure some or the other disease.

The conclusion drawn
   (a) definitely follows from the given statements
   (b) does not follow from the given statements
   (c) is probably true   (d) Can't say

36. Statements :   **(I. Tax & Central Excise, 1993)**
1. Water boils at 100°C.
2. Water freezes at 0°C.

Conclusion : At low pressure, water boils at lower temperatures.

The conclusion drawn is
   (a) definitely true   (b) definitely false
   (c) either probably true or probably false   (d) irrelevant

37. Statements :
1. During volcanic eruptions, molten lava oozes out in a stream.
2. The lava comes from under the crust of the earth.

Conclusion : The inside of the earth must be very hot.

The conclusion drawn is
   (a) definitely true   (b) probably true   (c) definitely false   (d) irrelevant

38. Statements :   **(I. Tax & Central Excise, 1994)**
1. Oxygen is a gas.
2. This cylinder contains gas.

Conclusion : This cylinder contains oxygen.

The conclusion drawn is
   (a) irrelevant   (b) definitely true
   (c) either probably true or probably false   (d) definitely false

39. Statements :
1. Pyramids date back to about 300 B.C.
2. Lots of gold and other valuables were found in them.
3. China has no pyramids.

Conclusion : China cannot claim a rich past.

The conclusion
   (a) follows from the given statements
   (b) does not follow from the given statements
   (c) is probably true   (d) is probably false

40. Statements :
1. Persons of modest means try to have a house of their own.
2. Since buying or constructing a house is an expensive affair, they try to save money in all possible ways.
3. After years of saving, they realise that although they have saved the amount they had planned to save, it is not sufficient now for constructing a house.

Conclusion :
Growing rates of land and building material shatter their dream.
The conclusion
(a) follows from the given statements
(b) does not follow from the given statements
(c) is irrelevant   (d) is probably false

41. **Statements :**   **(I. Tax & Central Excise, 1993)**
    1. Freedom fighters get 'tamrapatra'.
    2. Krishna was a freedom fighter.
    Conclusion : He got 'tamrapatra'.
    The conclusion drawn is
    (a) valid   (b) irrelevant   (c) invalid   (d) probably false

42. **Statements :**
    1. Only those young men smoke who do not go to colleges.
    2. Only those young men go to colleges who are not smart.
    Conclusion : Smart young men do not smoke.
    The conclusion drawn is
    (a) probably true   (b) definitely true   (c) probably false   (d) definitely false

43. **Statements :**
    1. Drugs obtained from herbs are very useful in curing diseases
    2. Some herbs are used by beauticians as well.
    Conclusion : Patients who take herbal drugs become beautiful.
    The conclusion
    (a) follows from the given statements
    (b) does not follow from the given statements
    (c) is probably true
    (d) None of these

44. **Statements :**
    1. Dogs do not bark on the arrival of friends of the family.
    2. When A entered B's house, B's dog started barking.
    Conclusion : A is B's enemy.
    The conclusion
    (a) follows from the given statements
    (b) is probably true
    (c) is probably false
    (d) does not follow from the given statements

45. **Statements :**
    1. The no-confidence motion is often allowed to be debated upon.
    2. There was a no-confidence motion last week.
    Conclusion : It was debated upon by the parties concerned.
    The conclusion drawn is
    (a) definitely true   (b) probably false   (c) definitely false   (d) Can't say

Directions (*Questions 46 to 50*) : *In each of the following questions, a conclusion is given followed by two statements labelled A and B. Give your answer as :*   (M.B.A. 1997)

(*a*) if statement A alone is needed to draw the conclusion;

(*b*) if statement B alone is needed to draw the conclusion;

(*c*) if both A and B are needed to draw the conclusion;

(*d*) if both A and B are not sufficient to draw the conclusion

46. He looks dangerous.

  A : He has a lean and hungry look.

  B : He thinks too much.

47. Shaving is smoother if some soap is applied with warm water.

  A : Brushing the soap to make lather increases the time it takes to shave.

  B : The face also gets a wash as it shaved.

48. Spices deteriorate after prolonged boiling.

  A : The essential oils in spices easily evaporate.

  B : Spices are put in pickles to add to the flavour.

49. Sometimes a single observation makes us recall innumerable events which have occurred in the past.

  A : Man has the gift of memory.

  B : Man is basically a dreamer.

50. Plants can also be sick.

  A : Only mammals can be ill.

  B : Improper nutrition will create aberrations in a plant's growth.

ANSWERS

1. (*d*)	**2.** (*b*)	**3.** (*c*)	**4.** (*c*)	**5.** (*c*)	**6.** (*d*)	**7.** (*d*)	**8.** (*c*)	**9.** (*d*)	**10.** (*e*)
11. (*b*)	**12.** (*e*)	**13.** (*d*)	**14.** (*d*)	**15.** (*d*)	**16.** (*b*)	**17.** (*c*)	**18.** (*c*)	**19.** (*b*)	**20.** (*b*)
21. (*d*)	**22.** (*c*)	**23.** (*d*)	**24.** (*d*)	**25.** (*d*)	**26.** (*b*)	**27.** (*c*)	**28.** (*a*)	**29.** (*d*)	**30.** (*d*)
31. (*b*)	**32.** (*a*)	**33.** (*d*)	**34.** (*a*)	**35.** (*d*)	**36.** (*d*)	**37.** (*a*)	**38.** (*c*)	**39.** (*b*)	**40.** (*a*)
41. (*a*)	**42.** (*d*)	**43.** (*b*)	**44.** (*d*)	**45.** (*d*)	**46.** (*a*)	**47.** (*a*)	**48.** (*a*)	**49.** (*a*)	**50.** (*b*)

6. DERIVING CONCLUSIONS FROM PASSAGES

In this section of logical deduction, the question consists of a brief passage followed by certain inferences based on it. The candidate is required to analyse the passage and grasp the desirable facts from it. Then, he has to consider each inference in context of the given passage, decide upon its degree of truth or falsity and then choose the best alternative provided accordingly.

ILLUSTRATIVE EXAMPLES

Directions : *Read the following passage and examine each inference given below it in the context of this passage.*

Mark your answer as :

(a) *if the inference is 'definitely true';*
(b) *if the inference is 'probably true';*
(c) *if the 'data provided is inadequate';*
(d) *if the inference is 'probably false'; and*
(e) *if the inference is 'definitely false'.*

Ex. 1. The space exploration has been done mainly by using unmanned satellites called space probes containing a large variety of latest scientific instruments on board. These space probes have provided us the close up pictures and other data about planets and other bodies in the outer space. The climax of the intensive American space programme came when Neil Armstrong became the first man to set foot on the moon on July 20, 1969. Originally, the artificial satellites were launched for studying the upper atmosphere of earth.

1. The space probes have increased our knowledge about space and the bodies in it.
2. Space probes are meant to study the upper atmosphere of earth only.
3. Neil Armstrong was the first man to go into space.
4. Space probes are provided with computers.
5. Moon has been explored by man.

Solution :

1. (a) : It is mentioned in the passage that the space probes have provided pictures and certain data of the outer space and the heavenly bodies. Thus, they have helped us increase our knowledge of outer space and the bodies in it.

2. (e) : According to the passage, the space probes were first designed to study the upper atmosphere of earth. But at present, they are also used to explore outer space and obtain more information about it.

3. (c) : It is given in the passage that Neil Armstrong was the first man to step foot on moon. But the first man to go into space is not being talked out.

4. (b) : According to the passage, space probes are provided with large variety of latest scientific instruments. Thus, computers may also be present.

5. (a) : The fact mentioned in the passage that Neil Armstrong was the first man to set foot on the moon clearly proves that moon has been explored by man.

Ex. 2. Ministry of environment and forest has granted environmental clearance to the Karkatla open-cast expansion project of the Central Coal Fields Ltd. in Bihar that envisages exploitation of non-cocking coal reserves. The present production level of 0.8 million tonnes is proposed to be expanded to 1.5 million tonnes per annum at an estimated cost of 67.82 crores under the project. The total land area requirement for the proposed mining activities is about 651 hectares which includes about one-sixth of it as foreign land.

1. The expansion plan would require about 100 hectares of forest land.
2. Karkatla open-cast mine is the only one of non-cocking coal in the country.
3. There is no demand for non-cocking coal.
4. The production cost of one tonne of non-cocking coal from Karkatla mine will be about Rs 450.
5. Environmental concern gets less priority over the need of the coal.

Solution :

1. (*a*) : According to the passage, land required for expansion plan = 651 hectares.

   Forest land $= \left(\frac{1}{6} \times \text{total land} \right) = \frac{1}{6} \times 651 = 108.5 = 100$ hectares (approximately).

2. (*c*) : It is mentioned only that Karkatla mine deals with exploitation of non-cocking coal reserves. But, it is not given that it is the only such mine.

3. (*a*) : The granting of environmental clearance to Karkatla mine shows that there is a demand for non-cocking coal.

4. (*a*) : Total estimated production = 1.5 million tonnes = (1.5×10^6) tonnes

   Total estimated cost = Rs 67.82 crores = Rs (67.82×10^7)

   Cost per tonne of coal = Rs. $\left(\frac{67.82 \times 10^7}{1.5 \times 10^6} \right)$ = Rs 452.13 = Rs 450 (approximately)

5. (*c*) : The given fact is neither mentioned in nor can be derived from the passage.

Ex. 3. A radical new surgery procedure, laughed at not long ago, is holding out fresh hope for patients of cardiac myopathy, or enlargement of the heart. The technique, now in India, allows patients to go home two weeks after the operation, to lead a near-normal sedantary life. Cardiac myopathy is a condition that has a variety of causative factors. An attack from one of the 20 identified viruses, parasite infection, long-term alcohol abuse and blood pressure could bring it on, and in rare cases, it could follow child birth and is even known to run in families. The condition is marked by an increase in the size of the heart's chambers and a decrease in the efficiency of pumping.   **(Bank P.O. 1997)**

1. Cardiac myopathy is hereditary.
2. The new technique was never tried in India in the past.
3. The cardiac myopathy slows down the heart beat.
4. Earlier the patients suffering from cardiac myopathy were required to travel abroad for such operation.
5. The efficiency of the heart is inversely proportional to the size of the heart.

Solution :

1. (*b*) : It is mentioned in the passage that in certain cases, cardiac myopathy was 'known to run in families'. So, it might be possible that it is hereditary.

2. (a) : The given conclusion can be clearly inferred from the line 'The technique, now in India, ...' which clearly means that the technique was previously not there in India.

3. (a) : It is clearly mentioned in the passage that cardiac myopathy is marked by 'a decrease in the efficiency of pumping'. This means that the heart beat is slowed down.

4. (c) : Nothing is mentioned about the time before the introduction of the new technique.

5. (a) : The given inference directly follows from the last line of the passage :'the condition is marked by an increase in the size of the heart's chambers and a decrease in the efficiency of pumping'.

Ex. 4. Though the state cultivates only 3.2 lakh tonnes of mangoes, they are of premium quality and with mangoes becoming second most consumed fruit in the world after grapes, the government has been trying exporting it through sea route which is cheaper. An experiment which was done in this regard last year has proved successful. **(Bank P.O. 1993)**

1. Quality of mangoes is an important factor in exports.
2. The state also exports good quality grapes.
3. There are some problems in exporting mangoes through sea route.
4. Most of the other exports are through sea routes which is cheaper.
5. The state also cultivates a large number of medium quality of mangoes.

Solution :

1. (a) : It is given in the passage that mangoes cultivated in the state are of good quality and the government is trying to export them. This implies the given fact.

2. (c) : Nothing about the production and export of grapes by the state is mentioned in the passage.

3. (e) : According to the passage, the government is trying to export mangoes through sea route which is cheaper. This clearly means that exporting mangoes through sea route does not entail any problems.

4. (b) : According to the passage, the government considers sea route a cheaper medium of export. Perhaps the other exports through sea route have given them this experience.

5. (e) : According to the passage, the state cultivates 3.2 lakh tonnes of mangoes, all of which are of premium quality.

EXERCISE 6A

Directions : *In each question below is given a passage followed by several inferences. You have to examine each inference separately in the context of the passage and decide upon its degree of truth or falsity.*

Mark your answer as :

(a) *if the inference is 'definitely true' i.e., it directly follows from the facts given in the passage;*

(b) *if the inference is 'probably true' though not definitely true in the light of the facts given;*

(c) *if you think the data are inadequate i.e., from the facts given you cannot say whether the inference is likely to be true or false;*

(d) *if you think the inference is 'probably false' though not definitely false in the light of the facts given; and*

(e) *if you think the inference is 'definitely false' i.e., it contradicts the given facts.*

Questions 1 to 5   (Bank P.O. 1996)

A recent survey shows that India has the lowest death rate for blood cancer. China, Thailand and Myanmar (countries that have taste for spices) also have low rates. Higher rates are found in U.S.A. where spices are not used. The typical American food remains chicken rolls, butter and beef.

1. Americans are unorthodox in their food habits.
2. Americans dislike spices.
3. Spices prevent blood cancer.
4. Spices promote forms of cancer other than blood cancer.
5. Chicken rolls, butter and beef promote cancer.

Questions 6 to 10

The basic thrust of the Government's policy is to provide price incentives to farmers to make them produce more food. But is a price-incentive system always efficient in ensuring incremental yields ? Our contention is that this incentive works only in persuading farmers to shift cultivation from one crop to another depending on which crop is more profitable at the given prices. But it would not be a sufficient condition in ensuring incremental output of all crops which is what is required.

6. This passage is taken from an article written by an expert on agricultural finance.
7. The author is advocating for more yield of various crops.
8. The Government is not ready to increase the procurement price of crops.
9. According to the passage, the farmers are not income-conscious.
10. Recently there was an agitation by farmers for increase in procurement price of crops.

Questions 11 to 16   (Bank P.O. 1998)

Urban services have not expanded fast enough to cope with urban expansion. Low investment allocations have tended to be underspent. Both public (*e.g.* water and sewage) and private (*e.g.* low-income area housing) infrastructure quality has declined. This impact of the environment in which children live and the supporting services available to them when they fall ill, seems clear. The decline in average food availability and the rise in absolute poverty point in the same unsatisfactory direction.

11. There is nothing to boast about urban services.
12. The public transport system is in the hands of private sector.
13. Birth rate is higher in urban areas as compared to rural areas.
14. Low-cost urban housing is one of the priorities.
15. The environment around plays an important role on the health status.
16. Though adequate provisions of funds were made but they remained unspent.

Questions 17 to 20

A tiger, when killing its natural prey, which it does either by stalking or lying in wait for it, depends for the success of its attack on its speed and, to a lesser extent, on the condition of its teeth and claws. When, therefore, a tiger is suffering from one or more painful wounds or when its teeth are missing or defective and its claws worn down, and it is unable to catch animals it has been accustomed to eating, it is driven by the necessity to killing human beings.

17. Human beings are the natural prey of tigers.
18. Sharp claws are needed by the tigers to kill animals in the forest.

19. Old age propels tigers to take to man eating.

20. Tiger kills man only when it has been incapacitated through wounds.

Questions 21 to 25 (Bank P.O. 1994)

The explosive growth in demand for castor oil abroad is bringing about a silent change in the castor seed economy of Gujarat. The State is well on its way to emerge as a strong manufacturing centre for castor oil relegating to background its current status as a big trading centre. The business prospects for export of castor oil which is converted into value-added derivatives are so good that a number of castor seed crushing units have already come up and others are on the anvil.

21. Gujarat used to supply castor seeds to the manufacturing units in the past.

22. Gujarat is the only State in India which produces castor seed.

23. India can produce enough castor oil to export after meeting the domestic demand.

24. The production of castor oil has become a profitable business proposition.

25. Manufacturing castor oil guarantees more surplus than selling castor seeds.

Questions 26 to 30

The water resources of our country are very much underutilised. The main reason of this underutilisation is the lack of capital and technology. A large portion of our water resources is wasted due to floods and unwise use of water for irrigation as well as domestic purposes. We can make full use of our water resources by building dams on rivers and by adopting policy of awareness among people not to waste water.

26. Our country has large areas to be irrigated and much water is wasted.

27. Building of dams is an essential step in the conservation of water resources.

28. Occurrence of floods adds to the water resources.

29. Some people do not use water resources in a judicious way.

30. The country does not have enough funds to develop water resources.

Questions 31 to 35 (Bank P.O. 1995)

The smaller pesticide formulation units in India operate under heavy constraints such as obsolete technology, small scale of operation and dependence on large units for raw materials. In view of the loss of expensive material by the smaller units it is important to either eliminate or reduce losses to the extent possible through innovative and sustainable waste minimisation techniques. Operating profit margins of the units are very low and small adverse conditions land these companies in trouble. Maximum losses suffered by these units are through poor house keeping, sub-optional operating practices, and lack of proper opportunities for recycling waste.

31. Smaller units should be operationally self-sufficient so as to minimise losses.

32. Recycling of wastes through modern techniques can set off large part of the losses incurred by the smaller units.

33. Pesticide units should necessarily be on a large scale to make them economically viable.

34. Waste management process in India needs modernisation.

35. Lack of funds compels smaller units to ignore house keeping.

Questions 36 to 39

The consumer movement in India is yet to make the grade. In the metropolitan areas, consumer organisations do exist but their role in the prevention of adulteration is limited. The position is worse in the countryside where the ignorance of the consumer is exploited by unscrupulous traders. The government's oldest remedy, which has been tried down the decades since 1947, is to enthuse the masses enlist themselves in consumer cooperatives besides encouraging industrial units or other establishment to set-up separate retail outlets solely for the benefit of their employees.

36. The consumer movement has not spread to the countryside.

37. The government has not cared to book the unscrupulous traders.

38. The consumer movement is doing well in other countries and the people are healthy there.

39. The people have not shown real interest in the government's plan.

Questions 40 to 44   (S.B.I.P.O. 1997)

The World Health Organisation has called for an improved surveillance to combat dengue and says the outbreak can be controlled in two weeks if all necessary steps are taken to stop the mosquitoes from breeding and break the transmission cycle. Dengue is already the most widespread mosquito-borne disease among humans. In the past 15 years, outbreaks in South and South-east Asia have been rapidly rising mostly due to falling environmental and public health standards during urbanisation. WHO reports that severe forms of the disease such as haemorrhagic fever (DHF) and shock syndrome (DSS) are putting more than 2.5 million people at risk worldwide each year. Importantly, 95% of the DHF cases are among children less than 15 years. Therefore, the disease has major impacts on public health and future generations.

40. If rate of urbanisation in South Asia is controlled, outbreaks of all diseases may be reduced.

41. World Health Organisation has not collected data of outbreak of dengue in the past.

42. There was no outbreak of dengue in the European countries in the recent past.

43. Over the last decade South Asian countries have not successfully stepped up mechanism to combat dengue.

44. DSS type dengue seems mostly to be affecting the adults.

Questions 45 to 50

Primary education in Bihar is in a poor shape. Pupils in over 50 percent of the schools read in the open throughout the year. Over six million children born to lower income group parents remain unlettered. Not even one percent of the 63,000 primary schools have facilities of furniture, toilet, drinking water and games. 3113 new teachers have been appointed in the current financial year out of which 2747 are women. Now each of the 13270 primary schools have at least two teachers.

45. 630 primary schools in Bihar have all the facilities like furniture, toilet, drinking water, games.

46. In Bihar, 90 percent of the primary teachers are women.

47. In Bihar, 50 percent of the children are illiterate.

48. A large number of primary schools in Bihar are one teacher schools.

49. There are six million parents belonging to lower income groups in Bihar.

50. Classrooms of most of the primary schools in Bihar are inadequate.

Questions 51 to 55   (Bank P.O. 1994)

More than a decade of erosion in budgetary support from the Union Government, has seriously affected Indian Railways' capacity to finance its plan expenditures. The situation has come to a pass where the railways must now think of innovative ways to get longer mileage from its investments. Significantly the resource crunch has had grievous impact on the railways. As a result, it will not be in a position to acquire necessary equipments and this will seriously affect the railways' capacity to serve the needs of the economy in future.

51. Railways had so far believed in traditional ways in generating income.

52. Government has shifted its priority from railways to other areas.

53. The Union Government has reduced drastically the budgetory support to railways during the last decade.

54. The fiscal position of railways in the earlier plan period was better than the current plan period.

55. During the current plan period, the railways will not be able to expand its network.

ANSWERS

1. (d) : It is mentioned that Americans have almost the same diet, with no intake of spices. This means that probably they cannot change diet easily and are orthodox in food habits.

2. (c) : Nothing about the reason for Americans not using spices in their diet is mentioned in the passage.

3. (a) : The fact that blood cancer is more prominent in America, where spices are not used while the rate is much lower in Asian countries where spices are used, makes the given conclusion valid.

4. (c) : Other forms of cancer have not been talked about in the passage.

5. (a) : It is mentioned that blood cancer is more prominent in America, where the typical diet comprises of chicken rolls, butter and beef.

6. (a) : Since the passage analyses the merits and demerits of the Government's new fiscal policy relating to agriculture, the given conclusion follows.

7. (a) : It is mentioned that the new policy will lead to a shift in cultivation and would not fulfill its real objective, which is to make farmers produce more food.
The last sentence of the passage also confirms the fact.

8. (e) : According to the passage, the Government is providing price incentives to farmers. This contradicts the fact given in the question.

9. (e) : According to the passage, the farmers would shift cultivation from the present crop to the more profitable one. This means that they are income-conscious.

10. (c) : The fact is neither mentioned in nor can be derived from the passage.

11. (a) : The first sentence of the passage verifies the given conclusion.

12. (c) : Nothing about the public transport system is mentioned in the passage.

13. (c) : The passage deals with deteriorating living conditions in urban areas. Nothing about the birth rate is mentioned.

14. (b) : Since the passage condemns the decline in quality of low-income area housing, it is probable that it is a vital aspect of urban services.

15. (a) : The conclusion directly follows from the statement 'The impact of the environment... seems clear' in the passage.

16. (e) : The phrase 'low investment allocations' in the passage implies that the funds provided were not adequate.

17. (e) : It is given in the passage that tigers take to killing human beings when they are unable to catch the animals they are used to eat. This violates the fact given in the question.

18. (a) : According to the passage, the success of a tiger in killing its prey depends on the condition of its claws. This implies the given fact.

19. (c) : The given fact is neither mentioned in nor can be derived from the given passage.

20. (*a*) : According to the passage, a tiger takes to killing man only when certain wounds render it incapable to kill its natural prey — the animals in the forest.

21. (*a*) : It is mentioned that Gujarat was uptil now not involved in manufacturing of castor oil, but was only a big trading centre. This implies that it used to supply castor seeds rather than processing them.

22. (*c*) : The given fact is neither mentioned in nor can be derived from the given passage.

23. (*a*) : The given fact directly follows from the last sentence of the passage.

24. (*a*) : It is mentioned that business prospects in the field of castor oil are good and the number of castor seed processing units is increasing. This implies the given fact.

25. (*a*) : It is mentioned that Gujarat has shifted from trading in castor seeds to manufacturing castor oil. This implies the given fact.

26. (*c*) : No mention of the land to be irrigated in India is there in the passage.

27. (*a*) : It is given in the passage that 'we can make full use of our water resources by building of dams'.

28. (*e*) : It is mentioned that much of our water resources are wasted due to floods.

29. (*a*) : It is mentioned that wastage of water takes place due to their unwise use for domestic purposes.

30. (*a*) : It is given in the passage that underutilisation of the water resources of our country is due to lack of capital or funds.

31. (*c*) : The given fact is neither mentioned in nor can be derived from the given passage.

32. (*a*) : It is mentioned in the passage that maximum losses suffered by the smaller units are because of lack of proper opportunities for recycling waste. This clearly implies the given fact.

33. (*b*) : From the first sentence of the passage, it is quite probable that operating on a large scale might make the pesticide units economically viable.

34. (*a*) : The fact directly follows from the sentence 'In view of the loss... waste minimisation techniques' in the passage.

35. (*b*) : It is mentioned in the passage that the profit margins of small units are low and so small adverse conditions land them in trouble. Thus, it is quite probable that lack of funds compels these units to ignore house keeping.

36. (*b*) : According to the passage the ignorance of the consumer is exploited in the countryside. So, it is quite probable that the consumer movement has not spread to the countryside.

37. (*b*) : It is mentioned in the passage that the ignorance of the consumer in the countryside is exploited by unscrupulous traders. So, it is probable that not much care has been taken to take any action against such traders.

38. (*c*) : Nothing is mentioned about the consumer movement in other countries in the passage.

39. (*b*) : It is mentioned in the passage that people need to be encouraged to enlist themselves in consumer cooperatives. So, it is quite probable that people do not have much interest in it.

40. (*b*) : It is mentioned in the passage that 'outbreaks in South and South-east Asia have been rapidly rising mostly due to falling environmental and public health standards during urbanisation. Thus, the fact in the question is quite probable.

41. (*e*) : The passage talks of outbreak of dengue during the past 15 years. This contradicts the fact given in the question.

42. (*c*) : The passage mentions the outbreak of dengue in Asian countries only and not the European countries.

43. (*a*) : It is mentioned in the passage that cases of outbreak of dengue are rapidly rising in South Asian countries since the last 15 years. This means that adequate steps to combat dengue have not been taken.

44. (*c*) : Nothing about the effect of DSS type dengue is mentioned in the passage.

45. (e) : According to the passage less than 1 percent of 63,000 primary schools have all the facilities. Thus, less than 630 primary schools have the facilities.

46. (c) : The given fact is neither mentioned in nor can be derived from the given passage.

47. (c) : The given fact is neither mentioned in nor can be derived from the given passage.

48. (e) : It is mentioned in the passage that each of the 13,270 primary schools have at least two teachers.

49. (a) : According to the passage, about six million children are born to lower income group parents. This clearly implies the given fact.

50. (b) : It is given in the passage that pupils in more than 50 percent of the schools read in the open. Perhaps this is because the classes provided are inadequate.

51. (a) : It is mentioned in the passage that railways now need to find 'innovative ways' to get bigger returns for their investments. This clearly implies the given fact.

52. (b) : According to the passage, budgetory support to the railways from the Union Government has declined. Perhaps this is because the Government has shifted its priority to some other areas.

53. (a) : The fact directly follows from the first sentence of the passage.

54. (a) : The fact that railways have now fallen in need of bigger returns from their investment, implies the given fact.

55. (a) : The given fact directly follows from the last sentence of the passage.

EXERCISE 6B

Directions : *In each question below is given a passage followed by some inferences. You have to examine each inference separately in the context of the passage and decide upon its degree of truth or falsity.*

Mark answer

(a) *if you think the inference is 'definitely true';*

(b) *if you think the inference is 'probably true' though not definitely true in the light of the facts given;*

(c) *if the data given is inadequate i.e., from the facts given you cannot say whether the inference is likely to be true or false;*

(d) *if you think the inference is 'probably false' though not definitely false in the light of the facts given; and*

(e) *if the inference is 'definitely false' i.e., it contradicts the given facts.*

Questions 1 to 5   **(Bank P.O. 1997)**

Despite the vast untapped export potential, the funding of sericulture development in the country has been found to be a very major stumbling block. Therefore, it is necessary that a scheme for providing free flow of credit to all those who are engaged in sericulture including silk weaving may be drawn up.

Further, taking into account the emerging trends to the Indian silk industry from global players like Korea and China, and also the serious challenges posed by the ongoing changes in the multi-fibre agreement and complete integration with GATT, it is necessary to formulate a new national silk policy. Another working group has to be constituted to evolve a long term import and export policy.

1. The formulation and implementation of long term import and export policy will only help Indian silk industry.

2. Extending free flow of credit may help Indian silk industry in some way.

3. Silk industries in China and Korea are totally supported by respective governments.

4. Indian silk industry had been facing very tough challenge from China and Korea.

5. So far there has been no National Silk Policy in India.

Questions 6 to 10

In the forties, nationalisation was considered the panacea for all socio-economic ills. Today, privatisation has become the buzz word that has been sweeping both the developed and the developing world for more than a decade now. Even in India, the idea has been gathering momentum. But before the idea is transplanted in India, there are several aspects of privatisation that need to be understood. It would be worthwhile, in this context, to look at the experiences of other countries.

6. Other countries which have adopted privatisation are considering now to change over to industrialisation.

7. Privatisation has been practised in USA since long.

8. India is also thinking of privatisation.

9. Nationalisation has failed to improve substantially the socio-economic situations of some countries.

10. India is the first country in Asian sub-continent to adopt privatisation.

Questions 11 to 15

(Bank P.O. 1995)

Laws governing the co-operative societies are uniform in all states. These laws give the member of a housing society the right to nomination during his life time. This is quite unlike the rule in other property related cases where nomination comes into force after the demise of the member. The question then arises that, can the nominee get full proprietorial rights over a flat merely because he has been nominated by a deceased member of the society. Many people are under the wrong impression that once a nomination form has been filled, their responsibility is over and that the nominee would have no problem acquiring the property. And, that the legal heirs of the member will pose no problem for the nominee.

11. The law that considers whether a person is a legal heir or not has some lacunae.

12. Nomination to property right need not be made to legal heirs only.

13. There is a need to educate the people on all aspects of laws governing the co-operative societies.

14. Co-operative movement had started with co-operative housing societies.

15. Property related laws are more or less same in all the states.

Questions 16 to 20

The bauxite deposits in India are widely distributed. Recently, deposits in Orissa have been developed and the largest plant of its kind in Asia has been set up to produce alumina and aluminium. Its annual capacity is 800,000 tonnes of alumina and 225,000 tonnes of aluminium. It uses the latest French technology. The ore is exported to Japan and European countries. In 1987, the output of bauxite was 2.6 million tonnes. The country's reserves are estimated at 270 million tonnes, of which 73 million tonnes are of high quality.

16. The plant set up in Orissa is the largest in India.

17. Aluminium is exported to Japan and European countries.

18. Orissa is the largest producer of bauxite in India.

19. The plant in Orissa was set up by financial aid from France.

20. 27% of total reserves of bauxite are of high quality.

Questions 21 to 25 (Bank P.O. 1996)

Of the roughly 4,40,000 children who currently languish in America's foster-care system, 20,000 are available for adoption, most of them are older children between the ages of 6 and 12. Among the adoptable children, 44% are white and 43% are black. But 67% of all families waiting to adopt are white, and many of them are eager to take a black child. The hurdles, however, are often formidable. Though only three US states — Arkansas, California and Minnesota — have laws promoting race matching in adoptions, 40 other favour the practice.

21. Children beyond 12 years of age are less suitable for adoption.

22. White children are being preferred for adoption by majority of black families.

23. Majority of the US states have laws that discourage the practice of adoption.

24. Among the adoptable children at least 10 percent are neither black nor white.

25. Two-third of the white families are waiting to adopt a black child.

Questions 26 to 30

In the overall economy of India, agriculture is the largest sector of economic activity. It plays a crucial role in the country's economic development by providing food to its people and raw materials to industry. It accounts for the largest share to the national income. The share of the various agricultural commodities, animal husbandry and ancillary activities has been more than 40 percent since independence. During the decade of the fifties, it actually contributed about half of the national output.

26. Agriculture is the mainstay of Indian economy.

27. The contribution of agricultural sector has decreased in recent years.

28. Agriculture is the only source of national income in India.

29. The contribution of agriculture to Indian economy rose substantially after independence.

30. Agriculture contributes to national income more than all other activities put together.

Questions 31 to 35 (Bank P.O. 1998)

Our country needs about nine to ten percent of yearly increase in power capacity. That means from the present 86000 MW we have today, we require an additional 8000 to 10000 MW every year. The private industries or foreigners may contribute by 1000 MW to 2000 MW. So, basically 90 percent of the capacity addition will have to be done by public sector companies. But Government cannot continuously give money for this. This means that the tariff has to be regulated to generate money, not based on the cost of 25 years ago. If this happens, optional utilisation of power will take place. It will not be wasted.

31. Presently some power is being wasted as the tariff is low.

32. The public sector enterprises in power generation have done a commendable job.

33. The private-industries are not willing to install big plants to generate power.

34. There is likelihood of increase in power tariffs in future.

35. Once we attain 10 percent increase in the present power capacity for few years we will have no problem.

Questions 36 to 40

The Government of India has urged the State Governments to create more job opportunities for women. All-out efforts are to be made to have more training facilities for women so that they can be gainfully employed. It is in pursuance of the recent policy decisions taken by the Government to make women self-reliant. The states have been asked to end discrimination against the fair sex so far new jobs are concerned. The same wage for women workers should also be strictly adhered to, it has been emphasised.

36. More job opportunities are being created for women to eradicate poverty among them.

37. The women have been benefited much by this government policy.

38. The Government emphasises on equality of men and women.

39. The Indian Government has arranged for proper education of women so that they can get good jobs.

40. Women should be given higher wages than men to make them self-reliant.

Questions 41 to 45   **(Bank P.O. 1991)**

The Haldia project, after being in a planning stage for many years, will ultimately become a reality with the joint participation of the Government of West Bengal and the House of Tatas. The letter of intent has been received in November 1991. The project will fulfill a long-felt need of modernisation of industry in Eastern India. The economic development of this region has also suffered a lot.

41. The planning of Haldia project started in the year 1984.

42. There is no industry in Eastern India.

43. Apart from West Bengal, other neighbouring states will also be benefited by the project.

44. Implementation work on the project has started.

45. The cost of the project would be equally shared by the Government of West Bengal and the House of Tatas.

Questions 46 to 50

The domestic market for electronic hardware in the country is likely to grow from Rs 1800 crore to about Rs 6500 crore per annum in the next few years. The Government is likely to further restrict foreign exchange needed for imports. So far, India has been importing about 80 percent of the components required for manu-facturing electronics gadgets. The country produced only 'passive components' like resistors, capacitors and conductors. Even integrated circuits (ICs) are being produced in a small way at high cost. Semi-conductors have remained India's weak spot.

46. Government is considering to further restrict foreign exchange needed for imports.

47. In India many manufacturers are reluctant to produce semi-conductors.

48. India does not have expertise in producing passive components like resistors, capacitors etc.

49. An increase of about 250 percent in India's domestic electronic market is pre-dicted during the next few years.

50. All the integrated circuits required for India are imported from U.S.A.

Questions 51 to 55   **(Bank P.O. 1997)**

In 1994-95, India consumed 65.3 million tonnes (mt) of petro products, out of which consumption of diesel was 28.3 million tonnes. The annual increase in diesel consumption from 1990-91 has been 8.5 percent as against 4.7 percent for all petro products.

As per 1993-94 data, 11 percent of diesel consumption is by industry, plantation etc., 8 percent by road transport, 5.5 percent by the railways and 75 percent by unspecified users. The consumption by farmers for tractors and irrigation pumps has been roughly 5.7 million tonnes valued at about Rs 5,500 crore. The agricultural produce in 1994-95 was valued at Rs 2,23,076 crore.

The consumption of diesel in 1995-96 is estimated at 32 million tonnes whereas consumption of petrol accounts for 14 percent of diesel consumption.

51. If the cost of diesel is increased along with small matching increase in procurement price, the farmer may be marginally affected.

52. The percentage increase in the consumption of diesel in India is equal to that of all petro products.

53. One rupee increase in diesel price will generate as much revenue as roughly seven rupee increase in petrol price.

54. The consumption of petrol by farmers for agricultural purpose is approximately 50 percent less than use of diesel.

55. The consumption of petrol for 1995-96 can be estimated to be in the range of 14 million tonnes.

ANSWERS

1. (a) : It is mentioned that taking into considerations the changes at the international level, India has to evolve a long term import and export policy. This clearly implies the given fact.

2. (a) : It is given in the passage that 'a scheme for providing free flow of credit to all those who are engaged in sericulture' is necessary. This implies the given fact.

3. (c) : Nothing about the management of silk industries in China and Korea is mentioned in the passage.

4. (a) : The statement is evident from the sentence '...the emerging trends...Korea' in the passage.

5. (e) : The passage talks of formulating 'a new National Silk Policy'. This means that one already existed.

6. (e) : It is clearly mentioned in the passage that the idea of privatisation has been sweeping both the developed and the developing world for more than a decade.

7. (c) : The passage does not contain any mention of U.S.A.

8. (a) : It is mentioned clearly in the passage that the idea of privatisation has been gathering momentum in India.

9. (a) : The passage says that earlier nationalisation was considered the remedy of socio-economic ills whereas at present, the idea of privatisation failed to improve the socio-economic situations of some countries.

10. (e) : It is clearly mentioned that the idea of privatisation is being promoted all over the world and has not been successfully transplanted in India.

11. (b) : According to the passage, even after the nomination form has been filled up by the deceased, the nominee faces difficulty in acquiring property, from the legal heirs. So, the given fact is quite probable.

12. (a) : It is mentioned in the passage that the nominee may face some problem from the legal heirs in acquiring a property. This clearly implies the given fact.

13. (a) : Clearly, such a training is necessary for people to justify nomination and overcome the problems faced by legal heirs.

14. (c) : Nothing about how cooperative movement started is mentioned in the passage.

15. (c) : The passage talks of similarity in laws of cooperative societies in all states and not the property related laws.

16. (*a*) : Since the plant set up in Orissa is the largest in Asia, it is evident that it is also the largest in India.

17. (*e*) : Not aluminium, but its ore is exported to Japan and European countries.

18. (*b*) : Since the largest bauxite producing plant is in Orissa, it is much possible that Orissa is the largest producer of bauxite.

19. (*e*) : The plant set up in Orissa uses French technology; it was not set up by financial aid from France.

20. (*a*) : Total reserves of bauxite = 270 million tonnes.

High quality reserves = 73 million tonnes.

Percentage of high quality reserves $= \left(\dfrac{73}{270} \times 100 \right)\% = 27\%$.

21. (*c*) : The passage talks of the children in the age group of 6 to 12 years only.

22. (*c*) : The passage mentions the attitude of white men only regarding adoption of a child and not that of black families.

23. (*e*) : According to the passage, only three U.S. states promote race matching in adoption, while 40 others favour the practice. This contradicts the fact given in the question.

24. (*a*) : According to the passage, among the adoptable children, 44% are white and 43% are black. Thus, the remaining *i.e.* 13% are neither black nor white.

25. (*c*) : It is mentioned that 67% of the families willing to adopt a child are white, but the percentage of white families willing to adopt a black child, is not given in the passage.

26. (*a*) : The given fact can be instantly derived from the first sentence of the passage.

27. (*c*) : Nothing is mentioned about the contribution of agricultural sector in recent years, in the passage.

28. (*e*) : It is given in the passage that agriculture accounts for the largest share to the national income. It implies that certain other activities contribute to the national income of India, too.

29. (*a*) : It is clearly mentioned in the passage that the contribution of agricultural sector increased from 40 percent at the time of independence to 50 percent during the next decade.

30. (*a*) : It is clear from the passage that agricultural sector is the largest contributor to national income. This implies the fact given in the question.

31. (*c*) : The given fact is neither mentioned in nor can be deduced from the passage.

32. (*d*) : It is mentioned that public sector enterprises lack the necessary funds to provide for the increasing need of power capacity.

33. (*e*) : The fact that private industries can contribute 1000 MW to 2000 MW of power, contradicts the fact given in the question.

34. (*a*) : According to the passage, the capacity of power generation ought to be increased every year and the funds must be collected by regulating the tariff accordingly. This implies the given fact.

35. (*a*) : The given fact is clearly evident from the first two sentences in the passage.

36. (*e*) : It is mentioned in the passage that more job opportunities are being provided to women to make them self-reliant.

37. (*c*) : Only the policy of the Government is mentioned in the passage and not the consequences.

38. (*a*) : It is given in the passage that the Central Government has asked the states to end the discrimination on grounds of sex.

39. (*c*) : Nothing is mentioned about the efforts of the Government as regards education of women, in the passage.

40. (*e*) : It is mentioned in the passage that men and women should be given equal wages for equal work.

41. (b) : It is mentioned in the passage that the Haldia project has been in a planning stage for many years. Since the letter of intent has been received in 1991, it is probable that its planning started some six to seven years ago in 1984.

42. (e) : From the passage, it can be deduced that there are industries in Eastern India but they are not modernised.

43. (b) : From the given passage, it can be said that the Haldia project will perhaps aid in the economic development of states of Eastern India.

44. (c) : It is not mentioned in the passage whether the construction of the project has started or not.

45. (c) : It is given in the passage that the project would be designed with the joint participation of the Government of West Bengal and the House of Tatas, but the distribution of cost between the two is not mentioned.

46. (a) : The fact is evident from the sentence 'The Government is likely to further restrict foreign exchange needed for imports' in the passage.

47. (b) : According to the passage, India manufactures only 'passive components' and most of the electronic components are being imported. The given fact seems quite probable from this.

48. (e) : It is given in the passage that India manufactures passive components like resistors, capacitors etc. This contradicts the fact given in the question.

49. (a) : Present value = Rs 1800 crore
Increase = Rs (6500 − 1800) = Rs 4700 crore.
$$\therefore \text{ Percentage of increase} = \left(\frac{4700}{1800} \times 100\right)\% = 261\%.$$

50. (e) : It is mentioned that ICs are also being produced in India. This means that not all of them are imported.

51. (c) : Nothing about the cost of diesel or the effect of its increase is mentioned in the passage.

52. (e) : It is mentioned in the passage that the annual increase in diesel consumption has been 8.5 percent as against 4.7 percent for all petro products. This contradicts the fact given in the question.

53. (a) : Consumption of diesel = 32 million tonnes.
Consumption of petrol = 14% of 32 million tonnes = 4.48 million tonnes.
Thus, the consumption of diesel is seven times the consumption of petrol. So, a one rupee increase in diesel price will generate as much revenue as roughly seven rupee increase in petrol price.

54. (c) : Nothing about the consumption of petrol by farmers in mentioned in the statement.

55. (e) : As estimated in Q.53, the consumption of petrol for 1995-96 is 4.48 million tonnes. This contradicts the fact given in the question.

EXERCISE 6C

Directions : *Below is given a passage followed by several possible inferences which can be drawn from the facts stated in the passage. You have to examine each inference separately in the context of the passage, decide upon its degree of truth or falsity and choose your answer accordingly from amongst the alternatives provided thereafter.*

Questions 1 to 5

Wind is an inexhaustible source of energy and an aerogenerator can convert it into electricity. Though not much has so far been done in this field, the survey shows that there is a vast potential for developing wind as an alternative source of energy. The wind survey has four components — direction, duration, speed and distribution. On this basis U.P. hill areas have been found an ideal place for setting up aerogenerators. In U.P. hills alone, as many as 58 sites have been identified.

1. Only the hilly areas of U.P. were surveyed for setting up aerogenerators.
    (a) Data inadequate   (b) Definitely true   (c) Probably false
    (d) Definitely false   (e) Probably true

2. The survey was conducted under the government of U.P.
    (a) Definitely true   (b) Probably true   (c) Data inadequate
    (d) Definitely false   (e) Probably false

3. Wind, as a source of energy, can replace exhaustible sources of energy.
    (a) Definitely false   (b) Data inadequate   (c) Probably true
    (d) Probably false   (e) Definitely true

4. Energy by wind is a comparatively new emerging field.
    (a) Probably true   (b) Probably false   (c) Definitely true
    (d) Data inadequate   (e) Definitely false

5. 58 sites identified in U.P. did not have electricity.
    (a) Definitely true   (b) Definitely false   (c) Data inadequate
    (d) Probably true   (e) Probably false

Questions 6 to 10   **(Bank P.O. 1995)**

    Indian granite industry is in peril in the absence of a uniform policy from the State Governments, despite the thrust given by liberalisation policies of the Union Government in the last two years. Compared to the remarkable progress in the field during the last three years, the absence of matching policies by State Governments had put granite quarry owners and others involved in the industry on the verge of collapse in the international market. The policies differed from state to state, had created problems as far as loyalty, dead rent and duration of lease were concerned.

6. The granite production is largely controlled by individuals.
    (a) Data inadequate   (b) Definitely true   (c) Probably true
    (d) Probably false   (e) Definitely false

7. The granite produced in India does not match with the quality of international level.
    (a) Definitely false   (b) Definitely true   (c) Probably false
    (d) Probably true   (e) Data inadequate

8. The Union Government's liberalisation policy became applicable to granite industry only during the last two years.
    (a) Definitely true   (b). Probably true   (c) Data inadequate
    (d) Probably false   (e) Definitely false

9. Each state having granite quarry has set up its own rules which are contrary to the interest of the industry.
    (a) Probably true   (b) Data inadequate   (c) Probably false
    (d) Definitely false   (e) Definitely true

10. Till three years ago, granite production in India was not profitable.
    (a) Data inadequate   (b) Probably true   (c) Definitely false
    (d) Probably false   (e) Definitely true

Questions 11 to 15

India is very poorly placed in regard to the reserves of gold ore. Currently, gold is mined at Kolar mines, the world's deepest and the Hutti mines — both in Karnataka. The other two mines in Anantpur and Chittoor districts of Andhra Pradesh have lately started functioning. The known reserves are placed at only 81000 kg of gold content. The annual production of gold has been dwindling. It has come down from 7000 kg in 1951 to 1931 kg in 1986.

11. The gold production has decreased by about 72% in 35 years.
   (a) Definitely true   (b) Probably true   (c) Data inadequate
   (d) Probably false   (e) Definitely false
12. Hutti mines are the deepest in the world.
   (a) Data inadequate   (b) Definitely false   (c) Probably false
   (d) Definitely true   (e) Probably true
13. India imports gold from other countries.
   (a) Probably true   (b) Definitely true   (c) Probably false
   (d) Definitely false   (e) Data inadequate
14. India does not have more than 81000 kg of gold reserves.
   (a) Definitely false   (b) Data inadequate   (c) Definitely true
   (d) Probably true   (e) Probably false
15. Kolar mines show the largest production of gold.
   (a) Definitely true   (b) Probably false   (c) Definitely false
   (d) Probably true   (e) Data inadequate

Questions 16 to 20   (Bank P.O. 1996)

The force of technological change will have an impact on the manufacturing industry. But the real effect will be on the information processing industry like software development, service industries like airlines, insurance and consulting — both technical and managerial, designing and executing jobs. Another feature of technological change by the end of century will be the resistance to change from within and outside the organisations. Satisfactory resolutions will require a high degree of mutual cooperation between Government and Industry, Industry and its users, Management and Unions and within organisations across functions.

16. The information processing industry has been less amenable to technological change than the manufacturing industry.
   (a) Data inadequate   (b) Definitely true   (c) Probably false
   (d) Definitely false   (e) Probably true
17. The technological change will affect only specific functions in an organisation leaving the others undisturbed.
   (a) Definitely true   (b) Data inadequate   (c) Definitely false
   (d) Probably true   (e) Probably false
18. As compared to service industry, the manufacturing industry will be less affected by the technological change.
   (a) Definitely true   (b) Probably true   (c) Data inadequate
   (d) Probably false   (e) Definitely false
19. Technological change has already set in.
   (a) Definitely false   (b) Probably false   (c) Data inadequate
   (d) Probably true   (e) Definitely true

20. People prefer status quo.
   (*a*) Probably true   (*b*) Probably false   (*c*) Definitely true
   (*d*) Definitely false   (*e*) Data inadequate

Questions 21 to 25

Dryland farming is the only way to not only combat recurring drought but also meet the increasing food requirements of India. About 45% of India's total crop production now comes from drylands. By the end of this century, this will have to increase to 60% if India is to provide adequate food for projected population of one billion by the turn of the century.

21. Dryland farming is important for India.
   (*a*) Data inadequate   (*b*) Definitely true   (*c*) Probably true
   (*d*) Probably false   (*e*) Definitely false

22. The per acre crop production in more in drylands than others.
   (*a*) Definitely false   (*b*) Definitely true   (*c*) Probably false
   (*d*) Probably true   (*e*) Data inadequate

23. India is self-sufficient in food production.
   (*a*) Definitely true   (*b*) Probably true   (*c*) Data inadequate
   (*d*) Probably false   (*e*) Definitely false

24. At present, India gets larger food production from wetlands.
   (*a*) Probably true   (*b*) Data inadequate   (*c*) Probably false
   (*d*) Definitely false   (*e*) Definitely true

25. In India, the rate of growth of population is 15 percent per year.
   (*a*) Data inadequate   (*b*) Probably true   (*c*) Definitely true
   (*d*) Probably false   (*e*) Definitely false

Questions 26 to 30   (S.B.I.P.O. 1995)

In the context of computers, the hardware specialities like the tendency of research connected with human factors, the design of the work stations, key boards, visual display etc. are being concentrated, though the literature connected with interface and software problems has recently been on the increase. There are two reasons for it. The first reason in the light of the increasing power of computers is that the designers have got an opportunity to select and organise that technique which the user follows in communicating the message. The second is that the human factors research organisations have deviated from physical specialities of self improving worksystem and gone to the psychological dimensions of the man-machine interaction.

26. In the field of computers, a change has taken place in the approach of the human factors research organisations.
   (*a*) Data inadequate   (*b*) Definitely true   (*c*) Probably true
   (*d*) Definitely false   (*e*) Probably false

27. The human factors research organisations do not help in designing the software system. They help only in the evaluation of ultimate production.
   (*a*) Definitely true   (*b*) Probably true   (*c*) Data inadequate
   (*d*) Probably false   (*e*) Definitely false

28. There has been a systematic progress in the basic computer technique.
   (*a*) Probably true   (*b*) Probably false   (*c*) Definitely false
   (*d*) Data inadequate   (*e*) Definitely true

29. The tools and methods of human research organisations have also undergone a change.

  (a) Definitely true   (b) Definitely false   (c) Probably false
  (d) Data inadequate   (e) Probably true

30. The human research organisations in the field of computers, had been started two decades ago.

  (a) Probably false   (b) Probably true   (c) Definitely true
  (d) Definitely false   (e) Data inadequate

Questions 31 to 35

The caffeine in one morning's coffee or tea may improve the complex reasoning ability of extroverts but has the opposite effect on introverts. More than 700 people were given caffeine equal to no more than three cups of coffee and then tested on word analogies, sentence completion, and identification of antonyms. The researchers believe that the caffeine was beneficial to the extroverts in the morning because they take longer to wake up. Introverts are more alert in the morning and become over-stimulated by the drug which interferes with their reasoning power.

31. The adverse effect on the reasoning power of introverts is not due to caffeine.

  (a) Definitely true   (b) Probably true   (c) Data inadequate
  (d) Probably false   (e) Definitely false

32. Caffeine has greater effect early in the morning.

  (a) Definitely false   (b) Definitely true   (c) Probably false
  (d) Probably true   (e) Data inadequate

33. Extroverts do not find caffeine beneficial in the evening.

  (a) Data inadequate   (b) Definitely true   (c) Definitely false
  (d) Probably true   (e) Probably false

34. Complex reasoning ability is made up of word analogies, sentence completion and identification of antonyms.

  (a) Probably false   (b) Probably true   (c) Definitely true
  (d) Data inadequate   (e) Definitely false

35. Caffeine affects reasoning ability of people who drink tea or coffee.

  (a) Probably true   (b) Definitely true   (c) Probably false
  (d) Definitely false   (e) Data inadequate

Questions 36 to 40   (U.T.I. 1993)

A survey in India indicated that in the core section of the companies, which were analysed, the compensation package for executives was divided into several fringe benefit groups. The number of items included in it rose as one ascended the management hierarchy. In many companies, provision was made for transportation and medical and housing assistance. A few companies also provided for children's education or permitted family allowance. Some of them have now adopted a specialised approach called the "cafeteria approach" in salary fixation. What is sought here is that the benefits must meet an executive's needs. Therefore, an appropriate selection has to be made of the benefits in terms of his needs after consulting him. Thus, this approach would individualise the system as the final choice is left to the executive concerned.

36. There is a standard universal compensation package for executives in most companies.

  (a) Definitely true   (b) Definitely false   (c) Probably true
  (d) Probably false   (e) Data inadequate

37. Fringe benefits offered by many companies take care of most of the basic physiological needs of the executives.

(*a*) Data inadequate   (*b*) Probably true   (*c*) Definitely true
(*d*) Probably false   (*e*) Definitely false

38. While designing the compensation package for executives, certain companies try to establish a match between needs and benefits.

(*a*) Definitely true   (*b*) Probably true   (*c*) Data inadequate
(*d*) Probably false   (*e*) Definitely false

39. Nowadays, most of the companies in India are designing their compensation packages on the lines of such packages offered by the companies in foreign countries.

(*a*) Definitely false   (*b*) Data inadequate   (*c*) Probably false
(*d*) Definitely true   (*e*) Probably true

40. The survey conducted in India on compensation package included employees working at different levels, including executives.

(*a*) Probably false   (*b*) Definitely false   (*c*) Probably true
(*d*) Definitely true   (*e*) Data inadequate

Questions 41 to 45

There is more bad news on food front. It now appears certain that there will be a shortfall of about 9 million tonnes in the food production in the current kharif season, which in turn means five million tonnes less than the production achieved in the last kharif season. However, rice procurement may only be partially affected since West Bengal and Andhra Pradesh have had sufficient rainfall while Punjab, the major contributor to the central pool is less dependent on rainfall. Still, the overall availability of rice may go down by more than four million tonnes. There may be worst news ahead.

41. There is no canal water facility in West Bengal and Andhra Pradesh.

(*a*) Definitely false   (*b*) Probably false   (*c*) Data inadequate
(*d*) Probably true   (*e*) Definitely true

42. The procurement price of rice will increase this year.

(*a*) Data inadequate   (*b*) Definitely true   (*c*) Probably true
(*d*) Definitely false   (*e*) Probably false

43. Rice is mainly produced in kharif season.

(*a*) Definitely true   (*b*) Probably false   (*c*) Definitely false
(*d*) Data inadequate   (*e*) Probably true

44. In the last year, there was a deficit production of rice by five million tonnes.

(*a*) Probably true   (*b*) Probably false   (*c*) Definitely false
(*d*) Definitely true   (*e*) Data inadequate

45. It is likely that production of rice will be below the normal level in the next year.

(*a*) Probably false   (*b*) Definitely false   (*c*) Data inadequate
(*d*) Definitely true   (*e*) Probably true

Questions 46 to 50   (Bank P.O. 1997)

Rabies is a disease transmitted to man and animals through the bite of a rabies-infected animal, most commonly by dogs. It is caused by a virus present in the saliva of the infected animal which gets deposited in the wound of the bite victim, multiplies and travels towards brain and spinal cord. If not treated, about half of such cases develop rabies. Symptoms of the disease start one to three months after the bite. Very few laboratory tests are available for the diagnosis of rabies in India. Precautionary measures include prompt washing of the dog bite wound with soap and water. The wound is also treated with cetavion : tincture of iodine or spirit.

46. The governments and local bodies should expedite measures to catch and kill stray dogs as a preventive measure.
    (a) Definitely false   (b) Definitely true   (c) Probably false
    (d) Probably true   (e) Data inadequate

47. Rabies can be transmitted from any animal to the other through open cuts and wounds.
    (a) Data inadequate   (b) Probably true   (c) Probably false
    (d) Definitely true   (e) Definitely false

48. The bite of rabies-infected animal to a healthy animal definitely results in spread of rabies.
    (a) Definitely true   (b) Probably true   (c) Data inadequate
    (d) Definitely false   (e) Probably false

49. The saliva of the house dogs should be periodically tested for the detection of rabies.
    (a) Probably true   (b) Probably false   (c) Definitely true
    (d) Data inadequate   (e) Definitely false

50. Western countries have well equipped laboratory tests to detect rabies.
    (a) Definitely false   (b) Data inadequate   (c) Probably true
    (d) Definitely true   (e) Probably false

ANSWERS

1. (c) : It is mentioned in the passage that the wind survey showed that there is a vast potential for harnessing wind energy. This means that an overall survey must have been made and not only of the hilly areas of U.P.
2. (b) : It may be true that the survey was conducted under the U.P. government as the areas of U.P. were also surveyed.
3. (e) : According to the passage, wind is an inexhaustible source of energy and efforts are being made to develop wind as an alternative source of energy. This clearly implies the given fact.
4. (c) : In the passage, it is given that not much has been done in the field of wind energy and efforts are on. Thus, it is clear that wind energy is a comparatively new emerging field.
5. (c) : In the passage, it is not mentioned whether the 58 sites identified in U.P. had the facility of electricity or not.
6. (b) : It is mentioned in the passage that the absence of matching policies by State Governments has put 'granite quarry owners' on the verge of collapse. This implies the given fact.
7. (e) : Nothing about the quality of granite produced in India is mentioned in the passage.
8. (a) : It is mentioned in the passage that the liberalisation policies of Union Government gave a thrust to the granite industry in the last two years. This clearly implies the given fact.
9. (e) : The given fact directly follows from the last sentence of the passage.
10. (a) : Nothing about profitability of granite industry three years ago is mentioned in the passage.

11. (a) : Total decrease in 35 years = (7000 − 1931) kg = 5069 kg.

$$\therefore \quad \text{Percentage of decrease} = \left(\frac{5069}{7000} \times 100\right)\% = 72.4\%.$$

12. (b) : It is mentioned that Kolar mines are the deepest in the world.

13. (e) : The given fact is neither mentioned in nor can be derived from the passage.

14. (e) : According to the passage, the known reserves of gold in India is 81000 kg. Perhaps, the country has more reserves also which are not known.

15. (d) : The fact given in the question may be true as Kolar mines are the deepest in the world.

16. (d) : According to the passage, technological change will have greater effect on the information processing industry than the manufacturing industry. This contradicts the fact given in the question.

17. (b) : The given fact is neither mentioned in nor can be derived from the given passage.

18. (a) : It is mentioned in the passage that the real effect of technological change would be on the service industries rather than the manufacturing industry. This clearly implies the given fact.

19. (d) : The passage talks of the effect of technological change by the end of the century. So, it is probable that it has already set in.

20. (e) : The given fact is neither mentioned in nor can be derived from the given passage.

21. (b) : The given statement can be derived from the first sentence of the passage.

22. (e) : Nothing about the per acre crop production in drylands in mentioned in the passage.

23. (c) : The fact is not mentioned in the passage.

24. (e) : At present, India gets 45% of its total crop production from drylands. Obviously, the rest is obtained from wetlands and is more.

25. (a) : The annual rate of growth of population is not mentioned in the passage.

26. (b) : The given fact directly follows from the last sentence of the passage.

27. (b) : In the first sentence of the passage, the human factors research organisations has been mentioned a hardware speciality. The given fact seems to be probably true in the light of this truth.

28. (d) : The given fact is neither mentioned in nor can be derived from the contents of the given passage.

29. (a) : The given fact directly follows from the last sentence of the passage.

30. (e) : The given fact is neither mentioned in nor can be derived from the contents of the given passage.

31. (e) : The given fact directly follows from the last sentence of the passage.

32. (d) : The passage talks of the effect of caffeine in early morning only. So, the given fact is quite probable.

33. (a) : Nothing about the effect of caffeine in the evening is mentioned in the passage.

34. (b) : The passage mentions the effect of caffeine on complex reasoning ability and then describes the results obtained from tests of word analogies, sentence completion and identification of antonyms. So, the given fact is probably true.

35. (b) : The given fact directly follows from the first sentence of the passage.

36. (b) : According to the passage, the compensation package in different companies includes different provisions.

37. (c) : The fact directly follows from the contents of the passage.

38. (a) : According to the passage, some companies have adopted the 'cafeteria approach' in which a selection of the benefits is made in terms of the executive's needs.

39. (b) : Nothing about the compensation packages provided in the foreign countries is mentioned in the passage.

40. (b) : It is mentioned in the first sentence of the passage that the survey conducted in India was on compensation package for executives only and not the employees at all levels.

41. (e) : According to the passage, the rice production in West Bengal and Andhra Pradesh would not be affected since they had sufficient rainfall. This implies that the farming there is dependent mainly on rain and no other irrigation facilities are available.

42. (c) : It is mentioned in the passage that rice production has gone down. This may lead to a rise in procurement price of rice.

43. (a) : The fact is clearly evident from the given passage.

44. (c) : According to the passage, there is a deficit production of rice by five million tonnes in the present year.

45. (e) : It is said in the passage : 'There may be worst news ahead'. There is no surety about the given fact. But it appears to be true according to the present trends.

46. (e) : It is not mentioned in the passage whether the bite of only stray dogs causes rabies. So, the given fact cannot be deduced from the passage.

47. (d) : The fact directly follows from the given passage.

48. (a) : The given fact directly follows from the first sentence of the passage.

49. (d) : The given fact is neither mentioned in nor can be derived from the passage.

50. (b) : Nothing about the laboratory tests in Western countries is mentioned in the passage.

7. THEME DETECTION

In this type of questions, a paragraph is given followed by certain statements which may or may not be inferred from the passage. The candidate is required to choose that statement which contains the jist or the theme of the passage *i.e.*, the idea that it conveys.

Example : Through advertising, manufacturing exercises a high degree of control over consumer's desires. However, the manufacturer assumes enormous risks in attempting to predict what consumers will want and in producing goods in quantity and distributing them in advance of final selection by the consumers. **(S.B.I.P.O. 1995)**

The paragraph best supports the statement that manufacturers —
- (a) distribute goods directly to the consumers.
- (b) can eliminate the risk of overproduction by advertising.
- (c) always take moderate and calculated risk.
- (d) can predict with great accuracy the success of any product they put on the market.
- (e) must depend upon the final consumers for the success of their undertakings.

Solution : According to the passage, it is very difficult for the manufacturer to predict the consumers' response to his products. But by advertising, he can stimulate the consumers to buy his product. So, the theme of the paragraph is best mentioned in (b). Hence, (b) is the answer.

- (a) is incorrect because it is mentioned in the paragraph that manufacturers distribute goods in advance of their demands and not directly to the consumers.
- (c) is wrong because according to the passage, manufacturers take 'enormous' and not 'moderate' risks.
- (d) is wrong because it is mentioned in the passage that manufacturers take great risk in predicting what the consumers want.
- (e) is a true statement but it does not depict the complete theme of the passage.

EXERCISE 7

Directions : *Each of the following questions contains a small paragraph followed by a question on it. Read each paragraph carefully and answer the question given below it :*

1. The virtue of art does not allow the work to be interfered with or immediately ruled by anything other than itself. It insists that it alone shall touch the work in order to bring it into being. Art requires that nothing shall attain the work except through art itself.
   (Bank P.O. 1996)

   This passage best supports the statement that :
   - (a) art is governed by external rules and conditions.
   - (b) art is for the sake of art and life.
   - (c) art is for the sake of art alone.
   - (d) artist realises his dreams through his artistic creation.
   - (e) artist should use his art for the sake of society.

2. Though the waste of time or the expenditure on fashions is very large, yet fashions have come to stay. They will not go, come what may. However, what is now required is that strong efforts should be made to displace the excessive craze for fashion from the minds of these youngsters.

The passage best supports the statement that :

(a) fashion is the need of the day.

(b) the excessive craze for fashion is detrimental to one's personality.

(c) the hoard for fashion should be done away with so as not to let down the constructive development.

(d) work and other activities should be valued more than the outward appearance.

3. Due to enormous profits involved in smuggling, hundreds of persons have been attracted towards this anti-national activity. Some of them became millionaires overnight. India has a vast coastline both on the Eastern and Western Coast. It has been a heaven for smugglers who have been carrying on their activities with great impunity. There is no doubt, that from time to time certain seizures were made by the enforcement authorities, during raids and ambush but even allowing these losses the smugglers made huge profits.

The passage best supports the statement that :

(a) smuggling hampers the economic development of a nation.

(b) smuggling ought to be curbed.

(c) authorities are taking strict measures to curb smuggling.

(d) smuggling is fast increasing in our country owing to the quick profit it entails.

4. The only true education comes through the stimulation of the child's powers by the demands of the social situations in which he finds himself. Through these demands he is stimulated to act as a member of a unity, to emerge from his original narrowness of action and feeling, and to conceive himself from the standpoint of the welfare of the group to which he belongs.

The passage best supports the statement that real education —

(a) will take place if the children imbibe action and feeling.

(b) will take place if the children are physically strong.

(c) is not provided in our schools today.

(d) comes through the interaction with social situations.

(e) comes from the self-centred approach of the students.   **(Bank P.O. 1996)**

5. Emerson said that the poet was landlord, sealord, airlord. The flight of imagination made the poet master of land, sea and air. But a poet's dream of yesterday becomes today an actual achievement and a reality for all men. Even those who invented, improved and perfected the aeroplane could hardly have dreamt of the possibility of flight into outer space.

The passage best supports the statement that :

(a) seemingly impossible imaginations make one a good poet.

(b) all imaginations become a reality some day.

(c) what man imagined has never been impossible; he has always turned it a reality through his conception of ideas and sheer hard labour.

(d) man has reached the climax of technological development with his exploration into outer space.

6. The prevention of accidents makes it necessary not only that safety devices be used to guard exposed machinery but also that mechanics be instructed in safety

rules which they must follow for their own protection, and that lighting in the plant be adequate. **(S.B.I.P.O. 1995)**

The passage best supports the statement that industrial accidents —

(a) are always avoidable.　　(b) may be due to ignorance.

(c) cannot be entirely overcome.

(d) can be eliminated with the help of safety rules.

(e) usually result from inadequate machinery.

7. It is upto our government and planners to devise ways and means for the mobilisation of about ten crore workers whose families total up about forty crore men, women and children. Our agriculture is over-manned. A lesser number of agriculturists would mean more purchasing or spending power to every agriculturist. This will result in the shortage of man-power for many commodities to be produced for which there will be a new demand from a prosperous agrarian class. This shortage will be removed by surplus man-power released from agriculture as suggested above.

The passage best supports the statement that :

(a) employment in production is more fruitful than employment in agriculture.

(b) Indian economy is in a poor shape basically due to improper mobilisation of man-power.

(c) a shift of labour from agricultural sector to the industrial sector would uplift the living standard.

(d) the industrial sector is labour-deficient while the agricultural sector is over-manned in our country.

8. To forgive an injury is often considered to be a sign of weakness; it is really a sign of strength. It is easy to allow oneself to be carried away by resentment and hate into an act of vengeance; but it takes a strong character to restrain those natural passions. The man who forgives an injury proves himself to be the superior of the man who wronged himself and puts the wrong-doer to shame.

The passage best supports the statement that :

(a) the sufferer alone knows the intensity of his sufferings.

(b) people tend to forgive the things happened in the past.

(c) natural passions are difficult to suppress.

(d) mercy is the noblest form of revenge.　　**(Bank P.O. 1996)**

(e) a person with calm and composed nature has depth of thought and vision.

9. Exports and imports, a swelling favourable balance of trade, investments and bank-balances, are not an index or a balance sheet of national prosperity. Till the beginning of the Second World War, English exports were noticeably greater than what they are today. And yet England has greater national prosperity today than it ever had. Because the income of average Englishmen, working as field and factory labourers, clerks, policemen, petty shopkeepers and shop assistants, domestic workers and other low-paid workers, has gone up.

The passage best supports the statement that :

(a) a country's economic standard can be best adjudged by per capita income.

(b) a country's balance of trade is the main criteria of determining its economic prosperity.

(c) a nation's economy strengthens with the increase in exports.

(d) English trade has continually increased since the Second World War.

10. Throughout the ages the businessman has helped build civilisation's great cities, provided people with luxuries and artists with patronage, and lift his fellow citizens to understand the standard of living. In the last few centuries the businessman has seeded the Industrial Revolution around the world.

The passage best supports the statement that the businessman —

(a) is accountable to the society.

(b) lives luxurious and comfortable life.

(c) is the beneficiary of the Industrial Revolution.

(d) is capable of raising his standard of living.

(e) has contributed to the growth of civilisation.   **(S.B.I.P.O. 1995)**

11. Industrial exhibitions play a major role in a country's economy. Such exhibitions, now regularly held in Delhi, enable us to measure the extent of our own less advanced industrial progress and the mighty industrial power and progress of countries like the U.K., U.S.A. and Russia whose pavilions are the centres of the greatest attention and attractions.

The passage best supports the statement that industrial exhibitions —

(a) greatly tax the poor economies.

(b) are more useful for the developed countries like U.S.A. whose products stand out superior to those of the developing countries.

(c) are not of much use to the countries who are industrially backward.

(d) boost up production qualitatively and quantitatively by analytical comparison of a country's products with those of the developed countries.

12. Satisfaction with co-workers, promotion opportunities, the nature of work, and pay goes with high performance among those with strong growth needs. Among those with weak growth needs, no such relationship is present — and, in fact, satisfaction with promotion opportunities goes with low performance.

This passage best supports the statement that :

(a) satisfaction is an inevitable organisational variable.

(b) job satisfaction and performance are directly and closely related.

(c) relationship between job satisfaction and performance is moderated by growth need.

(d) every organisation has few employees having weak growth need.

(e) high performance is essential for organisational effectiveness.

13. The attainment of individual and organisational goals is mutually interdependent and linked by a common denominator — employee work motivation. Organisational members are motivated to satisfy their personal goals, and they contribute their efforts to the attainment of organisational objectives as means of achieving these personal goals.   **(S.B.I.P.O. 1995)**

The passage best supports the statement that motivation —

(a) encourages an individual to give priority to personal goals over organisational goals.

(b) is crucial for the survival of an individual and organisation.

(c) is the product of an individual's physical and mental energy.

(d) is the external force which induces an individual to contribute his efforts.

(e) makes organisation and society inseparable.

14. The consumption of harmful drugs by the people can be prevented not only by banning their sale in the market but also by instructing users about their dangerous effects which they must understand for their safety. Also the drug addicts may be provided with proper medical facilities for their rehabilitation. This will help in scaling down the use of drugs.   **(Bank P.O. 1996)**

The passage best supports the statement that consumption of harmful drugs —

(a) are on increase in the society.   (b) can always be reduced.

(c) are due to lack of medical facilities.

(d) can be eliminated with the help of banning their sale.

(e) may be channelised through proper system.

15. The future of women in India is quite bright and let us hope that they will justify their abilities by rising to the occasion. Napolean was right when he declared that by educating the women we can educate the whole nation. Because a country can never rise without the contribution of 50% of their population.

The passage best supports the statement that :

(a) India is striving hard for the emancipation of women.

(b) all women should be well educated.

(c) a nation can progress only when women are given equal rights and opportunities as men.

(d) women ought to be imparted full freedom to prove their worth and contribute to the progress of the nation.

16. The school has always been the most important means of transferring the wealth of tradition from one generation to the next. This applies today in an even higher degree than in former times for, through the modern development of economy, the family as bearer of tradition and education has become weakened.

This passage best supports the statement that for transferring the wealth of tradition from one generation to the next —   **(S.B.I.P.O. 1995)**

(a) there are means other than the school.

(b) several different sources must be tried.

(c) economic development plays a crucial role.

(d) modern technology must be put to use.

(e) family, as ever, is the most potent means.

17. One of the important humanitarian by-products of technology is the greater dignity and value that it imparts to human labour. In a highly industrialized society, there is no essential difference between Brahmin and Dalit, Muslim and Hindu; they are equally useful and hence equally valuable, for in the industrial society individual productivity fixes the size of the pay cheque and this fixes social status.   **(Bank P.O. 1996)**

The passage best supports the statement that :

(a) technology decides individual's social status.

(b) castes and religions are man-made.

(c) human labour has dignity and value.

(d) all individuals, irrespective of caste and creed, are born equal.

(e) industrial society is a great leveller of men.

18. **The paragraph above also supports the statement that :**
    (a) there are individual differences in industrial productivity.
    (b) there are numerous side-effects of technology.
    (c) size of the pay and social status contradict each other.
    (d) labour force is treated well in modern day industries.
    (e) division of labour based on caste was justified.

19. The press should not be afraid of upholding and supporting a just and righteous cause. It should not be afraid of criticising the government in a healthy manner. The press has to be eternally vigilant to protect the rights of the workers, backward and suppressed sections of the society. It should also give a balanced view of the things so that people can be helped in the formation of a healthy public opinion.

    The passage best supports the statement that :
    (a) press has a great role to play in a democracy.
    (b) the press is the only means to project to the masses the policies of the government.
    (c) the freedom of press is essential for the proper functioning of democracy.
    (d) the press can be used by the governments as an effective media for the upliftment of the backward sections of society.
    (e) all the information given by the press should be well-articulated so as to gain a good opinion towards the ruling party.

20. There is a shift in our economy from a manufacturing to a service orientation. The increase in service-sector will require the managers to work more with people rather than with objects and things from the assembly line.

    This passage best supports the statement that : (Bank P.O. 1996)
    (a) managers should have a balanced mind.
    (b) assembly line will exist in service organisations.
    (c) interpersonal skills will become more important in the future work place.
    (d) manufacturing organisations ignore importance of people.
    (e) service organisations will not deal with objects and things.

ANSWERS

1. (c)	**2.** (c)	**3.** (d)	**4.** (d)	**5.** (c)	**6.** (d)	**7.** (b)	**8.** (d)	**9.** (a)	**10.** (e)
11. (d)	**12.** (c)	**13.** (a)	**14.** (d)	**15.** (d)	**16.** (c)	**17.** (c)	**18.** (a)	**19.** (c)	**20.** (c)

8. QUESTION — STATEMENTS

This section consists of problems in which a particular question is given followed by certain statements containing facts providing clues to answer the question. The candidate is required to find out which of the given statements is/are sufficient to answer the given question.

If the answer can be derived from statement I alone, we write (a); if the answer can be derived from statement II alone, we write (b); if the answer can be derived from either of the statements I and II, we write (c); if the answer cannot be derived even from both the statements taken together, we write (d); and if the answer can be derived from both the statements taken together, we write (e).

Ex. Has decrease in infant mortality rate increased the life span of human beings ?

    I. The average life span of tribals is 85 years.

    II. Women outlive men in younger age groups.

Sol. Clearly, none of the statements I and II alone or together lead to the answer to the question. So, the answer is (d).

EXERCISE 8

Directions : *Each question given below has a problem and two statements numbered I and II giving certain information. You have to decide if the information given in the statements is sufficient for answering the problem. Indicate your answer as*

(a) *if the data in statement I alone are sufficient to answer the question;*

(b) *if the data in statement II alone are sufficient to answer the question;*

(c) *if the data either in I or II alone are sufficient to answer the question;*

(d) *if the data even in both the statements together are not sufficient to answer the question; and*

(e) *if the data in both the statements I and II are needed to answer the question.*

1. Why haven't Indian scientists made much headway in any field after independence ?

    I. Indian scientists are not provided with up-to-date laboratory facilities.

    II. Indian scientists regard that knowledge of western science advances is enough for a nation to advance.   **(U.D.C. 1995)**

2. What time does the office start working ?   **(Bank P.O. 1995)**

    I. Some employees reach office at 9.30 a.m.

    II. Some employees reach office at 4.30 p.m.

3. Is Srikant eligible for an entry pass to the company premises ?

    I. The company does not allow strangers to enter the company.

    II. All employees are eligible to get a pass.

4. Is Nitin entitled to free studentship ?   **(S.B.I.P.O. 1994)**
    I. The school offers free studentship to those who are under 12 years of age
        and have secured 60 percent marks in the last final examination.
    II. Nitin has secured 85 percent marks in the last final examination.
5. How many children in a room are boys ?
    I. 50% of the children are in white dress.
    II. Only boys are in white dress.
6. Did Arvind lose money in the school ?   **(Assistant Grade, 1992)**
    I. Children are not expected to carry money with them in the school.
    II. His father gave him money in the morning.
7. What is the exact duration of the course ?   **(S.B.I.P.O. 1997)**
    I. It has three semesters but there is internship in between second and third
        semester.
    II. Duration of the internship varies as per the report of the professor.
8. Who is the best salesman in the company ?
    I. Rohit sold maximum number of air conditioners this summer.
    II. The company made the highest profit this year.
9. Is exercise good for health ?
    I. Most of the people, who exercise regularly, keep fit.
    II. Health is worth preserving.
10. There were 54 members of a cooperative society. How many members attended
    the recent Annual General Meeting (AGM) ?   **(Bank P.O. 1996)**
    I. Normally two-third members attend the meeting.
    II. One-sixth of the members were out of the town on AGM's day.
11. How many matches will be played between A and B in this tournament ?
    I. A has already won three matches against B and with this third win he has
        won the tournament.
    II. The fifth match will be played next week.
12. Out of A, B, C and D, who was selected by the interview panel ?
    I. C's interview was much better than A and D.
    II. B had better qualification and experience than the remaining three.
                                                                        (Bank P.O. 1998)
13. Who is a better artist — Abid or Hussain ?
    I. Abid had more art exhibitions.
    II. The number of paintings sold by Hussain is more.
14. Is cigarette smoking injurious to health ?
    I. Non-smokers have a longer life-span.
    II. The incidence of heart attacks is more in smokers.
15. Did the author of this novel die before 1956 ?
    I. Transistors were invented in 1957.
    II. There is a reference to transistors in this novel.
16. How many flats are there in this housing complex ?   **(Bank P.O. 1997)**
    I. Each wing has 16 flats which is incidentally equal to the total number of
        buildings.
    II. Each building has 4 wings — A, B, C and D.

17. What is the colour of the curtains on the stage ?
  I.   The curtains have the same colour as the walls of the hall which are green.
  II. The colour of the curtains is quite appealing.

18. Does the use of labour-saving devices tend to make us lazy ?
  I.   No labour-saving device has done mankind any good.
  II. Laziness is more appealing to people.   **(Assistant Grade, 1992)**

19. Does television viewing affect the performance of students ?
  I.   The number of failures in Class XII is more this year.
  II. Television watching is harmful to the eyes.

20. Does drinking coffee lead to headache ?   **(C.B.I. 1995)**
  I.   Overstimulation of pancreas leads to headache.
  II. Coffee contains caffeine which excessively stimulates pancreas.

21. Does intelligence predict the child's ability to learn ?
  I.   Intelligence is unaffected by bad teaching or dull home environment.
  II. Children from poor home backgrounds do not do well in their school work.

22. The cost of the kit is solely based on number of leaves. The kit has how many leaves ?   **(Bank P.O. 1995)**
  I.   The cost of the kit of medium size is Rs 850.
  II. The small size kit contains 55 leaves.

23. How many rooms does your house have ?
  I.   The number of rooms is the same as in our house.
  II. The number is sufficient to accommodate our family members.

24. On which day of the week did Arun reach Bombay ?   **(Bank P.O. 1995)**
  I.   Arun reached one day after Jai reached Bombay.
  II. Arun's mother left Bombay on Thursday two days before Jai reached Bombay.

25. Is the number of girl students more in the B.Ed. course ?
  I.   The girls' performance in the annual examination is better than boys.
  II. The proportion of female teachers has been increasing over the last two years.

26. Did less than 500 people see the magic show ?
  I.   Less than 700 people saw the show.
  II. Not more than 400 people saw the show.

27. When will the prices of the air coolers be the lowest ?   **(Bank P.O. 1998)**
  I.   From July till January end companies offer 15 percent off-season discount.
  II. During November, the prices will be 20 percent less than off-season prices and 30 percent less than February to June prices.

28. Are women more emotional ?
  I.   Women believe that men's way of thinking cannot help them solve their problems.
  II. The reality confronted by women is entirely different from the reality men have to struggle with.

29. Can a democratic system operate without effective opposition ?
  I.   The opposition is indispensable.
  II. A good statesman always learns more from his opponents than from his fervent supporters.

30. A ground plus four storeyed residential building has 3 wings namely A, B and C. How many flats are there in the building ? **(Bank P.O. 1996)**

    I. Each floor has equal number of flats.

    II. All the three flats on the ground floor of wing A are unoccupied.

31. Why is it that most of the eminent music maestros are Muslims ?

    I. Religions other than Islam do not encourage fine arts.

    II. Muslims did not go in for western type of education. **(U.D.C. 1995)**

32. How many cups of tea did Satish take yesterday in office ? (Presume that he paid for the tea taken by him.)

    I. He paid Rs 15 for the day for tea and snacks.

    II. Tea in his office costs Re 1 per cup.

33. A girl had to pass in both English and Mathematics to be promoted. Was any girl promoted ?

    I. 40 girls passed in English and 30 girls passed in Mathematics.

    II. There were totally 60 girls in the class.

34. Does investment in education guarantee a bright future ?

    I. Educated people are generally better off.

    II. Educated people are better employed than uneducated.

                                                   (Assistant Grade, 1992)

35. How old is Tarun ? **(Bank P.O. 1998)**

    I. Tarun could not appear for the final examination because he was short by two months for the stipulated 18 years of age in January this year.

    II. He will become eligible for casting his vote, where minimum age limit is 18, in March this year.

36. How many doctors are practising in this town ? **(Bank P.O. 1997)**

    I. There is one doctor per seven hundred residents.

    II. There are 16 wards with each ward having as many doctors as the number of wards.

ANSWERS

1. (a)   **2.** (d)   **3.** (d)   **4.** (d)   **5.** (d)   **6.** (d)   **7.** (d)   **8.** (a)   **9.** (a)   **10.** (d)

11. (e)   **12.** (d)   **13.** (b)   **14.** (c)   **15.** (e)   **16.** (e)   **17.** (a)   **18.** (d)   **19.** (d)   **20.** (e)

21. (d)   **22.** (d)   **23.** (d)   **24.** (e)   **25.** (d)   **26.** (b)   **27.** (e)   **28.** (d)   **29.** (c)   **30.** (d)

31. (d)   **32.** (d)   **33.** (e)   **34.** (e)   **35.** (c)   **36.** (b)

---

9. MISCELLANEOUS LOGICAL PUZZLES

Directions (Questions 1 to 3): In each of the following questions, examine the given statements carefully and find out which two of the statements cannot be true simultaneously, but can both be false.

1. 1. All animals are carnivorous.
    2. Some animals are not carnivorous.
    3. Animals are not carnivorous.
    4. Some animals are carnivorous.   **(S.C.R.A. 1993)**
    (a) 1 and 2   (b) 2 and 3   (c) 1 and 3   (d) 3 and 4

2. 1. All children are inquisitive.
    2. Some children are inquisitive.
    3. No children are inquisitive.
    4. Some children are not inquisitive.   **(I.A.S. 1995)**
    (a) 1 and 3   (b) 1 and 4   (c) 2 and 3   (d) 3 and 4

3. 1. Some nations wish for peaceful coexistence.
    2. All nations wish for peaceful coexistence.
    3. Some nations are not wishing for peaceful coexistence.
    4. No nations are wishing for peaceful coexistence.
    (*a*) 1 and 2   (*b*) 1 and 3   (*c*) 2 and 4   (*d*) 3 and 4

4. Examine the following statements regarding a set of balls
    1. All balls are black.
    2. All balls are white.
    3. Only some balls are black.
    4. No balls are black.:   **(I.A.S. 1997)**
    Assuming that the balls can only be black or white. which of the two statements given above can both be true, but cannot both be false?
    (*a*) 1 and 3   (*b*) 1 and 4   (*c*) 2 and 3   (*d*) 2 and 4

Directions (Questions 5 to 9): In each of the following questions, there are several statements which are followed by a conclusion. Read the statements and the conclusion carefully and indicate your answer as:

    (a) if the conclusion follows from the given statement;
    (b) if the conclusion contradicts the given statement;
    (c) if the conclusion neither follows from nor contradicts the given statement.
statement.   **(M.B.A. 1997)**

5. No experienced engineer is incompetent.
   Rohan is always blundering.
   No competent person is always blundering.
   Therefore, Rohan is not an engineer.
6. No one takes in 'The Times' unless he is well educated.
   No hodgepogs can read.
   Those who cannot read are not well educated.
   Therefore all hodgepogs take in 'The Times'.
7. Boys are illogical.
   Nobody is despised who can manage a dog.
   Illogical persons are despised.
   Therefore, boys cannot manage dogs.
8. Everyone who is sane can do logic.
   No lunatics are fit to serve on the jury.
   None of your sons can do logic.
   Therefore, none of your sons are fit to serve on a jury
9. My plates are the only things I have that are made of glass.
   I find all your presents very useful.
   None of my plates are of the slightest use.
   Therefore, your presents to me are made of glass.
10. Try this coaching class and you will not repent later. Which of the following, if true, would support and strengthen this statement? **(Bank P.O. 1997)**
    (*i*) The class is centrally located.
    (*ii*) Some teachers who teach in the class have good background.
    (*iii*) All the teachers in the class teach the subject very well.
    (*iv*) Students get personal attention and feedback.
    (*v*) The class gifts a calculator to first 100 students.
    (*a*) Only (*i*), (*ii*) and (*iii*) (*b*) Only (*i*) and (*ii*)
    (*c*) Only (*i*), (*ii*) and (*v*) (*d*) Only (*iii*) and (*iv*)
    (*e*) Only (*iv*) and (*v*)
11. Which of the following statements are facts?
    1. Peacock is a beautiful bird.
    2. There are seven stages of human life.
    3. There are seven days in a week.
    4. 'A thing of beauty is a joy for ever. **(Asstt. Grade, 1994)**
    (*a*) 1 and 3 (*b*) 3 only (*c*) 3 and 4 (*d*) All four

Directions (Questions 12 to 16): The following four statements are about the composition of participants in five different get-togethers: **(M.B.A. 1997)**
   (a) The number of male participants is the same as the number of female participants but is not quite so large as the number of child participants.
   (b) The number of male participants is larger than both the number of female and that of the child participants.

(c)   The number of child participants is larger than the number of male which is larger than the number of female participants.

(d)   The number of female participants is the same as the number of male participants but the number of child participants is less than that of female participants.

Each of the following questions contains a statement which is logically equivalent to one and only one. For each of the questions, select which of the above four statements is its logical equivalent.

12.   The number of female participants is less than the number of male participants which is not as large as the number of child participants.

13.   The number of female participants is less than that of male participants which is larger than that of the child participants.

14.   The number of female participants is the same as the number of male participants but is not so small as the number of child participants.

15.   The numbers of male and female participants are both less than the number of child participants and the former two numbers are same.

16.   The number of male participants is larger than that of the chile participants and is equal to the number of female participants.

ANSWERS

1. (c)   2. (a)   3. (c)   4. (b)   5. (a)   6. (b)   7. (a)   8. (a)   9. (b)   10. (d)
11. (b)   12. (c)   13. (b)   14. (d)   15. (a)   16. (d)

S. CHAND'S BOOKS FOR COMPETITIONS

GENERAL KNOWLEDGE

R.S. Aggarwal
Advanced Objective General Knowledge

S. Chand's Question Bank in General Studies

C.S. Bedi
S. Chand's General Studies for Central Civil Services

Mani Ram Aggarwal
General Knowledge Digest & General Studies with latest G.K.

आर. के. जैन
सामान्य ज्ञान तथा तर्क शक्ति परीक्षा

GUIDES FOR MEDICAL ENTRANCE EXAMINATIONS

Vinay Kumar
Biology for Pre-Medical/Pre-Dental Entrance Examination
Harjinder Kaur
Objective Chemistry

Mahesh Jain
Objective Physics

P.S. Varma & P.C Srivastava
Objective Zoology

S.R. Singh
Objective Botany

REASONING
R.S. Aggarwal
A Modern Approach to Verbal Reasoning

A Modern Approach to Non-Verbal Reasoning

A Modern Approach to Verbal & Non-Verbal Reasoning

Advanced Non-Verbal Reasoning For Bank Recruitment Test and other Competitions

Modern Approach to Logic Reasoning

NUMERICAL ABILITY
R.S. Aggarwal & Deepak Aggarwal
Mathematics for M.C.A. Entrance Examination

R.S. Aggarwal
Mathematics for N.D.A. Entrance Examination

Mathematics for C.D.S. Entrance Examination

Mathematics for MBA

Maths for BBA

Objective Arithmetic (Numerical Ability Test)

For Railways, Banks, Insurance, Police, Forest,

Defence, Revenue Services & Other Competitive Examinations

Quantitative Aptitude

For Bank Probationary Officers, G.I.C./ L.I.C.A.A.O., Assistant Grades, NDA/ C.D.S.,M.B.A./C.A.T., Excise/Income Tax Inspectors Examinations (Fully Solved)

An Advanced Approach to Data Interpretation

Arithmetic (Subjective and Objective for Competitive Examinations)

अंक गणित : प्रतियोगी परीक्षाओं के लिए (वस्तुनिष्ठ प्रश्नों सहित)

प्रतियोगी परीक्षाओं के लिए वस्तुनिष्ठ अंक गणित (पूर्ण हल सहित)

संख्यात्मक अभिरुचि (प्रतियोगी परीक्षाओं के लिए)

REFERENCE BOOKS
Vishnoo Bhagwan and Vidya Bhusan
Indian Administration

A Textbook of Public Administration

LANGUAGE
T. Saran
Precis Writing and Drafting

R.S. Aggarwal & Monika Aggarwal
Objective General English

Objective General Hindi

A.N. Kapur
A Guide to Business Correspondence

Chand's Dictionary of English-Hindi Usage & Technical

Terminology for Competitive Examinations

General English for Competitions

COMPLETE GUIDES
K.L. Kumar
Your Interview

R.S. Aggarwal & Deepak Aggarwal
A Complete Guide for MCA Entr. Exam.

A Complete Guide for Bank P.O. Exam.
Bank Clerical Guide

S.S.C. Clerk's Grade Kit (Fully Solved)

बैंक क्लर्क गाईड

G.D. Maheshwari
Complete Guide to Career Planning

GUIDES FOR I.I.T. ENTRANCE EXAM.
Mahesh Jain
Physics for IIT-Jee and other Engg. Entrance Exams

Objective Physics

Harjinder Kaur
Objective Chemistry

J.N. Gurtu, Rakesh Kapur & V.B. Rana
I.I.T. Chemistry(For All Engineering Examinations)

J.N. Gurtu, R. Kapur, V.B. Rana & A. Kapur
Numerical Chemistry (For Entrance Examinations of I.I.T. (JEE), Roorkee, MLNREC, Aligarh, AFMC, AIIMS, BHU & allother Engineering & Medical Competitive Examinations, U.P. Board, CBSE, ISC